# Ethnicity and
the New Family Economy

# Social Inequality Series
## Marta Tienda and David B. Grusky, Series Editors

*Ethnicity and the New Family Economy:*
*Living Arrangements and Intergenerational Financial Flows,*
edited by Frances K. Goldscheider and Calvin Goldscheider

FORTHCOMING

*Equality and Achievement in Education,* James S. Coleman

*Getting Started: The Transition to Adulthood*
*in Great Britain,* Alan C. Kerckhoff

*Social Stratification: Class, Race, and Gender*
*in Sociological Perspective,* edited by David B. Grusky

# Ethnicity and the New Family Economy

Living Arrangements and Intergenerational Financial Flows

EDITED BY
Frances K. Goldscheider and
Calvin Goldscheider

Westview Press
BOULDER, SAN FRANCISCO, & LONDON

*Social Inequality Series*

This Westview softcover edition is printed on acid-free paper and bound in library-quality, coated covers that carry the highest rating of the National Association of State Textbook Administrators, in consultation with the Association of American Publishers and the Book Manufacturers' Institute.

All rights reserved. No part of this publication may be reproduced or transmitted in any form or by any means, electronic or mechanical, including photocopy, recording, or any information storage and retrieval system, without permission in writing from the publisher.

Copyright © 1989 by Westview Press, Inc.

Published in 1989 in the United States of America by Westview Press, Inc., 5500 Central Avenue, Boulder, Colorado 80301, and in the United Kingdom by Westview Press, Inc., 13 Brunswick Centre, London WC1N 1AF, England

Library of Congress Cataloging-in-Publication Data
Ethnicity and the new family economy : living arrangements and intergenerational financial flows / edited by Frances K. Goldscheider and Calvin Goldscheider.
  p. cm. — (Social Inequality Series)
  ISBN 0-8133-7856-7
  1. Family—United States—Cross-cultural studies. 2. Households—United States—Cross-cultural studies. 3. Intergenerational relations—Economic aspects—Cross-cultural studies. 4. Minorities—United States—Case studies. I. Goldscheider, Frances K. II. Goldscheider, Calvin. III. Series.
HQ536.E84 1989
306.87—dc20                                                              89-35687
                                                                           CIP

Printed and bound in the United States of America

∞ The paper used in this publication meets the requirements of the American National Standard for Permanence of Paper for Printed Library Materials Z39.48-1984.

10  9  8  7  6  5  4  3  2  1

To the Maxcy Hall Community

# Contents

List of Tables xi
List of Figures xiv
Preface xv

## CHAPTER ONE

**The New Family Economy: Residential and Economic Relationships Among the Generations** 1
*Frances K. Goldscheider and Calvin Goldscheider*

The Modernization of the Family Economy 1
Family Changes and the Life Course 3
Ethnic Variation and its Explanation 6
The Research Studies 9
Research Implications 11
References 14

## PART I

## CHAPTER TWO

**Nonfamily Living Arrangements Among Black and Hispanic Americans** 17
*Luis Lazaro Hernandez*

Modernization Theory and the Family 18
Constraints, Resources, and Preferences 19
Hypotheses 22
Data and Methods 23
Ethnic and Racial Differences 25
Discussion 31
References 34

## CHAPTER THREE

**The Asian-American Traditional Household**     39
   *Wilawan Kanjanapan*

Changes in Immigration to the U.S.     39
Ethnic Differentials in Living Arrangements     41
Data, Definitions, and Measurement     42
Household Types     45
Household Size and Composition     46
Nonfamily Living Versus Family Extension     48
Nonfamily Living     50
Family Extension     51
References     54

## CHAPTER FOUR

**Nonfamily Households and Housing Among Young Adults**     57
   *Patricia B. Christian*

Background: Nonfamily Living     58
Housing and Income     59
Hypotheses     60
Data and Methods     61
Dependent Variables     62
Independent Variables     62
Predicting Nonfamily Living     64
Predicting Marriage and Family Living     67
Conclusions     70
References     71

## CHAPTER FIVE

**Living Arrangements Among the Older Population:
Constraints, Preferences, and Power**     75
   *Calvin Goldscheider and Mali B. Jones*

Autonomy and Dependence Among the Elderly     75
Data     78
Living Arrangements of Older Persons     81
Availability     83
Feasibility     86
Preferences     87
Discussion     88
References     90

Contents ix

## CHAPTER SIX

**Are Mormon Families Different? Household Structure and Family Patterns**    93
  *Anne Castleton and Frances K. Goldscheider*

| | |
|---|---|
| Religion and Family Patterns | 94 |
| Individualism and Family Patterns | 96 |
| Hypotheses, Methods, and Data | 97 |
| Family Patterns of Religious Groups | 99 |
| Discussion | 104 |
| References | 107 |

## PART II

## CHAPTER SEVEN

**Children Leaving Home and the Household Economy**    111
  *Frances K. Goldscheider*

| | |
|---|---|
| The Transition to Adulthood | 111 |
| Data | 113 |
| Nestleaving and Schoolleaving | 114 |
| Resource Flows Between the Generations | 118 |
| Discussion | 123 |
| References | 125 |

## CHAPTER EIGHT

**Family Transfers and Household Living Arrangements Among the Elderly**    127
  *Carol Shuchman*

| | |
|---|---|
| Income Sources, Family Transfers, and Living Arrangements | 128 |
| Family Transfers and Public Transfers | 129 |
| Data and Methods | 132 |
| Living Arrangements and Income | 134 |
| Discussion | 140 |
| References | 142 |

## PART III

## CHAPTER NINE

**Household Structure and Living Alone in Israel**     147
  *Frances K. Goldscheider and Zara Fisher*

Data, Hypotheses, and Operationalization     149
Ethnic Origin and Living Arrangements     152
Life Cycle, Socioeconomic, and Ethnic Factors     154
Age, Sex, and Education: Interactions with Ethnicity     156
Implications     158
References     160

## CHAPTER TEN

**Intergenerational Household Extension in Japan**     163
  *Hiroshi Kojima*

Theoretical Framework     166
Data and Method     170
Household Extension     171
Discussion     178
References     181

## CHAPTER ELEVEN

**Ethnicity and the New Family Economy:
Synthesis and Research Challenges**     185
  *Frances K. Goldscheider and Calvin Goldscheider*

An Emergent Research Model of Living Arrangements     185
Demographic Constraints     188
Economic Factors and Resources     189
Preferences and "Tastes"     191
Modernization or Westernization?     194
Methodological and Theoretical Conclusions     195

List of Contributors     199

# Tables

| | | |
|---|---|---|
| 2-1: | Age Patterns of Nonfamily Living Arrangements for Whites, Blacks, and Hispanics in the United States, 1980 | 26 |
| 2-2: | Evaluation of a Living Arrangements Model for Whites, Blacks, and Hispanics in the United States, 1980: Factors in Living Away from Family | 27 |
| 2-3: | Evaluation of a Living Arrangements Model for Mexicans, Puerto Ricans, and Cubans in the United States, 1980: Factors in Living Away from Family | 29 |
| 3-1: | Legal Immigrants Admitted to the United States, by Region of Birth | 40 |
| 3-2: | Asian Immigrants, by Race, Ancestry, Place of Birth, and All Three Variables Combined | 44 |
| 3-3: | Percentage Distribution of Some Selected Variables by Race, Ancestry, Place of Birth, and All Three Variables Combined | 45 |
| 3-4: | Living Arrangements of Asian Immigrants by Household Type, 1980 | 46 |
| 3-5: | Household Size and Composition of Asian Immigrants, 1980 | 47 |
| 3-6: | Living Arrangements of the Unattached by Sex: Asian Immigrants, 1980 | 50 |
| 3-7: | Percent Nonfamily by Age and Sex: Unattached Asian Immigrants, 1980 | 51 |

| | | |
|---|---|---|
| 3-8: | Percent Living in Extended Families by Age: Recent and Long-Term Unattached Asian Immigrants, 1980 | 52 |
| 4-1: | Regression Coefficients Estimating Proportion Nonfamily, Both Sexes, Controlling for Marriage | 65 |
| 4-2: | Regression Coefficients Estimating Percent Married of All 25-29 Year Olds | 68 |
| 5-1: | Measures of Living Arrangements by Ethnic Origin, Age, and Marital Status: Rhode Island Population 50 Years of Age and Older, 1980 | 82 |
| 5-2: | Models of Living Arrangements for the Older Population of Rhode Island, 1980 | 84 |
| 5-3: | The Effect of Number of Children Ever Born on Living Arrangements of the Older Population: Logistic Coefficients | 85 |
| 7-1: | Age of Leaving Home by Ethnicity and Sex | 115 |
| 7-2: | Educational Attainment by Ethnicity and Sex | 116 |
| 7-3: | Sequence of Leaving Home and Finishing School by Ethnicity and Sex | 117 |
| 7-4: | Resource Flows Between Parents and Children by Ethnicity and Sex | 119 |
| 7-5: | Percent Contributing to Household Income Among Those Who Remain at Home After Finishing School by Ethnicity and Sex | 120 |
| 7-6: | Percent Receiving Aid from Parents Among Those Leaving Home Before Finishing School | 121 |
| 7-7: | Age of Leaving Home for College Attendees by Ethnicity and Sex | 122 |
| 8-1: | Percent Living Alone by Age, Sex, and Race | 134 |
| 8-2: | Living Arrangements and Mean Income by Sex and by Category of Income | 136 |

Tables                                                                     xiii

8-3:   Mean Values of Family Transfers by Living
       Arrangement, Sex, and Receipt of Public
       Income                                                              139

9-1:   Variation in Marital Status and Living
       Arrangements by Age, Sex, and Ethnicity:
       Israel, 1972                                                        151

9-2:   Basic Models of the Proportion Living Outside
       of Families: Israel, 1972                                           154

9-3:   Significant Ethnic Interactions in the
       Proportion Living Outside of Families:
       Israel, 1972                                                        157

10-1:  Trends in Household Structure: Japan, 1955-85                       164

10-2:  Living Arrangements of the Elderly: Japan, 1985                     164

10-3:  Logistic Regression Coefficients for Deter-
       minants of Coresidence of Heads with Parents:
       Japan, 1985                                                         172

10-4:  Logistic Regression Coefficients for Deter-
       minants of Coresidence of Heads with a
       Married Child: Japan, 1985                                          174

# Figures

| | | |
|---|---|---|
| 6-1: | Percent Ever Married, Women Aged 20-24 and 40-44: 1950-1980 | 100 |
| 6-2: | Children Ever Born for Women Aged 20-24 and 45-49: 1960-1980 | 100 |
| 6-3: | Proportion of Ever Married Women Ever Divorced by Age 49: 1970-1980 | 102 |
| 6-4: | Percent of Women Currently Divorced, Aged 20-49: 1950-1980 | 102 |
| 6-5: | Headship Rates for Unmarried Women Aged 20-24: 1950-1980 | 105 |
| 6-6: | Headship Rates for Married Women, 1980 | 105 |
| 7-1: | Percentage of Respondents' Children Living with Them by Age and Sex of Child, 1979 | 114 |
| 10-1: | Analytical Framework for Determinants of Coresidence of Married Male Household Head with Parents and with a Married Child | 167 |
| 10-2: | Definition of Variables Used in Regressions | 176 |

# Preface

The focus of this volume is on the way the family economy is being shaped both by changes in living arrangements and in intergenerational financial flows. Increasing proportions of adults are living alone or in other nonfamily households. As a result, the family has become less important as a mechanism for redistributing resources to its members within the household, making it necessary to examine resource flows between households. We address issues of variations in these processes in the United States, particularly differences among ethnic, racial, and religious communities. We focus on Blacks and Hispanics but also examine variation among Hispanics, Asian Americans, and religious groups (including Mormons and Catholics). In order to increase the generality of our findings and to make cross-societal comparisons, we have included two studies of living arrangements and household structure that share the theoretical orientation of the American research projects: One is a study of the household patterns of ethnic and religious groups in the State of Israel; the other examines household extension in Japan as an illustration of a non-Western industrialized nation.

Nine research studies are presented, which all analyze household and family patterns emerging around 1980. Each represents research directions begun in graduate seminars under the direction of the senior editor, primarily at Brown University but also at the Hebrew University in Jerusalem. Most of the projects were completed independently by the students; some were carried to completion jointly with faculty. The research studies have been thoroughly edited and revised for this volume and in several cases have been rewritten by the editors to insure comparability of style and scholarly standards. None of these studies has been published before, although almost all of them have been presented at professional meetings of sociologists, demographers, and historians. The orientation of these studies has been worked out over the years by the editors of this volume in a series of publications and continues to inform their current research. The studies investigate the socio-demographic factors lying behind the new patterns of family and household structure, with particular emphasis on variation and change among ethnic, racial, and religious subpopulations.

The volume begins with an overview of changes in family structure and intergenerational financial exchanges, placing these research studies in the theoretical and substantive contexts of ethnic change and variation in modern societies. The first research study, by Luis Hernandez in Chapter Two, focuses on Hispanics and was originally part of a larger study he prepared while completing a joint B.A./M.A. degree at Brown under the direction of the senior editor of this volume and Martin U. Martel of the Department of Sociology. Chapter Three is a revised version of a paper on Asian Americans that Dr. Wilawan Kanjanapan prepared for the conference on "The U.S.: A Decade After the Vietnam War," Institute of American Culture, Academia Sinica, Taipei, June 1986. She earned her doctorate at Brown with a study of household structure in Thailand, under the direction of the senior editor. The research reported here was carried out while she was a postdoctoral fellow at the Population Studies and Training Center, Brown University, and subsequently at the School of Urban and Regional Planning, University of Southern California. In addition to working with the editors, Dr. Kanjanapan received help from Professor Alden Speare, Jr., of Brown University, who made the data available for the project; Professor Peter Gordon of the University of Southern California read an earlier version.

Patricia Christian's research on housing (Chapter Four) was originally part of a longer master thesis in the Department of Sociology, under the direction of the the senior editor and Alden Speare, Jr. The research reported in Chapter Five by Mali Jones and the co-editor of this volume deals with the elderly and was carried to completion as part of the research apprenticeship program in demography in the Department of Sociology at Brown. An earlier version was presented at the American Sociological Association meetings in Chicago, August 1987. The paper benefitted from the comments of Mark Hayward of the University of Southern California and from those of Sally Findley of the Rockefeller Foundation. Alden Speare, Jr., helped prepare the data files for the analysis.

Chapter Six introduces the religious dimension by focussing on Mormons; it is part of a project initiated by Anne Castleton while she was completing her M.A. degree in the Program in American Civilization at Brown University and later expanded together with the senior editor of this volume. It was presented at the Population Association of America meetings, New Orleans, 1988. The original paper that forms the basis of Chapter Seven on intergenerational resource flows in early adulthood was presented by Frances Goldscheider at the Social Science History Association meetings in Rochester, New York, in 1980. The paper was linked with a related paper by N. Grey Osterud, then a graduate student in American Civilization at Brown, who was completing a doctoral dissertation under the guidance of the senior editor. Chapter Eight examines resource flows to the elderly and was presented by Carol Shuchman at the 1983 annual meetings of the Population Association of America. That research project was directed by the senior editor of this volume, with helpful support by Alden Speare, Jr.

The materials on Israel in Chapter Nine were prepared jointly with Zara Fisher, who was working on her M.A. thesis at the Hebrew University in Jerusalem when the senior editor was there on a Fulbright Teaching Fellowship in the Departments of Demography and Sociology for the academic year 1983-84. An earlier version was presented at the demography section meetings of the 1985 World Congress of Jewish Studies conference in Jerusalem. The research findings on Japan reported in Chapter Ten were presented by Hiroshi Kojima at the 1987 meetings of the Population Association of America meetings in Chicago and were revised with helpful comments from Alden Speare, Jr., Sidney Goldstein, Roger Avery, John Casterline, Gregory Elliot, and Sara Millman from Brown University and Susan De Vos of the University of Wisconsin.

We edited these chapters and wrote Chapter One during our stay at The RAND Corporation as the first part of our 1988-89 sabbatical from Brown University. The research in the volume reflects our long-standing interests in the demography of households and families, which have been further shaped by our research colleagues and friends at RAND. Linda Waite, Julie DaVanzo, Jim Smith, and Peter Morrison have stimulated our research efforts, critically evaluated our papers, and worked with us jointly on our various research projects. They have made our research activities at RAND efficient and productive. We could not ask for more supportive colleagues, good friends, and facilitators. Overlooking the beaches of Santa Monica, watching a sunset, and often a sunrise, we have been able to formulate our research agenda and carry it out at RAND. We are grateful to our colleagues and friends for making it all happen there.

John Quinn, Dean of the Faculty at Brown University, was supportive of this project and provided the senior editor with a small grant from the Faculty Development Fund to support some of the technical preparation of the manuscript. As in previous ventures, we have depended on Carol Walker at Brown University to type portions of the manuscript. Janice Green of the Social Science Data Center of Brown University helped her to convert and reformat papers prepared on three other word processing systems. The tables were expertly and professionally prepared by the publication office at RAND on very short notice. We are particularly grateful to Janet DeLand and Patricia Bedrosian at RAND who were extremely helpful and efficient. At Westview we are grateful to Dean Birkenkamp for being our staunch supporter. We want particularly to express our gratitude to the authors and co-authors of the materials in this volume for allowing us to incorporate their work and to colleagues, students, and friends at all our institutions for helping us complete this project.

We dedicate this volume to our community in Maxcy Hall, Brown University--our sociology colleagues, our graduate students, the support staffs of the Population Studies and Training Center, Social Science Data Center, and the Department of Sociology. It is a first-rate team, of which we are justly proud.

Frances K. Goldscheider and Calvin Goldscheider
Santa Monica, California

# 1

# The New Family Economy
## Residential and Economic Relationships Among the Generations

FRANCES K. GOLDSCHEIDER
AND CALVIN GOLDSCHEIDER

**The Modernization of the Family Economy**

Major changes are revolutionizing the modern family. Divorce rates are increasing rapidly, young adults are deferring marriage and living away from their parental home and its family-oriented lifestyle before they marry, the elderly are increasing in absolute number and relative to the younger population, and more and more people are living alone in nonfamily households. Adults in most modern societies spend less of their adult years in families than ever before. As a result the role of the family as a central conduit of resources from men to women, from parents to children, and from grown children to aging parents has declined substantially.

These major changes in the structure and functions of the family are the most conspicuous indicators of the diminishing family orientation of modern society. These changes have been linked to increasing affluence, to new social and economic opportunities, to the transformation of women's and men's roles, and to changes in traditional family values. • Family structural changes have occurred in conjunction with high and increasing rates of labor force participation of women (even those with young children at home). They have been associated with major demographic transitions, particularly the decline in fertility, delays in first marriage, increases in non-marriage and in remarriages, extension of life into the older ages, differential mortality of men and women, and changing patterns of urbanization and housing.

While these general changes have occurred in most western societies as they have modernized, family changes did not occur all at once or equally among all populations. They have evolved over time, often slowly, and initially among those whose values and economic circumstances were undergoing the most rapid transformation. Some groups, for example traditional ethnic and religious communities, have resisted these family changes, and of course not all groups have participated equally in the general increase in affluence. It is likely that the emerging middle classes were altering their family patterns earlier than the lower classes; children of immigrants were more likely than the native born to break with their families of origin and their "old world" values; urban residents and the more educated were often in the forefront of the family revolution. Similarly, some industrializing nations experienced family changes more intensively and earlier than others; others appear to resist them to a great extent (Goode, 1984; Morgan and Hirosima, 1983).

Thus, while the revolution in family structure and values appears ubiquitous, a more systematic and careful examination suggests a range of family changes and a diversity of responses to the broad and general family revolution that has come to typify modern, westernized societies in general. Hence, our analytic question shifts from identifying the contours of the general revolution in family patterns characteristic of all modernizing societies to particular contexts, and to specifying which factors reinforce traditional family patterns as societies modernize and which factors result in more rapid family change. In particular, we look at the family unit in the context of community to isolate and identify the factors that contribute both to family change and continuity.

Changes so radical over time, in such a fundamental institution of society as the family, cannot but be expected to have major ramifications for the linkages between the family and other institutions--social, political, cultural, and particularly economic. Indeed, one of the master themes in the study of the transformations associated with the modernization of western societies has been the importance of structural differentiation. In premodern communities, the family and economic spheres were tightly integrated, so that economic consumption and production took place in a family context and, along with functions associated with socialization and cultural transmission, the family became the central institution around which other activities revolved. In the modern period, as the institutions of the family and the economy are transformed, critical changes have occurred in the relationships between these spheres of activity. The differentiation between family and economic activities and the separation of family and economic roles results in their realignment and newly formed reintegration. Thus, in modern societies, the family is not fully independent of economic activities, nor is the economy without important family connections. Rather the relationships between family and economic processes have changed. These new relationships, subsumed under the broad concept "the new family economy" are the focus of the research studies in this volume.

One aspect of these family and economic changes and the relationships between them relates to changes across the generations. In particular, an often neglected research issue is the degree to which family values are transmitted intergenerationally and the extent to which complex family ties are maintained. Some of these intergenerational linkages are residential, i.e., parents and adult children sharing the same household; others are the exchanges of resources and mutual assistance between the generations.

One of the themes of stratification research has been the intergenerational transfer of wealth and the maintenance of the social class structure and the opportunities for social mobility. However, as young adults move away from the parental home to set up an independent household before marriage, as older persons live alone, as fewer years are spent by everyone in nuclear family households, as families become complex through divorce, remarriage, blending and stepparenthood, the intergenerational transfer of resources becomes more complex. These new forms of interfamily income flows are further complicated by the changing roles of nonfamily agencies, local and national governments that have increasingly substituted for traditional family patterns by providing assistance to those in nonfamily situations.

To introduce these themes of social class and ethnic variation in family change and in the new linkages between the generations and the economy, we review below some of the major issues that will be examined in the research reported in this volume. We then suggest how these themes are treated in the research on the new family economy that are detailed in the ensuing chapters. Emerging from our review are a series of theoretical arguments about the interrelationships among demographic, economic, and socio-cultural determinants of family changes and a set of consequences of these family changes for the new connections between family and economy in modern societies.

## Family Changes and the Life Course

The dimension of family change that we particularly focus on in these studies is the decline in household size and its potential impact on family financial relationships within and between households. This process has usually been referred to as "the decline in family extension" in the literature on modernization and structural differentiation. However, the few studies of family structure that spanned any length of time (e.g., Pryor, 1972; Laslett, 1972) found little evidence for such a decline. They discovered that relatively few families in Western, currently economically developed countries were in fact actually extended in the period prior to industrialization.

Nevertheless, massive changes were in progress during the periods being studied, but which were obscured. In part, the changes were masked by demographic forces which were operating in the opposite direction, increasing the likelihood that families would be extended. The critical demographic change was the decline in mortality, which together with the decline in fertility resulted in the rapid aging of the population. In a preindustrial demographic regime of high fertility and mortality, few *families* would have any surviving elderly relatives available with whom to coreside for any length of time. High fertility rates would have given the surviving elderly many options for coresidence with the families of their adult offspring, and few adults survived to ages beyond their children's reaching adulthood. Modern demographic regimes, in contrast, create the potential for substantial family extension, since the elderly have few children with whom to live and most survive not only through their children's family-building years but often into their grandchildren's adulthood. Recent historical analyses have confirmed that some increase in family extension actually occurred in the early years of rapid demographic change (Ruggles, 1988). Nevertheless, few modern families now realize these opportunities for family extension because their elderly relatives are not living in families at all, and hence are ignored totally in studies of *family* changes (as opposed to research on household structure); they are living alone. From the point of view of the surviving elderly, their likelihood of extending a family has dropped dramatically. It was only from the point of view of their children that little or no increase in family extension occurred.

The accelerating pace of separate living in adulthood became increasingly visible, then, only when it began to affect other age groups. When young adults began leaving home at an earlier age and when levels of divorce began to rise dramatically, it became easier to realize that families were being increasingly denuded of their "extra" adults--the widowed mothers, adult children, unmarried aunts and uncles, and even the fathers--coming down to what are now called "minimum" households (Ermisch and Overton, 1985). And it has taken even more time to move beyond identifying the emerging patterns and to begin to assess the consequences of these processes.

One key consequence of the decline in the coresidence of related adults is its impact on the role of the coresident family as a means for redistributing economic goods and services--food, shelter, and care--among its members. This is one of the most important functions of the family. The adult members of a family provide not only for the socialization but also for the physical rearing of dependent children, who are the next generation. Adults also have provided care for each other when they became ill or disabled, helping them to return to health if at all possible, thereby extending the useful life of older family members and prolonging their ability to contribute knowledge, experience, and wisdom to the community. On the one hand, it has become less necessary for family members to take care of one another as other institutions within the welfare state substitute for the family. At the younger end of the life course, these institutions have encouraged a longer period of childhood and an extension of dependence among young adults on the family, as there are greater needs for investments in the education and career of the next generation.

The distributional function of the coresident family group is such a pervasive one that many of our economic concepts reflect it. Most welfare programs--including SSI, food stamps, and AFDC--are adjusted to reflect the level of resources coming into the coresident family as a whole, thus assuming that all have access to them. Aggregate measures such as "per capita family income" are calculated by taking total family incomes and dividing them by family size. At the same time, our concepts and measures assume that there is little or no economic redistribution *between* families and households; that the unit of redistribution is the coresident group.

Both the assumption of equal distribution within coresident family groups and the assumption of no redistribution between such groups are clearly incomplete. Despite the ideals in modern cultures of equality between husband and wife, or "companionate marriage," of equal treatment of children, such as the rejection of primogeniture, and even of companionship and democracy in parent-child relationships, hierarchies of power, control, and access to resources exist within families. Under pressure, the adults may even act to rid themselves of unproductive dependents, as our myths about Hansel and Gretel suggest and our anthropological reports on the abandoned elderly of the Eskimo confirm. And close members living in separate households regularly find ways to transcend the barriers of space and convenience to provide needed care and support for each other.

Nevertheless, as adults increasingly separate out from each other residentially, the family's ability to redistribute from its more to its less able members is reduced. To a large extent, it is likely that residential independence is a reflection of the greater ability of the less able members to live independently, and their greater reliance on nonfamily sources for economic support and other forms of care. But they have relinquished the potential benefits of coresidence in their decision to spare themselves the costs of coresidence.

The greater vulnerability that results from adults' decisions not to live with other related adults appears to be particularly critical for three groups. One group is the dependent children of separating couples, who have been documented to suffer financially as they lose access to their father's incomes. This results because male earning power is usually greater, fathers usually do not keep physical custody, and their "interhousehold" contributions of child support have proved unreliable. In some sense, children become the passive "victims" of their parents' decisions about their own and their family's welfare (Weitzman, 1987; Hoffman and Duncan, 1988).

The other groups whose lives have been changed by the transformation in the family economy are themselves adults--the youngest and oldest adults--who are increasingly living separately at the extremes of the adult life course. These are the life course points where household separation and household consolidation are at issue: when young adults are beginning their adult, independent lives and when the elderly are confronting increasing dependency. For each of them, independence may be possible, but continuing contributions from their kin are necessary. As a result, interhousehold transfers take on increasing importance as family members live separately from each other. A major concern is whether residential independence has, at least in some cases, been achieved at the cost of access to family backup.

Thus, family changes over time and variations in the life course are linked. The traditional "normal" adult life course pattern (Glick, 1947) started with marriage, continued through the "honeymoon" period when the married couple lived together before having children, was followed by the period of childbearing and childrearing (full nest), by the empty nest when the youngest child got married and left home, and finally by widowhood, when one spouse (most often the wife) remained. This life course pattern has changed dramatically with the broader transformation of the family. While in the past, only widowhood had been viewed as the period of possible nonfamily living, the empty nest is currently earlier than the marriage of the last child, as nonfamily living has become a more common feature of early adulthood. The family life course has changed and household composition has been altered with the emergence of large numbers of one-parent reconstituted or blended families. So the rise in nonfamily households at both ends of the adult life course, along with increases in complex family structures and quasi-nuclear one-parent families, have led to new adult life course patterns that do not fit the traditional transitions that were the norm in the past.

## Ethnic Variation and its Explanation

While increases in income and education have been associated with family changes, as have demographic changes at the macro level, changes in ethnic, racial, and religious group identification have also been related to family structure and family norms. Often these ethnic, racial, and religious factors are of no less importance than economic, educational, or demographic factors. Large differences in average marriage age, proportions marrying, and divorce have been documented among white religious groups, Protestants, Catholics, and Jews, and among Catholic ethnic subpopulations (Kobrin and Goldscheider, 1978). Significant variation in extended family ties and in the prevalence of households headed by women characterize Blacks, Hispanics, and whites (Frisbie et al., 1982; Tienda and Angel, 1982; Angel and Tienda, 1982; Cooney, 1979). Moreover, the probability of nonfamily living differs among groups of European language origins in the United States: Polish, Greek, Russian, and Yiddish (Kobrin and Goldscheider, 1982). And there has been an extensive literature on the family patterns of Black Americans, focusing on non-marriage, childbearing outside of marriage, female-headed households, and family-kinship support networks. In turn, these family patterns have been linked to the economic circumstances of Blacks in the United States, to the structure of opportunities, to government programs, as well as to racial discrimination in America (see among others Farley, 1986; Moynihan, 1986; Schoen and Kluegel, 1988).

Ethnic, racial, and religious differences are reflected in attitudes and expectations about the timing of marriage and of childbearing, contraceptive usage, and family size (Goldscheider and Goldscheider, 1985; Mosher and Hendershot, 1984; Goldscheider and Mosher, 1988).

Differences have also been documented for premarital residential independence among young adults. Asian Americans, for example, tend to leave home later than others (Goldscheider and DaVanzo, 1989), and Hispanics and Blacks are less likely than white nonHispanics to establish an independent household before marriage (U.S. Bureau of the Census, 1980).

Research on the normative aspects of premarital residential independence as expressed by young adults has also shown major ethnic and religious group variation: Hispanics, for example, are less likely than others to expect to live independently before marriage, no matter how late they expect to marry or what their socioeconomic status is. Likewise, traditional Protestants (e.g., Baptists) and Catholics from southern Europe are also less likely to expect to leave home before marriage; a higher proportion of Blacks than others expect not to marry and they have distinctive patterns of leaving the parental home (Goldscheider and Goldscheider, 1987; 1988).

The normative and behavioral variation in family patterns reflects three processes. First there is an overlap between socioeconomic status and ethnic, racial, and religious group membership. Second, the variation among ethnic, racial, and religious groups may be indicative of differential values and preferences. Such value differences are not usually measured directly, and are often inferred from behavior and attributed to "culture." Third, differences in family patterns may be related to ethnic community networks and the institutional transmission of family values.

Our theories of why ethnic and racial groups are characterized by different family patterns draw on several research traditions. The first is an explicitly cultural approach, which places these differences in the context of immigration and the cultural "baggage" that accompanied immigrant groups to America (Gordon, 1964; Glazer and Moynihan, 1970). In this view, cultures vary on many dimensions, and the immigrant generation is closer in time to the sources of ethnic values. The argument is that as ethnic groups move further from the immigrant generation, their unique family oriented patterns should decline, since modern societies are assumed to integrate and assimilate immigrant groups, and the residual ethnic factor in family patterns should be weaker over time. Indeed, only when there remains an overlap of ethnic group membership and social class should ethnicity (and race) affect family patterns. The primary emphasis of this framework is on ethnic and racial categories as proxies for social class or as a transitional influence operating during the process of ethnic acculturation and assimilation.

In part, a similar argument can be made with regard to religious group membership. In modern, urban, industrialized societies, religion appears to be but a fading legacy of the past; in secular societies, religion is treated as a weak differentiator of family patterns. As with the cultural legacy of the ethnic past, religion is also expected to weaken over time. Hence, as with increasing levels of education and affluence, growing secularization results in the decline in religious variation in family patterns.

Another research tradition has focused primarily on the structural-ecological dimensions of racial, ethnic, and religious groups. This structural approach stresses the regional or neighborhood concentration of ethnic groups as a basis for linking individuals and their families to the community (Yancey et al., 1976, 1985; Goldscheider, 1986; Lieberson, 1980; Portes and Bach, 1985). Geographic concentration implies a relatively large ethnic community and, hence, the possibility of developing more extensive ethnic networks based on communal interaction. The key theoretical concern is to treat ethnic, racial, and religious groups in the context of communities--communities of shared spatial location, social interaction, and shared culture. Institutions, such as churches or schools, reinforce and maintain traditional family norms. Likewise, other institutions can transmit and reinforce traditional culture and thereby account for the persistence of traditional family values. Family norms and lifestyles may be transmitted through interaction among those who share similar social networks.

When there are overlapping ethnic and religious communities, as for example, among Italian Catholics and Jews, networks and institutions reinforce ethnic communal cohesion. When community and networks are sustained by common lifestyles or shared economic circumstances, or reinforced by external constraints, such as discrimination and racism, the internal cohesion of the racial, ethnic, and religious community is strengthened.

Ethnicity and religiosity therefore combine both structural and cultural components. Speaking a foreign language implies a closeness to the cultural origins of the past as well as the continuing salience of community interaction. Likewise, geographic concentration and church attendance imply both community interaction and the transmission of culture; each contributes to the maintenance of distinctive communities, racial, religious and ethnic. Accordingly, the examination of ethnic, racial, and religious variation in family patterns may be interpreted in the context of both the structure of social networks--the multiple ways members of these communities are involved and interact formally and informally with each other--and the values transmitted within them, to discover how they are linked to traditional family norms. Our inquiry into the determinants and consequences of the new family economy bears on the process of ethnic, racial, and religious change in modern society and the factors affecting the maintenance of group continuity and change. In these ways, the family changes resulting in new linkages between economic and family patterns and the general social changes transforming ethnic, racial, and religious communities are related processes. Distinctive communities are likely to have distinctive family patterns; continuing ethnic, religious, and racial differences in family-economic linkages are likely to result in the transmission of these family patterns and values to the next generation.

## The Research Studies

The research studies that are presented in this volume focus on ethnic, racial, and religious variation in family-related processes within the United States, with Japan and Israel as comparative cases. We begin by examining Black and Hispanic variation in nonfamily living (Chapter Two). Using U.S. census data, the analysis shows that economic factors do not account wholly for the distinctive ethnic and racial patterns of living arrangements. Nevertheless, resources are important factors within both the Black and Hispanic populations. Hernandez documents variation among Hispanics--Cubans, Mexicans, and Puerto Ricans--and speculates that a national Hispanic minority may be emerging in the United States.

While Asian Americans as a group have distinctive family patterns (Chapter Three), there is also a great deal of internal subgroup variation. Changes brought about by economic, demographic, and immigration patterns to the United States have led to sharp variation among recent Asian immigrants. Kanjanapan observes patterns of convergence in family patterns among Asian American subpopulations, as length of stay and exposure to broader American values intensifies.

Isolating the younger end of the adult life course, Patricia Christian uses census data on metropolitan areas to examine regional and community level influences on nonfamily living arrangements (Chapter Four). She is able to identify factors that determine living alone compared with living with roommates among young adults and demonstrating the limitation of a strictly economic interpretation of family processes. She shows how factors influencing nonfamily living differ for men and women when marriage and living with parents are considered together. Moreover, she demonstrates the enormous value of contextual analysis for understanding family patterns by documenting the importance of population composition by race in living arrangement patterns.

The effects of both community- and individual-level variables are demonstrated further when we focus on the elderly segment of the life course (Chapter Five). C. Goldscheider and Jones show how census data can be used to test the relative importance of availability, feasibility, and preferences in the living arrangements of ethnic and racial groups in one community. Racial and ethnic variation in living alone and in family extension go beyond issues of disadvantage and resources and do not appear to be wholly transitional, since much later generations of Italians and Irish continue to have distinctive family patterns.

Variation in family processes is characteristic of some religious subpopulations as well. The analysis in Chapter Six shows the substantial differences between Catholics and Mormons as well as the importance of regional, western patterns. These are documented by examining family processes of "states," given the unique concentration of Catholics in Rhode Island and Mormons in Utah, and the role of California as the epitome of an open, modern, nonfamily-oriented community. As Castleton and F. Goldscheider show, Catholics and Mormons have had different responses to changing family and sex roles patterns, indicating that not all religious traditions relate to family patterns in the same way.

Coresidence is one of the ways that the generations are related. Another is through the direct exchange of resources. Census data are not as useful for studying intergenerational financial flows as they are for living arrangements. To explore these intergenerational financial flows, the two studies in Part Two use specially collected survey data. In Chapter Seven, F. Goldscheider uses data from the Rhode Island Survey to examine life cycle transitions, inferring changes over time from the rich data on ethnic variation. Resources flow very differently between the generations among ethnic and religious communities. Some groups subsidize their children's leaving home to obtain higher levels of education and help them set up an independent residence, while receiving little contribution from their children to the family economy. In others, parents do not subsidize the education of their children, while their children may sacrifice education to family obligations. The importance of these different generational perspectives and the diverse patterns among groups living in the same community emerges from this project.

At the other end of the adult life course, Shuchman focuses on family transfers to the elderly in Chapter Eight. She analyzes data from the Panel Study of Income Dynamics to broaden the range of resources considered in studying the economic well-being of older people. She shows how these resources are used to purchase privacy and independence among older persons.

In Part III we move away from an exclusive focus on ethnic, racial, and religious differences in the United States as a basis for inferring how preferences about family and household relationships are shaped by social and economic structures. The two research studies reported in Chapters Nine and Ten allow us to take the next comparative step. Examining ethnic variation in household structure in the State of Israel, F. Goldscheider and Fisher show how structural factors are associated with living alone. Ethnic groups within Israel range enormously in their national origins, from the most traditional to the most modern. Some of the features of ethnic variation are particular to the circumstances of immigration to Israel and are specific to the national origins and emerging culture of the Israeli population. Nevertheless, the set of factors that determine living arrangements among Israel's ethnic mosaic have strong parallels to the patterns of living arrangements among groups within the American ethnic mosaic.

Japan is an additional contrast to the American pattern of family change. In Chapter Ten, Kojima discusses Japan as an example of a modern industrialized nation that is non-western, with a strong tradition of family continuity and cohesion. This case study allows us to compare commonalities and differences and to uncover those factors that sustain continued family cohesion in the context of industrialization and modernization. While again there is much that is specific to Japan, the factors that mark the Japanese family have similarities to other western countries. The issue is not the convergence of Japanese family structure to the western model, but rather the identification of the particular matrix of factors specific to the traditions of one society and culture to learn about patterns and prospects for change there and clarify the elements that are unique and those that are more generalizable, cross-nationally and cross-cuturally.

These research studies document a range of variation in family patterns and should be viewed in the context of a broader theory of family change as well as a more general theory of ethnic continuity and change. Such theories with regard to the family should stress the multiplicity of determinants of family processes for different segments of the life course. The major categories of determinants of family processes can be conveniently grouped into demographic, economic, and cultural factors. But the priorities among these factors remain uncertain, and the relative importance of specific elements varies among groups and for the particular family processes examined.

**Research Implications**

The value of a series of studies illustrating these common themes rests with their contribution to the cumulative understanding of family changes. The findings of these research projects are of great potential value since they also form the background for new research questions and generate new study designs attempting to address emerging issues. Four sets of research themes appear to us to emerge from these studies and to require further research attention.

(1) Clearly, new patterns of intergenerational relations have emerged over the last several decades. We do not yet know how intrafamily flows work. How do we get into the black box of the family economy to see more about why some adults leave the household when they get more income (wives, mothers, adult children) and others seek greater coresidence through marriage (adult males)? Similarly, we need to learn more about interfamily and interhousehold flows. We have very few existing data sources to help us understand interhousehold exchanges, both actual or potential.

(2) We have learned to exploit census and other official data sources to learn more about family processes and identify some of the major contours of family change and variation. These data sources often contain details not elsewhere available for small subpopulations and areas. Nevertheless, they, along with one-time cross-sectional surveys, cannot fully address the in-depth analytic questions we ask. Clearly, the processes of interfamily relationships unfold over the life course and therefore require

research studies designed to capture the longitudinal nature of these processes. Similarly, our research designs need to study the generations directly: Parents and children along with other family members of different generations have different perspectives on their family situation. Factors that determine one generation's family patterns may or may not be identical to the factors affecting the other generation; the consequences of family relationships for one are unlikely to be identical to those for the other.

(3) Our research questions and our study designs need to reflect the combined impact of personal and family characteristics along with community level variables. We have been able, for example, to study the effects of income on living arrangements and the impact of race on female headed households. We have also researched the impact of community characteristics, such as the proportion Black or the percent with low income, on the family patterns in those communities. We have rarely designed our studies to be able to combine these micro- and macro-level characteristics. Are the family patterns of Blacks living in neighborhoods of high Black population concentration similar to Blacks with otherwise comparable characteristics, living in more integrated racial neighborhoods? Are the family patterns of those with low incomes living in poor areas different from those living in better-off neighborhoods? or than those living in extended families? These and other questions that combine individual and family level variables, together with community level (i.e., contextual) effects require new, carefully designed data collection efforts.

(4) We have consistently reported on ethnic, racial, and religious differences in family patterns. We need to direct our future research efforts to uncover how and why these factors work as they do to reinforce family values. We need to systematically incorporate in our studies questions that go beyond the categorical variables of group membership to obtain insight into ethnicity, religiosity, and racial concentration. We need to identify, directly rather than by inference, the factors that are specific to the values and the institutions of these communities. These questions are of particular importance in modern pluralistic societies, where ethnic, religious, and racial identification is unlikely to disappear and where new minority groups are being formed through immigration and related processes.

The focus on the generations is a clear theme in the new family economy. It is, as well, the central focus of studies of change and continuity among ethnic, race, and religious groups. Combined, the set of questions that we address include the following: Will family patterns and norms persist or change into the next generation--and if so, how? To what extent are the family-economy linkages transmitted across generations and what social structural conditions are conducive to that transmission? And in these processes of family change and continuity, do the distinctive ethnic, racial, religious patterns change as well? Do they merge for the same reason that the general patterns are changing or are there factors that continue to differentiate these communities and make them distinctive? Racial, ethnic, and religious group assimilation is a frequent outcome of increased exposure to the norms and institutions of modern societies. Yet these processes are not inevitable. We need to study the mechanisms that sustain and reinforce traditional family values among young adults and that persist throughout the life course, as well as those factors that result in change and convergence. Ethnicity and religiosity are variables that change over time and in response to different community contexts; they also vary over the life course. How these two processes--family and group membership--are linked to each other and are affected by economic factors remains one of the continuing challenges of social science research.

The studies reported in this volume, each in their way, attempt to sort out the combination of factors--structural and cultural--that maintain racial, ethnic, and religious communities and thereby continue to influence family values and preferences among the generations. The results set the stage for further inquiries, more studies that will sharpen the questions we can ask. They will clarify patterns that have been observed, so that we will be able to better understand those that may occur in the future. Some of these new research directions and study designs are underway among current research projects. Data sources are increasingly available to allow us to answer some of these new questions. And we shall continue to study variation and change in the new family economy so that we are better able to understand both family and economic processes and the linkages between them over the generations for the variety of communities and groups in our society.

## REFERENCES

Angel, R. and M. Tienda. 1982. "Determinants of Household Structure: Cultural Patterns or Economic Need?" *American Journal of Sociology* 87:1360-1383.

Cooney, Rosemary. 1979. "Demographic Components of Growth in White, Black and Puerto Rican Female-Headed Families: A Comparison of the Cutright and Ross/Sawhill Methodologies." *Social Science Research* 8:144-158.

Ermisch J. and E. Overton, 1985. "Minimal Household Units: A New Approach to the Analysis of Household Formation." *Population Studies* 39:33-54.

Frisbie, Parker, et al. 1982. "Household/Family Structure and Socioeconomic Differentials: A Comparison of Hispanics, Blacks, and Anglos." University of Texas Population Research Center Paper Series. No. 4.009.

Farley, Reynolds. 1986. *Blacks and Whites: Narrowing the Gap*. Cambridge: Harvard University Press.

Glazer, Nathan and Daniel P. Moynihan. 1970. *Beyond the Melting Pot*. Cambridge, MA: MIT Press.

Glick, Paul. 1947. "The Family Cycle." *American Sociological Review* 12:164-174.

Goldscheider, Calvin. 1986. *Jewish Continuity and Change: Emerging Patterns in America*. Bloomington, IN: Indiana University Press.

Goldscheider, Calvin and Frances Goldscheider. 1985. "Family Size Expectations of Young American Jewish Adults." Papers in Jewish Demography. Jerusalem, Israel: The Hebrew University.

Goldscheider, Calvin and Frances Goldscheider. 1987. "Moving Out and Marriage: What Do Young Adults Expect?" *American Sociological Review* 52:278-285.

Goldscheider, Calvin and Frances Goldscheider. 1988. "Ethnicity, Religiosity, and Leaving Home: The Structural and Cultural Bases of Traditional Family Values." *Sociological Forum* 3:525-547.

Goldscheider, Calvin and William Mosher, 1988. "Religious Affiliation and Contraceptive Usage: Changing American Patterns, 1955-82." *Studies in Family Planning* 19:48-57.

Goldscheider, Frances, and Julie DaVanzo. 1989. "Pathways to Independent Living in Early Adulthood: Marriage, Semiautonomy, and Premarital Residential Independence." *Demography* Volume 26.

Goode, William. *The Family*. Englewood Cliffs, N.J.:Prentice-Hall.

Gordon, Milton. 1964. *Assimilation in American Life*. New York: Oxford University Press.

Hoffman Saul and Greg Duncan. 1988. "What are the Economic Consequences of Divorce?" *Demography* 25:641-645.

Kobrin, Frances E. and Calvin Goldscheider. 1978. *The Ethnic Factor in Family Structure and Mobility*. Cambridge, MA: Ballinger Publishing Co.

Kobrin, Frances E. and Calvin Goldscheider. 1982. "Family Extension or Nonfamily Living." *Western Sociological Review* 13:103-118.

Laslett, Peter. 1972. "Introduction: The History of the Family" in Peter Laslett and Richard Wall (eds.) *Household and Family in Past Time*. Cambridge:Cambridge University Press.

Lieberson, Stanley. 1980. *A Piece of the Pie*. Berkeley, CA: University of California Press.

Morgan, S. P. and K. Hirosima. 1983. "The Persistence of Extended Family Residence in Japan: Anachronism or Alternative Strategy?" *American Sociological Review* 48:269-281.

Moynihan, Daniel P. 1986. *Family and Nation*. New York: Harcourt Brace Jovanovich, Publishers.

Mosher, William and G. Hendershot. 1984. "Religious Affilation and the Fertility of Married Couples." *Journal of Marriage and the Family* 46:671-77.

Portes, Alejandro and Robert Bach. 1985. *Latin Journey: Cuban and Mexican Immigrants in the United States*. Berkeley, CA: University of California Press.

Pryor, Edward. 1972. "Rhode Island Family Structure: 1875 and 1960," in Peter Laslett and Richard Wall (eds.) *Household and Family in Past Time.* Cambridge: Cambridge University Press.

Ruggles, Steven. 1987. *Prolonged Connections: The Rise of the Extended Family in Nineteenth Century England and America.* Madison: University of Wisconsin Press.

Schoen, Robert and James Kluegel. 1988. "The Widening Gap in Black and White Marriage Rates: The Impact of Population Composition and Differential Marriage Propensities." *American Sociological Review* 53:895-907.

Tienda, Marta and Ronald Angel. 1982. "Headship and Household Composition among Blacks, Hispanics and Other Whites." *Social Forces* 61:508-53.

U.S. Bureau of the Census. 1980. Marital Status and Living Arrangements: March 1979. P-20, no. 349, February.

Weitzman, Lenore. 1985. *The Divorce Revolution.* New York: The Free Press.

Yancey, W., et al. 1976. "Emergent Ethnicity: A Review and Reformulation." *American Sociological Review* 41:391-402.

Yancey, W., et al. 1985. "The Structure of Pluralism." *Ethnic and Racial Studies* 8:94-116.

# PART I

# 2

# Nonfamily Living Arrangements Among Black and Hispanic Americans

LUIS LAZARO HERNANDEZ

Historical and comparative research has shown the relative invariance of household size, the prevalence of nuclear household structure, and the concentration of household extension in only limited segments of the life course. These findings do not contradict the claim that extended kinship ties beyond the household may decline with modernization, but they have led to more refined theories about the decline of extended households and the rise of the nuclear family (Levy, 1965; Burch, 1970; Laslett, 1972).

How can family structure remain relatively unchanged when there have been dramatic changes in broader social, economic, and demographic processes? In part new combinations among these processes have taken place. Thus some have suggested that "two societies or subgroups could have similar proportions nuclear despite very different family systems and/or economic levels" (Kobrin and Goldscheider, 1982:104). On the other hand, differences in the extent of nonfamily living may simply reflect differences in the availability of relatives, rather than normative differences or broader factors associated with modernization (Freedman et al., 1978).

The central issue therefore is the analysis of the changing constraints and preferences in living arrangements, focusing on those who have a variety of choices in living arrangements--who are nonparenting and unmarried (since they have no constraints posed either by a spouse and/or children). The research carried out at this level documents the rise of alternatives to extended household patterns, particularly the increase in one-person households in the United States (Kobrin, 1976). These trends have been explained in terms of a combination of rising levels of affluence that has made independence and privacy increasingly affordable in modern societies and changes in norms, residence rules, and tastes.

The theoretical basis for the hypothesis that rising income is primarily responsible for the increases in living alone derives from a consumer demand model in which unmarried persons are assumed to desire privacy in living arrangements. Higher income means that persons can afford to buy the autonomy and privacy that comes from living alone; those with lower incomes must reduce monetary costs by sharing living arrangements (Michael et al., 1980; Hughes and Gove, 1981). Thus as the income of the population increases, the demand for living alone increases as well.

Alternatively, the effect of income has been explained by structural changes in tastes for living alone since only recently has income been used for autonomy and privacy rather than for other goods (Beresford and Rivlin, 1966). Others argue that the decline of the extended family and the residential segregation of generations have made norms, preferences, and residence rules more supportive of living alone in advanced industrial societies (Burgess, 1960; Kobrin, 1981). This normative emphasis suggests that increases in income, before changes in tastes for privacy and autonomy had occurred, did not result in a higher proportion living alone. But changes in preferences have increased the probability of persons living alone independent of increases in income levels (Pampel, 1983).

## Modernization Theory and the Family

Modernization theory has often been used by demographers to interpret changes in family structure. According to this approach, "wherever the economic system expands through industrialization, family patterns change. Extended kinship ties weaken, lineage patterns dissolve, and a trend toward some form of the conjugal system generally begins to appear--that is, the nuclear family becomes a more independent kinship unit" (Goode, 1963:6). This conjugal family is characterized by the relative exclusion of other relatives from its everyday affairs, i.e., there is very little extension of the kin network. Thus, some have argued that there is "...a historic trend to whittle down the size of the kinship units in the general direction of isolating the nuclear family" (Parsons, 1961:257).

It has been further suggested that the conjugal family "fits" the needs of industrialization and urbanization well. Mainly, it fits the need for placing individuals in their jobs on the basis of merit rather than family position. But we cannot assume a causal relationship between industrialization and the rise of the conjugal family (Goode, 1963; cf. Elder, 1978). The classical linkage between modernization and family changes would argue that industrialization, complemented by the spreading ideology of the conjugal family, puts pressure on the traditional family structure as follows:

> (1) Generating opportunities that result in movement from one locality to another, thereby decreasing the frequency and intimacy of contact among members of a kin network;

> (2) Creating class differential mobility, resulting in the more rapid mobility of some kin creating differences in lifestyles, tastes, and incomes among kin and thus decreasing kin contact;

(3) Undermining large corporate kin groupings, so that urban and industrial systems of agencies and organizations handle the problems that were solved within the kin network;

(4) Creating a value structure that recognizes achievement more than ascription, reducing what kin can offer an individual in exchange for his/her commitment;

(5) Creating new specialized jobs, making it less likely for an individual to obtain a job through kinspersons.

An extension of the trend away from the extended family with close kin ties to the more isolated nuclear family is the pattern for the "unattached," characterized by independent living arrangements (Kobrin, 1976; Michael et al., 1980). A version of modernization theory argues that modern economic development isolates the unattached from family resources and social support. Since relations with kin and others are defined within the conjugal family system, the unattached become more isolated. In contrast to the kin network that pressures children and other family members to provide shelter and physical care for parents and unattached relatives, the conjugal family system imposes fewer obligations between relatives or between parents and children, once the children have established their own households. The assumption is that the spread of the conjugal family system is responsible for the changing living arrangements of the unattached. Research has indicated that factors associated with modernization--higher income, higher education, and reduced fertility--have been associated with living alone (Belcher, 1967; Chevan and Korson, 1972; Soldo, 1977). Thus, it is may be argued that as populations become wealthier, better educated, and less fertile, residential isolation of the unattached increases (Kobrin, 1981).

Another version of modernization theory sees extended family living as a function of poverty, illiteracy, and high fertility. Accordingly, "increases in living alone...can be interpreted as better informed choices on how to spend increased resources, unburdened by the heavy demands of kin" (Kobrin, 1981:371). After all, living alone represents privacy and a high degree of independence in household and personal affairs--aspects of a conjugal family system. If modernization has increased residential isolation through individual-level effects and also through changes in norms and preferences in living arrangements, then increases in living alone should occur even among the poorer and less educated segments of society (Kobrin, 1981).

## Constraints, Resources, and Preferences

The decision facing the unattached is whether to live with relatives or live alone (or with nonrelatives) As with other consumer choices, an individual's decision will reflect income, the price of the goods, and the taste for that good relative to alternative goods. Moreover, the choice of living in family or nonfamily households varies over the life course. Thus, the factors influencing the unattached's living arrangements may be separated into constraints, resources, and preferences (Kobrin and Goldscheider, 1982:104-105):

> (1) The availability of households that contain relatives. If there are no or few relatives available, the choice of living arrangements is limited.
>
> (2) Whether it is economically feasible to live alone, since living alone may involve greater costs than living with relatives.
>
> (3) The issue of family norms and preferences. The choices that are made depend on the desirability of family extension.

Thus, in modern societies the choice of living arrangements among the unattached is not only dependent on the demographic availability of households to attach to, or the economic constraints requiring such extension but is closely tied to the relative desirability of family extension versus independent living. Premodern societies are characterized by ideal-typical conditions where demographic and economic constraints are powerful and thus limit living arrangement choices (Kobrin and Goldscheider, 1982). The normative emphasis on family extension thus characterizes societies where demographic and economic constraints limit the expression of these norms; when these constraints are no longer as powerful, family extension preferences and norms change (Levy, 1965).

These theoretical issues can be addressed comparatively by using racial/ethnic minority groups in the United States that are hypothesized to exhibit different group preferences (Hispanics and Blacks) from those of the total population. Thus, by focusing on the living arrangements choices made by the unattached at one point in time, race and ethnic differences may be viewed as an indicator of family norms and preferences.

The Black family has often been portrayed as plagued by instability, disintegration, weakness, or pathology (Moynihan, 1965; Frazier, 1966; Grier and Cobbs, 1968). This traditional focus has created the impression that instability and pathology are characteristic of most Black families. Yet kinship relations tend to be stronger among Black than white families (Cohen and Hodges, 1963; Bott, 1964; Feagin, 1968). These stronger kinship relations have also been explained as more prevalent among low-income than middle-income families (perhaps accounting for the stronger kinship ties among Black families). More recent studies that have controlled for income and education in examining extended living arrangements have nonetheless found considerable variation among racially and ethnically distinct populations (Aschenbrenner, 1973; Cooney, 1979; Staples and Mirande, 1980). Without dismissing an economic or class explanation, these studies suggest that cultural factors among Blacks are vital in making living arrangement choices. Thus it is quite reasonable to accept the argument that a major strength of the Black family is strong kinship bonds (Hill, 1971).

There is a tendency to characterize Hispanic families as more familistic than the general population (Keefe, 1980). Hispanics are perceived as valuing family relationships so that collective familial needs take precedence over individual needs. Moreover, the Hispanic family is often portrayed as an extended family of several generations, including cousins. Some have noted that the Latin American family extends to godparenting ("compadrazgo"), which serves as a method of binding the community together and of formalizing friendship ties (Hayner, 1954). This characterization of the Hispanic family dominates the early literature, but it has recently been reevaluated (Mirande, 1977; Moore and Pachon, 1985).

One major problem with the conception of the traditional Hispanic family is that traditionalism is also a function of class status. In one study of San Antonio and Los Angeles (Moore, 1976:131) respondents were asked: "Is it important to live near the parents, even if it means losing a good job opportunity?" and, "Is it better to hire a relative rather than a stranger?" The majority disapproved of familism at the expense of economic efficiency. But poorer Chicanos were more likely than middle-income Chicanos to emphasize familism. Familism is thus often explained as economically helpful in the poorer areas of large cities, and in rural communities where people are tied to the land. Tienda and Angel (1982) emphasized economic factors in arguing that the incorporation of nonnuclear members into households encouraged creative income strategies to cope with economic hardship. Similarly, evidence available shows that the presence of nonnuclear adults in the household facilitates the labor force participation of women by relieving domestic burdens (Tienda and Glass, 1985).

It is unrealistic to expect "traditional" values to solely account for how Hispanics behave in major social institutions (e.g., the family). But it is equally unrealistic to overlook the fact that for Hispanics, the family is a significant source of pride. Although traditionalism is also a function of class status, research shows that Hispanics are more traditional relative to native whites, have more traditional values, and perceive themselves as being more traditional. In a study of Chicano heroin addicts, Moore and Mata (1982) asked if they agreed with the statement, "Girls with a bad reputation as a teenager will have a hard time changing it." Only 27 percent agreed. But when asked what they thought "most Chicanos" would think, 59 percent felt that other Chicanos would agree. The same disparities were found when asked about work roles and the primacy of the family.

Caring for the elderly is a good example of the continuation of family respect and attention to the aged members of Hispanic families. In Los Angeles, Mexican Americans are far more likely than the white or Black elderly to interact with children and grandchildren, and the same is true for

Puerto Rican elderly in New York City (Bengtson, 1979; Cantor, 1979). It was also found that Puerto Rican elderly receive more help from their children than do Black or white elderly.

The minority experience may be at least as significant in affecting values as is the particular cultural heritage. In a study of Chicano, Black and Anglo migrants to Wisconsin, Shannon and Shannon (1973) reported that Mexican-American and Black migrants have a very similar world view, and it is dramatically different from the world view of Anglo Americans. In a pilot study of living arrangement choices among Puerto Ricans, Blacks, and whites in New York, I found that Puerto Ricans and Blacks made similar living arrangements choices, but differently from whites. Both studies found the same results when income was controlled. These studies suggest that although cultural value patterns are highly responsive to economic circumstances, Blacks and Hispanics still exhibit different family values than do whites.

## Hypotheses

Taken together, our argument has been that the monetary costs of housing represent a major constraint on living arrangements. Access to relatives reduces this constraint because relatives may be able to offer housing below market costs. Since the availability of relatives decreases with age (Kobrin, 1981), younger adults should be less likely to live alone or with nonrelatives. Moreover, the availability of relatives varies by marital status, since marriage creates new family bonds. Thus, the formerly married should more frequently live with relatives.

Since separate households are more expensive to maintain, access to resources is a central factor in living arrangement choices. Personal income is an appropriate indicator of financial ability to maintain a separate household. For individuals with low levels of income, living with relatives may present a strategy for escaping poverty. Alternatively, it is expected that those with more income will be more likely to live alone.

Education is an important social resource in modern society. It is likely that higher levels of educational attainment will increase one's ability to find housing and manage the responsibilities associated with maintaining an independent household. Chevan and Korson (1975) maintain that education promotes individualism over family-oriented values, and show that the proportion of women living alone increases with education, even when controlling for income. But others (Christenson and Slesinger, 1986) find little difference among educational levels in the likelihood for widows to live alone. When considering the unattached as a whole (as opposed to only widows) and the fact that education and ability to speak English are closely tied for many Hispanic groups, education is likely to have a significant effect on living arrangement choices.

Finally, different norms and preferences represent the third component in determining living arrangements. Kobrin (1981: 372) suggests that gender is an indicator of this dimension since "research shows that women take more responsibility for maintaining family ties than men." But of primary interest is the suggestion that cultural traditions differentially encourage individuals to live with family rather than live alone or with nonrelatives. Ethnic and racial variations in family norms may encourage differential preferences for living alone, since the family systems of minority groups may retain the traditional protective functions associated with the extended family, when minority groups are slower to modernize their family systems (Chevan and Korson, 1975:510).

Individuals who have immigrated to the United States, particularly recent immigrants, are less likely to live in a nonfamily arrangement than the native-born, since they are more dependent on family ties for emotional and social support. By placing a greater emphasis on family relationships (e.g., family reunification) as a basis for selection of immigrants, the 1965 Immigration Act inevitably reinforced dependence on family ties (Keely, 1980). Christenson and Slesinger (1986) indeed found that recency of immigration negatively influences the likelihood of living alone for widows in the United States. Ability to speak English should also be an important factor in choosing living arrangements; individuals who have difficulty using English should be less likely to live alone or with nonrelatives.

Another factor we want to consider for Hispanics is place of residence. Hispanics consist of Mexican Americans concentrated in the Southwest, Puerto Ricans living mainly in New York and New Jersey, Cubans concentrated in Florida, and "Other Hispanics" scattered throughout (Davis et al., 1983). Do Mexican Americans in the Southwest make living arrangement choices differently from those of Mexicans living elsewhere? Do Cubans in Florida make different housing choices compared with Cubans in non-Cuban areas? And how about Puerto Ricans? One might hypothesize that in areas of Mexican, Puerto Rican, and Cuban concentration, individuals will be less likely to live alone or with nonrelatives. In these areas, the family's control over individuals and cultural traditions in favor of family living are much stronger. Moreover, there are likely to be more relatives to live with in these areas.

## Data and Methods

To test these hypotheses, we use data from the one percent sample of U.S. households recorded in the A-sample of the Public-Use micro-data (PUMS) file of the 1980 Census. The individuals selected from the file live in households, are over age 25, and are neither married, nor the head of a family or subfamily with own children less than age 18. Persons in school are excluded. A random sample of individuals that oversamples smaller minority groups was drawn from the PUMS file. This procedure was based on a random selection of 25 percent of non-Hispanic whites, but 100 percent of Hispanics and non-Hispanic Blacks. The resulting sample consists of 8,596 persons.

This selection process was based on the argument that "unattached" individuals, by being less constrained by other choice or characteristics, will have a variety of choices in living arrangements (Kobrin, 1981). Individuals over age 25 were selected since most children will have left the parental home by then. Married persons and those with minor children were excluded as were students. The married tend to maintain separate households; students tend to be younger and living with parents, and the financial limitations of student status is an additional constraint on living arrangements choices.

The dependent variable was constructed as a dichotomy, distinguishing between family and nonfamily living arrangements. Individuals may either live alone or with nonrelatives in a nonfamily living arrangement or may join or form families of related persons.

The factors affecting this choice are personal income, gender, marital status, age, education, ability to speak English, nativity, place of residence (for Hispanics), and racial/ethnic origin. Income includes all earned and other income in 1979 and was treated as the natural logarithm to reduce skewness. Gender is treated as a dummy variable with males as the reference group.

Marital statuses identified by the Census include never married, divorced, separated, and widowed. The separated and the divorced are combined and the never married were used as the reference group. Age is divided into five categories: Young (25-44), Middle Age (45-64), Young Old (65-74), Old (75-84), and Old Old (85+). The reference category is middle age. Since age and living arrangements tend to show a strong nonlinear relationship, we treat age categories as dummy variables.

Education is indicated by four categories based on the highest year of school attended: 0 to 8 years of education; 9 to 11 years of education (some high school); 12 years of education (high school graduates) the reference category; and those who finished 13 or more years of education.

Self-reporting of English speaking ability in the Census includes five categories ranging from speaking only English to not speaking English at all. We dichotomized responses into those who reported that they only spoke English, or spoke English well or very well, under "English" (the reference category) and those who responded that they did not speak English at all or did not speak it well, categorized under "No English." Nativity is divided into the native-born and four categories of foreign-born, indicating recency of immigration. Born in the U.S. (native-born) serves as the reference group.

Racial/ethnic origins are coded into three main categories: Blacks, Hispanics, and whites. Blacks and whites are non-Hispanic, while the Hispanics are of various racial origins. Hispanics were categorized by national origin--Cuban, Mexican, Puerto Rican, and Other. Cubans living in Florida were coded as living in a Cuban region; Mexicans living in California, Arizona, New Mexico, Colorado, or Texas were coded as living in Mexican regions. Puerto Ricans living in New York or New Jersey were coded as living in Puerto Rican regions. For the three variables constructed

(Cuban Region, Mexican Region, and Puerto Rican Region), living in the respective non-ethnic region (e.g., Cubans in non-Cuban areas) serves as the reference group.

The analysis applies a multivariate regression model of living arrangement choices to each of the main racial/ethnic groups independently. The equation permits an estimation of the effects of income, marital status, gender, age, education, ability to speak English, and nativity on the probability of living alone or with nonrelatives rather than living with relatives for Blacks, Hispanics, and whites. The equation for Hispanics also includes national origin (Puerto Rican as reference group) to test for variations among Hispanics. The model is applied to each of the main Hispanic groups (Cubans, Mexicans, and Puerto Ricans) independently, in order to further investigate how each group makes living arrangement choices. The model is not applied to Other Hispanics since this group is much too heterogeneous to derive any reasonable generalizations from the analysis. In addition, in data not presented, the full model was applied to the entire population in order to test statistically for differences between racial/ethnic groups in the ways other factors affect living arrangements. This allows us to find whether the factors affecting living arrangement choices differ for Blacks and Hispanics in comparison to whites.

The multivariate analyses used are based on ordinary least squares (OLS). OLS estimation with dummy dependent variables may present difficulties and logistic regression can be used to avoid these problems (Hanushek and Jackson, 1977). However, differences between OLS and logistic regression are likely to be large only when the dependent variable is skewed--with one category having less than 20 percent of the cases (Goodman, 1976). Since the means for nonfamily living in our population vary between 46 and 65 percent by racial/ethnic group, the two types of estimates are not expected to differ greatly. Thus OLS is used for simplicity, and in order to utilize the R squared(s) (not available with logistic regression) as a measure of the model's sensitivity to each of the racial/ethnic groups.

## Ethnic and Racial Differences

Table 2-1 presents variation in nonfamily living arrangements by age and racial/ethnic origin. About half of the total group lives alone or with nonrelatives, with moderate racial/ethnic variation ranging from 64.6 percent overall for whites to 49.2 percent for Hispanics. The three groups follow a similar age pattern in their living arrangements: there are increases in living away from family from age 45 through age 74, and then a decline occurs. Overall, Blacks seen most sensitive to age, Hispanics least, and whites intermediate. But these similarities and differences may be accounted for by the composition of these populations or by the structure of the relationships. In order to get a better picture, the full living arrangements model is applied to each group.

### Table 2-1

**AGE PATTERNS OF NONFAMILY LIVING ARRANGEMENTS FOR WHITES, BLACKS, AND HISPANICS IN THE UNITED STATES, 1980**

|  | Percent Living Away from Family | | |
|---|---|---|---|
| Age | Whites | Blacks | Hispanics |
| Young (25–44) | 65.3 | 48.2 | 49.0 |
| Middle age (44–64) | 63.5 | 51.1 | 48.8 |
| Young old (65–74) | 71.5 | 61.1 | 54.8 |
| Old (75–84) | 62.5 | 56.3 | 46.0 |
| Old old (85+) | 48.6 | 32.7 | 34.4 |
| Total | 64.6 | 51.4 | 49.2 |
| N | 3,115 | 4,189 | 1,292 |

NOTE: Individuals in households who are over 25 and who are neither married nor the head of a family or subfamily with own children less than 18. Persons in school are excluded.

SOURCE: 1980 PUMS A-Sample for the United States.

In comparing results among Blacks, Hispanics and whites, some major differences appear. Table 2-2 shows that, as expected, income has a strong and significant effect on the choice to live in a nonfamily arrangement. For whites, an increase of one unit in the natural log of income increases the probability of living away from family by 5.2 percent; this same change produces a 3.5 percent increase for Hispanics or Blacks. Sex did not have a significant impact on whites, but Hispanic and Black females were 12.3 percent and 10.2 percent less likely to live in a nonfamily arrangement than were males. Each of these differences is significant in the pooled analysis.

The divorced are more likely to live away from family than are the single, with no significant differences among the three racial/ethnic groups. The widowed are also more likely than the unmarried to live away from family, but only among Blacks and Whites. For Hispanics, widowhood has no significant effect on living arrangements.

Age seems to largely produce the same general curvilinear pattern observed in Table 2-1 for all three groups. Being young is not significantly different from being middle age in terms of living arrangements for any of the groups. Nonetheless, the regression coefficients for Young are negative for Blacks and Hispanics, as expected, and Black and Hispanic youths are more likely than are Whites to live with relatives (although only the Black

## Table 2-2

**EVALUATION OF A LIVING ARRANGEMENTS MODEL FOR WHITES, BLACKS, AND HISPANICS IN THE UNITED STATES, 1980: FACTORS IN LIVING AWAY FROM FAMILY**

| Variable | Unstandardized Regression Coefficient | | |
|---|---|---|---|
| | Whites | Blacks | Hispanics |
| Income[a] | .05217* | .03510* | .03335* |
| Female | −.02061 | −.10193* | −.12333* |
| Divorced | .13540* | .10877* | .12400* |
| Widowed | .17100* | .08331* | .05310 |
| Young | .03837 | −.02870 | −.03205 |
| Young old | .08865* | .11200* | .10967* |
| Old | −.00250 | .08932* | .01501 |
| Old old | −.09701* | −.12230* | −.07354 |
| 0–8 yrs education | −.03335 | .01164 | .00529 |
| 9–11 yrs education | .01347 | .00293 | .02885 |
| 13+ yrs education | .08774* | .09582* | .07824 |
| No English | −.14431 | −.02160 | −.07710* |
| Imm. early[b] | .07813 | −.07974 | .05085 |
| Imm. 1950–59 | .20386* | .01135 | −.03093 |
| Imm. 1960–69 | .10976 | .03733 | .12073* |
| Imm. 1970–80 | −.01799 | .13608* | .09084 |
| Mexican | — | — | −.08885* |
| Cuban | — | — | −.12494* |
| Other | — | — | −.03150 |
| Intercept | .06457 | .20372* | .27816* |
| $R^2$ | .09567 | .07127 | .08843 |
| F | 20.48359* | 20.01122* | 6.49437* |
| N | 3,115 | 4,189 | 1,292 |

[a]Natural logarithm of income.
[b]Before 1950.
*Significant at .05 level.
NOTE: Same population as Table 2-1.
SOURCE: Same as Table 2-1.

interaction is significant). The young-old are significantly more likely to live alone or with nonrelatives than the middle aged, with no significant differences among the three groups; the old-old reverses the life course patterns of increase for all three groups.

Individuals with higher levels of education were expected to be more likely to live alone. When compared with high school graduates, those who had 13 or more years of education (e.g., at least some college) were found to be significantly more likely to live in a nonfamily arrangement. Whereas whites and Blacks with 13 or more years of education were 8.8 percent and 9.6 percent more likely to live alone or with nonrelatives than their counterparts who only completed 12 years of education, no significant education effect was found for Hispanics. However, this appears to reflect differences in size among the three groups, since there are no significant differences among them in the effect of education (data not presented.) Not being able to speak English reduces the likelihood of living with relatives for all groups, although only significantly for Hispanics. Hispanics who did not speak English were 7.7 percent less likely to live alone or with nonrelatives than were Hispanics who spoke English.

Recency of immigration showed no clear influence on the living arrangement process. Although those who had immigrated to the U.S., particularly recent immigrants, were expected to be less likely to live in a nonfamily arrangement than native-born individuals, the data show that recency of immigration operated in the opposite direction, with somewhat different patterns for the different groups. For whites, those who immigrated to the U.S. between 1950 and 1959 were, in fact, 20.4 percent *more* likely to live in a nonfamily arrangement than were the native-born. Hispanics immigrating to the U.S. between 1960 and 1969 were 9.1 percent more likely to live alone or with nonrelatives than were native-born. Blacks who immigrated to the U.S. between 1970 and 1980 were 13.6 percent more likely to live in a nonfamily arrangement than were native-born Blacks. However, Hispanics are the only group where recency of immigration is a significant factor: those who immigrated between 1950 and 1959, were significantly less likely to live away from family than were their white counterparts.

Among Hispanics, national origin exhibited significant variations. Being Cuban or Mexican is significantly different from being Puerto Rican when choosing living arrangements. When everything else is held constant, Mexicans and Cubans are more likely than are Puerto Ricans to live with family members. Other Hispanics were not significantly different from Puerto Ricans.

In order to get a better picture of the variation among Hispanics, the full living arrangements model was applied to Mexicans, Puerto Ricans, and Cubans separately. As before, differences among these groups have been tested in the full model pooling Mexicans, Cubans, and Puerto Ricans; these data will be discussed but not presented in tabular form.

Data in Table 2-3 shows that, as expected, income has a significant effect on living arrangements choices for all three major Hispanic groups,

## Table 2-3

**EVALUATION OF A LIVING ARRANGEMENTS MODEL FOR MEXICANS, PUERTO RICANS, AND CUBANS IN THE UNITED STATES, 1980: FACTORS IN LIVING AWAY FROM FAMILY**

| Variable | Unstandardized Regression Coefficient | | |
|---|---|---|---|
| | Mexicans | Puerto Ricans | Cubans |
| Income[a] | .02249* | .04305* | .05136* |
| Female | −.12324* | −.18392* | −.09445 |
| Divorced | .17221* | .17528* | .04411 |
| Widowed | .14314* | .02589 | −.12323 |
| Young | −.03294 | −.07261 | −.00182 |
| Young old | .09037 | .24169 | .19620 |
| Old | .03492 | −.10863 | −.01019 |
| Old old | −.12969 | .22587 | −.05909 |
| 0–8 yrs education | −.08777 | −.08247 | .11379 |
| 9–11 yrs education | −.09332 | .14965 | .00986 |
| 13+ yrs education | .09727 | .10058 | .05962 |
| No English | .00455 | −.07275 | −.04628 |
| Imm. before 1950 | .04223 | — | .15867 |
| Imm. 1950–59 | −.21121* | .38309 | .08094 |
| Imm. 1960–69 | .17766 | −.15423 | .12352 |
| Imm. 1970–80 | .10195 | .44030* | .08933 |
| Mexican region | −.06945 | — | — |
| Puerto Rican region | — | .02456 | — |
| Cuban region | — | — | −.24416* |
| Intercept | .34086 | .20077 | .10012 |
| $R^2$ | .09408 | .18726 | .20760 |
| F | 3.84228* | 2.47692* | 1.78764* |
| n | 647 | 189 | 134 |

[a]Natural logarithm of income.
*Significant at .05 level.
NOTE: Same population as Table 2-1.
SOURCE: Same as Table 2-1.

although the differences that appear among these groups (showing that Mexicans are less responsive to income) are not significant. Mexican and Puerto Rican women are much less likely to live away from family than are their male counterparts, while gender matters little for Cubans. Again, these differences are not statistically significant.

Marital history shows some interesting differences among Hispanics. On the one hand, divorce produces a nonfamily effect for all groups (although only statistically significant for Mexicans and Puerto Ricans). Widowhood, however, has sharply different effects, increasing nonfamily living for Mexicans, relative to the single, but leading Cuban widows to be more likely to live with relatives than single Cubans, a significant difference.

Living in an ethnic region was only significant for Cubans, distinguishing them from the other groups. Cubans who live in Florida are much less likely to live alone or with nonrelatives than are Cubans who live in other parts of the U.S. But for Mexicans and Puerto Ricans, living in Mexican or Puerto Rican regions has no effect on living arrangement choices compared with living in non-Mexican or non-Puerto Rican regions.

Recency of immigration seems to significantly influence Mexicans who entered the U.S. between 1950 and 1959, and Puerto Ricans who entered between 1970 and 1980. The former are much less likely to live away from family than are native-born Mexicans, while the latter are much more likely to live away from family than are native-born Puerto Ricans. However, neither age, education, nor ability to speak English was significant for any of the three groups. Caution should be exercised in dismissing these effects because of the small number of cases, especially for Puerto Ricans and Cubans. For example, the unexpected regression coefficient for the Puerto Rican old old of .226 is due to the fact that only one observation is found for Puerto Ricans in that age group. No observations for Puerto Ricans entering the U.S. before 1950 were available. Moreover, in the equation for Hispanics in Table 2-2, Other Hispanics are included. These may account for some of the discrepancies between the equation for Hispanics in Tables 2-2 and Table 2-3.

Taking into account the limitations of the data, the findings point to differences among Mexicans, Puerto Ricans and Cubans in making living arrangement choices. Clearly it is misleading to analyze Hispanics as a whole when considering living arrangement choices. While income, sex, being divorced, and immigrating to the U.S. between 1950 and 1959 have similar effects on Cubans, Puerto Ricans, and Mexicans, widowed Cubans make living arrangement choices differently than Mexicans and Puerto Ricans: widowhood has a positive nonfamily effect for Mexicans and Puerto Ricans but a negative nonfamily effect for Cubans.

## Discussion

The results presented provide support for the argument that there are racial and ethnic variations in family norms and preferences for living alone. The fact that Blacks and Hispanics have different living arrangements than whites suggests the importance of group norms and preferences in determining choice of living arrangements. For all groups, the effect of resources on living arrangements is strong: those with higher income were more likely to live alone or with non-relatives, as were those with some college education. Also, there are general increases by age in living away from family which are consistent with the declines in close kin ties. But economic feasibility and availability of kin do not fully account for the observed patterns of living arrangements. Other factors affect the choice of whether to live with relatives or not, even when income is sufficient and relatives are available.

Thus, economic feasibility and kin availability cannot totally account for ethnic and racial variation in living arrangements. The divorced, having more available relatives than the never married, are less likely to live with relatives than are the single, even when controlling for income. Except for Cubans, the widowed are also less likely to live with family than are the single. These patterns suggest that the experience of marriage reinforces preferences for independence from extended family living for all but Cuban widows. Differences in living arrangements seem to reflect a set of family values and norms tied to ethnic communities which operate even when income and relatives are available.

The two-way interaction analysis suggests that Blacks and Hispanics are less likely to use economic resources to purchase privacy than are whites and widowhood operates less as a break from family for Hispanics and Blacks than it does for whites. Females are also more likely to live with family among Hispanics and Blacks, as are the younger Blacks. Older Blacks are more likely to live away from family than are their white counterparts. Such differences in living arrangements point to the need to go beyond demographic and economic factors to explore group norms and preferences in the complex process of living arrangements choices.

The analysis also suggests that a similar set of values and norms may be increasingly common to all Hispanic groups in the United States. The fact that Cubans, Mexicans, and Puerto Ricans generally make similar choices about living arrangements supports this conclusion, as well as the argument that Hispanics have become a national minority. Nevertheless, some of the differences among these Hispanic subgroups are quite significant. Each group has become part of the larger American population in a different manner. Each lived through different economic, political, and social conditions, and each has a different sense of its own identity. Mexican Americans became a minority not by immigrating or being brought to this country as slaves, but by conquest. Thus, many Hispanics in the Southwest trace their ancestry directly to Mexico. Others, such as the Hispanos of New Mexico, are descendants of the 16th century Spanish

Conquistadores and see themselves quite different from other "Mexican Americans." But the majority of today's Mexican-American population is the result of immigration in the 20th century, beginning in the 1900s with immigrants attracted north to work in the farmlands and to build the railroads of the Southwest. In the 1940s, the "bracero" program was designed to bring temporary workers in order to alleviate U.S. labor shortages during World War II. The program brought in 4.8 million Mexicans before its end in 1964 (Moore and Pachon, 1985). Fueled by legal and illegal immigration plus relatively high fertility, the Mexican-American population has continued to grow. The 1980 Census reports 8.7 million persons who identified themselves as Mexican American; they make up about 60 percent of the total Hispanic population of the U.S. (Davis et al., 1983).

Puerto Ricans have been U.S. citizens since the Jones Act of 1917, and can therefore travel freely between the island and the mainland. Yet less than 70,000 Puerto Ricans had settled on the mainland by the time the 1940 Census was taken (Davis et al., 1983). The sudden appearance of surplus airplanes and low-cost flights from Puerto Rico to New York City after World War II led to a burst of movement. Unemployment was rising on the island, whereas unskilled jobs were plentiful in the New York City area. The Puerto Ricans population on the mainland quadrupled between 1940 and 1950 and tripled again by 1960 (Rodriguez, 1974). The 1980 Census reports about two million Puerto Ricans living on the mainland, primarily in New York and New Jersey (Davis et al., 1983).

Before Castro overthrew the regime of Flugencio Batista in 1959, fewer than 50,000 Cubans lived in the U.S. But the first wave of exiles after the Cuban Revolution brought an estimated 260,000 largely affluent, professional Cubans to the United States. Cuban immigration was temporarily ended in 1962, following the Cuban missile crisis. An airlift agreed upon by Castro and the Johnson Administration in 1965 brought in 344,000 additional Cubans, until Castro ended emigration in 1973. Thousands more arrived by small boats or through Mexico or Spain in the subsequent years. A third wave of 125,000 Cubans arrived in the Mariel boatlift of 1980. The Cubans who arrived in the United States after more than a decade of socialism were noticeably different from the earlier immigrants. There were more black Cubans, and people of lower-middle-class and blue-collar backgrounds predominated (Perez, 1980). As a result, Cubans living in the U.S. have come more and more to reflect the pre-revolutionary Cuban social class structure. The 1980 U.S. Census reported about 800,000 Cubans living in the United States, with over half in Florida (Davis et al., 1983).

Hispanics as a whole are younger and have higher fertility than the total U.S. population. Whereas the median age for the Hispanic population was 23 years, compared to 30 years for the total U.S. population in 1980, the median age for Cubans was 41 years (Davis et al., 1983). Cubans have lower fertility than other Hispanics and below that of non-Hispanic women. Some of these demographic differences may partially explain why only the Cuban widowed (in contrast to other Hispanic groups and Blacks and whites) are more likely to live with relatives than are the single. It may well be that an older and lower fertility population is more willing and able to take care of the elderly and the widowed than a younger and higher fertility population. Despite these demographic differences, there seem to be enough similarities in the life experiences of Hispanic Americans to argue that they increasingly represent one large national minority.

All Hispanic groups lag behind the U.S. averages in occupational status and educational attainment and all segments of the Hispanic population are predominantly urban, facing problems common to urban-based immigrant minorities. Moreover, Hispanics are beginning to disperse outside of their traditional areas of residence. Mexican Americans are increasingly located in northern industrial cities, such as Chicago and Detroit, as well as in the Southwest; Puerto Ricans are increasing living in industrial cities in the Northeast and Midwest outside of New York. Cubans are residing in large colonies in New York, New Jersey, Chicago, and Los Angeles, as well as in Florida (Moore and Pachon, 1985).

Perhaps most importantly, the Hispanic populations are increasingly being treated by the larger society as one ethnic group, with common problems and concerns. As a result, Hispanics are beginning to think of themselves as sharing common problems. Political interest in bilingual education is a good example of how distinct Hispanic populations have worked together to benefit all Hispanics.

Given these trends, it is not surprising that Cubans, Mexicans, and Puerto Ricans generally have similar living arrangements. These findings suggest that the distinct Hispanic minorities in the United States are converging toward one Hispanic model. Processes of minority convergence have analytic importance as well as critical political and social implications that require detailed research.

## REFERENCES

Aschenbrenner, J. 1973. "Extended Families Among Black Americans." *Journal of Comparative Family Studies* 4:257-268.

Belcher, J.C. 1967. "The One-person Household: A Consequence of the Isolated Nuclear Family?" *Journal of Marriage and the Family* 29:534-540.

Bengtson, V. 1979. "Ethnicity and Aging: Problems and Issues in Current Social Science Inquiry," in Gelfand and Kutzik, eds. *Ethnicity and Aging*. New York: Springer.

Beresford, J.C. and A.H. Rivlin. 1966. "Privacy, Poverty, and Old Age." *Demography* 3:247-258.

Bott, Elizabeth. 1964. "Conjugal Roles and Social Networks," in R.L. Coser, ed., *The Family: Its Structure and Functions*. New York: St. Martin's Press.

Burch, T.K. 1970. "Some Demographic Determinants of Average Household Size: An Analytic Approach." *Demography*, 7:61-70.

Burgess, E.W. 1960. "Aging in Western Culture," in Ernest W. Burgess, ed. *Aging in Western Societies*. University of Chicago Press.

Cantor, M. 1979. "The Informal Support System of New York's Inner-city Elderly: Is Ethnicity a Factor?" in Gelfand and Kutzik, eds., *Ethnicity and Aging*. New York: Springer.

Chevan, Albert and J.H. Korson. 1972. "The Widowed Who Live Alone: An Examination of Social and Demographic Factors." *Social Forces*, 51:45-53.

Chevan, Albert and J.H. Korson. 1975. "Living Arrangements of Widows in the United States and Israel, 1960 and 1961." *Demography*, 12:505-518.

Christenson, B.A. and D.P. Slesinger. 1986. "Effect of Race, Ethnicity, and Poverty on the Living Arrangements of Widows in the United States." Paper prepared for the 1986 Annual Meeting of the Population Association of America, San Francisco, California.

Cohen, A.K. and H.M. Hodes. 1963. "Characteristics of the Lower-Blue-Collar Class." *Social Problems* (Spring):303-334.

Cooney, R. 1979. "Demographic Components of Growth in White, Black and Puerto Rican Female Headed Families: A Comparison of the Cutright & Ross and Sawhill Methodologies." *Social Science Research* 8:144-158.

Davis, D.C., Carl Haub and Joanne Willette. 1983. "U.S. Hispanics: Changing the Face of America." *Population Bulletin* Vol. 38, No. 3, Population Reference Bureau, Inc.: Washington, DC.

Elder, Glen H., Jr. 1978. "Approaches to Social Change and the Family," in John Demos and Sarane Boocock, eds., *Turning Points*. Chicago: University of Chicago Press.

Feagin, Joe. 1968. "The Kinship Ties of Negro Urbanities." *Social Science Quarterly* 49 (December):660-665.

Frazier, E. F. 1966. *The Negro Family in the United States*. Chicago: University of Chicago.

Freedman, Ronald et al. 1978. "Household Composition and Extended Kinship in Taiwan." *Population Studies* 32 (1):65-80.

Goode, William J. 1963. *World Revolution and Family Patterns*. New York: Free Press.

Goodman, C.A. 1976. "The Relationship between Modified and Usual Multiple-Regression Approaches to the Analysis of Dichotomous Variables," in D. Heise, ed., *Sociological Methodology*. San Francisco: Jossey-Bass.

Grier, W.H. and P.M. Cobbs. 1968. *Black Rage*. New York: Basic Books.

Hanushek, E.A. and J.E. Jackson. 1977. *Statistical Methods for Social Scientists*.

Hayner, N.S. 1956. "The Family in Mexico." *Marriage and Family Living* 16:369-373.

Hill, Robert B. 1971. *The Strength of Black Families*. New York: Emerson Hall Publishers.

Hughes, M. and W.R. Gove. 1981. "Living Alone, Social Integration, and Mental Health." *American Journal of Sociology* 87:48-74.

Keely, Charles. 1980. "Immigration Policy and the New Immigrants, 1965-1975," in Roy S. Bryce-Laporte, ed., *Sourcebook on the New Immigration*. Brunswick, NJ: Transaction Books.

Kobrin, F.E. 1976. "The Fall in Household Size and the Rise of the Primary Individual in the United States." *Demography* 13(1):127-138.

Kobrin, F.E. 1981. "Family Extension and the Elderly: Economic, Demographic, and Family Cycle Factors." *Journal of Gerontology* 36(3):370-377.

Kobrin F. and C. Goldscheider. 1982. "Family Extension or Nonfamily Living: Life Cycle, Economic, and Ethnic Factors." *Western Sociological Review* 13(1):103-118.

Laslett, P. 1972. "Introduction: The History of the Family," in P. Laslett, ed., *Household and Family in Past Time*. London: Cambridge University Press.

Levy, M. 1965. "Aspects of the Analysis of Family Structure," in A.J. Coale et al., eds., *Aspects of the Analysis of Family Structure*. Princeton: Princeton University Press.

Lopata, Helena. 1971. "Living Arrangements of American Urban Widows." *Social Forces* 5:41-61.

Michael, Robert T., Victor R. Fuchs, and Sharon R. Scott. 1980. "Changes in the Propensity to Live Alone: 1950-1976." *Demography* 17:39-53.

Mirande, A. 1977. "The Chicano Family: A Reanalysis of Conflicting Views." *Journal of Marriage and the Family* 39 (November):747-756.

Moore, Joan. 1976. *Mexican Americans*. Englewood Cliffs, NJ: Prentice-Hall.

Moore, J. and Alberto Mata. 1982. *Women and Heroin in Chicano Communities*. Los Angeles: Chicano Pinto Research Project.

Moore, J. and Harry Pachon. 1985. *Hispanics in the United States*. Englewood Cliffs, NJ: Prentice-Hall.

Moynihan, D.P. 1965. *The Negro Family: A Call for National Action*. Washington: U.S. Department of Labor.

Pampel, Fred C. 1983. "Changes in the Propensity to Live Alone: Evidence from Consecutive Cross-Sectional Surveys, 1960-1976." *Demography* 20(4):433-447.

Parsons, Talcott and Winston White. 1961. "The Link Between Character and Society," in S. M. Lipset and Leo Lowenthal, eds., *Culture and Social Character*. Glencoe, IL: The Free Press.

Perez, Lisandro. 1980. "Cubans," in Stephan Thernstrom, ed., *The Harvard Encyclopedia of American Ethnic Groups*. Cambridge, MA: Belknap Press of Harvard University.

Rodriguez, Clara. 1974. *The Ethnic Queue in the U.S.: The Case of the Puerto Ricans*. San Francisco: R & E Associates.

Shannon L. and M. Shannon. 1973. *Minority Migrants in the Urban Community: Mexican-American and Negro Adjustments to Industrial Society*. Beverly Hills, CA: Sage.

Soldo, B. 1977. "Demographic Composition and Source of Temporal Variation in the Living Arrangements Among the Elderly." Paper presented at the 1977 Annual Meeting of the Population Association of America, St. Louis, Missouri.

Staples, R. and A. Mirande. 1980. "Racial and Cultural Variations Among American Families: A Decennial Review of the Literature on Minority Families." *Journal of Marriage and the Family* 42 (November): 887-903.

Tienda, Marta and R. Angel. 1982. "Headship and Household Composition among Blacks, Hispanics and Other Whites." *Social Forces* 61(2):508-531.

Tienda, Marta and Jennifer Glass. 1985. "Household Structure and Labor Force Participation of Black, Hispanic, and White Mothers." *Demography* 22(3):381-394.

# 3

# The Asian-American Traditional Household

## WILAWAN KANJANAPAN

Immigrants originating in Asia comprise a relatively large proportion of those who settled in the United States during the past two decades. Changes in American immigration laws in 1965 and the more recent arrival of refugee groups from Indochina have resulted in rapid growth for the Asian population. Asian Americans consist of over twenty groups, each differing in language, culture, and other attributes of ethnicity. The largest subgroups include the Chinese, Filipino, Japanese, Asian-Indian, Korean, and Vietnamese. The living arrangements patterns of these diverse groups of Asian Americans will be investigated in this chapter.

### Changes in Immigration to the U.S.

In order to provide some background, it is helpful to review immigration patterns to the United States. There has been a significant increase in the total number of legal immigrants admitted to the United States in the recent period and there have been changes in the national origins of immigrants. In this context, there has been a dramatic increase in the number of Asian immigrants and in their proportion to the total immigrant population.

Data in Table 3-1 show that the annual numbers of legal immigrants increased almost two-fold during the twenty-year period from 1961 to 1981. It rose from an average annual number of approximately 290,000 in the 1961 to 1965 period to about 547,000 from 1978 to 1981. This trend of rising immigration to the United States has been viewed as a result of three major developments (Massey, 1981). First, the implementation of the 1965 Amendments to the Immigration and Nationality Act abolished the discriminatory national origin quota system and replaced it with an ethnic-blind preference system. Second, the fall of American-supported governments in Cuba and Indochina produced a large number of refugees seeking entry to the United States. Third, a world-wide pattern of international labor migration emerged.

### Table 3-1

**LEGAL IMMIGRANTS ADMITTED TO THE UNITED STATES, BY REGION OF BIRTH**

| Region | 1961–1965 | 1966–1968 | 1969–1973 | 1974–1977 | 1978–1981 |
|---|---|---|---|---|---|
| Average Annual Number of Immigrants (in thousands) | | | | | |
| Europe | 122 | 133 | 103 | 79 | 68 |
| Asia | 22 | 54 | 104 | 152 | 235 |
| North America | 119 | 165 | 140 | 166 | 188 |
| South America | 24 | 21 | 21 | 27 | 38 |
| Africa | 3 | 4 | 7 | 8 | 13 |
| Oceania | 1 | 2 | 3 | 4 | 4 |
| Total | 290 | 380 | 377 | 436 | 547 |
| Percentage Distribution for Each Period | | | | | |
| Europe | 42 | 35 | 27 | 18 | 12 |
| Asia | 8 | 14 | 28 | 35 | 43 |
| North America | 41 | 43 | 37 | 38 | 34 |
| South America | 8 | 6 | 6 | 6 | 7 |
| Africa | 1 | 1 | 2 | 2 | 2 |
| Oceania | 0 | 1 | 1 | 1 | 1 |
| Total | 100 | 100 | 100 | 100 | 100 |

NOTE: The sums of the subtotals are slightly different from the total due to rounding error.
SOURCE: U.S. Department of Justice (1981, 1975, 1974, 1973, 1972, 1970).

In addition to the increase in absolute numbers of immigrants, there have been significant changes in the region of origin of immigrants. In the period prior to the 1965 Immigration Act, about 122,000 European immigrants arrived annually. However, in the more recent period (1978-1981), European immigration declined to about 68,000 per year, from 42 percent of the total immigrant population in the pre-1965 period to 12 percent in more recent years (1978-1981).

During these two decades, a dramatic shift occurred in Asian immigration, in numbers as well as in proportions of the total immigrant population. Pre-1965 Asian figures were at about 22,000 per year, only 8 percent of the total immigration stream. In the most recent period (1978-1981), the average annual Asian immigration rate increased significantly to about 235,000 per year, accounting for 43 percent of the total immigration population. This figure represents the highest proportion of immigrants from any region in the world.

The basic change in immigration patterns in the recent period occurred as a result of alterations in U.S. immigration policy. It began with the new Immigration Act of 1965, which was a comprehensive restructuring of U.S. immigration legislation. The new act replaced the biased and restrictive National Origins Quota Act of 1924 and further elaborated the preference system of the McCarren-Walter Act of 1952. Family reunification was the main target of preferred immigration, with secondary allowances for occupational skills and refugee status. More specifically, the 1965 Amendments assigned annual quotas of 120,000 persons for the Western Hemisphere regions and 170,000 persons for the Eastern Hemisphere areas. Within this general quota system, there is no national origin quota other than a limitation of 20,000 annual visas for each Eastern Hemisphere country.

The principal Asian beneficiaries of these new immigration regulations were natives from China (including Taiwan and Hong Kong), India, Japan, Korea, and the Philippines. Their share of the immigrant flow to the United States increased from approximately 5 percent between 1961 and 1965 to over 20 percent during the 1978-1981 period (U.S. Department of Justice, 1961-1977). The proportionate and numerical increases of immigrants born in these countries reflect the chain-migration of family members and relatives as well as manpower mobility (Boyd, 1974).

## Ethnic Differentials in Living Arrangements

Asian immigrants deserve increased attention not only because of their mounting visibility, but also because a large proportion of them are new arrivals, different in character from older immigrants (Wong, 1985). Although it may be informative to discuss Asian immigrants in general, there are important differences among the Chinese, Japanese, Filipino, Korean, Asian Indian, Vietnamese and others in their socio-economic and demographic characteristics as well as their language and customs (Wong and Hirschman, 1983). Placing these different groups into one category of "Asian immigrants" masks their diversity in various characteristics and adjustment processes.

The examination of ethnic differentials in household composition and living arrangements patterns is very complex. Groups differ in their age-sex structure, their social and economic characteristics, as well as their family-related norms and values. Therefore, ethnic differences in residential choices may reflect any or all these factors. It has been found, for example, that white-nonwhite differences in family structure are mainly due to socio-economic class (Carliner, 1974; Ross and Sawhill, 1976). Differences in the family patterns of white ethnics in the United States have been linked to geographic mobility (Kobrin and Goldscheider, 1978), and great variation in factors underlying preference for family extension among persons of eastern European origin has been documented (Kobrin and Goldscheider, 1982). Detailed analyses of Spanish origin groups in American society have found a significantly greater probability of co-residence, especially for male-headed households (Angel and Tienda, 1982; Tienda and Angel, 1982). It is therefore important to investigate factors which determine residential choices for the more recently formed Asian-

American ethnic groups.

In the United States, highly diversified living arrangements patterns have emerged. This is especially true for people without the immediate family tie of a spouse and/or minor child. Whereas almost all married couples maintain a separate household (Kobrin, 1976), and most single-parent families do the same (Sweet, 1972), adults who are not in these categories still exhibit a variety of household patterns, including living alone, joining others to extend their families, or combining with friends or acquaintances.

One model of household composition and living arrangements postulates that three sets of factors affect residential choices of non-nuclear adults over the life cycle (Kobrin and Goldscheider, 1982): constraints, resources, and preferences. The first set refers to the availability or accessibility of households that contain relatives. If there are no relatives available, the choice of living arrangements is reduced. The availability of relatives varies over the stages of life cycle--by age and marital status. Secondly, even if households with relatives are available for the non-nuclear family adult, the question is whether it is economically feasible to live independently. Forming a separate household may prove to be more costly than living with relatives. The degree of economic feasibility varies as well with life cycle stage and gender. The third dimension involves the issue of family norms and preferences. Preference for family cohesiveness may encourage co-residence of related persons while considerations emphasizing independence or privacy may make family extension less likely.

Previous investigations of living arrangement patterns of Asian ethnics have not incorporated each of these three sets of variables into the analyses, tending to overemphasize the existence of traditional values and norms related to family extension. Key variables such as age and marital status are often ignored. Moreover, there has been no effort to distinguish individual immigrants with the immediate family tie of a spouse and/or minor child from adults who are not nuclear family members in this sense. The present study will examine ethnic differentials in residential choices among non-nuclear adult immigrants of Asia origin, controlling for life cycle stage. Attempts will also be made to investigate whether choices of nonfamily living arrangements versus family extension are linked to duration of residence in American society (i.e., recent and long-term immigration).

**Data, Definitions, and Measurement**

The data for this analysis are drawn from the 1980 U.S. Census Public Use Microdata Sample (PUMS). This dataset comprises a one-percent sample of the foreign born U.S. population. For the purpose of the present study, only foreign born of Asian origins were selected. Consideration was also given only to individual immigrants in private households. Those who resided in group quarters or who were in institutions were excluded from the analysis. The sample yielded 22,106 individual immigrants originating in Asia.

This chapter uses the following definitions adopted in U.S. censuses:

*Household.* A household comprises all persons who occupy a "housing unit," that is a house, an apartment, or other group of rooms, or a single room that constitutes "separate living quarters." Households can be divided into:

1. *Family Household.* A family household includes the related family members and all unrelated persons, if any, such as lodgers, foster children, wards, or employees who share the housing unit.

2. *Nonfamily Household.* This term refers to a person living alone or a group of unrelated persons sharing the same housing unit.

The census categories that can be used to operationalize living arrangement types are fairly straightforward. Those living alone are primary individuals who are heads of separate households with no one else living in the housing unit. Nonrelatives include those living in households who are unrelated to the household head, and those primary individuals living with others. "Other relatives" are both all other relatives of the head (except child or spouse), and those, although unmarried and living with no own children, are heads of a family, consisting of one or more adult relatives. Children of the household head are treated as a separate category since their behavior is distinct from those who are "other relatives."

There are at least three criteria for classifying Asian ethnicity: race, ancestry, and place of birth. Previous studies often rely upon one of these criteria (for example, race - Gardner et al., 1985; place of birth - Boyd, 1974; ancestry - Pereira, 1985). These alternative bases of classification raise questions about reliability and validity. Since these categories are based on self-identification, how do they relate in different ways to social processes? Are there better ways to measure Asian immigrants to the United States? Moreover, given the complex nature of ethnicity, does reliance on a single measure distort reality? What are the possible combinations of ethnic variables derived from the census which can be used to study various Asian ethnic groups?

The population who identify themselves as Asian by race is homogeneous with respect to racial origin, ancestry, and place of birth as well as these three variables combined. The data show that out of the 2,087 foreign born persons who identified themselves as being Japanese by race, 1,958 or 94 percent reported having Japanese ancestry, and 1,981 persons or 95 percent were recorded as being born in Japan. When these three variables are combined so that ethnicity is defined as including not only race but also ancestry and place of birth, the proportion Japanese is reduced to 86 percent of those Japanese by race. The degree of homogeneity varies for other Asian groups. The analysis reveals that the Chinese, Vietnamese, and Asian Indians are less homogeneous than Korean, Japanese, and Filipino (Table 3-2).

Table 3-2

ASIAN IMMIGRANTS, BY RACE, ANCESTRY, PLACE OF BIRTH, AND ALL THREE VARIABLES COMBINED

| Ethnicity | Race Only (1) | Ancestry Only (2) | Place of Birth Only (3) | All Three Variables Combined (4) | Percent of Race (5)=(4)/(1) |
|---|---|---|---|---|---|
| Japanese | 2,087 | 1,976 | 1,981 | 1,812 | 86.7 |
| Chinese[a] | 5,187 | 5,249 | 4,430 | 4,123 | 79.5 |
| Filipino | 5,159 | 4,339 | 4,950 | 4,193 | 81.3 |
| Korean | 2,978 | 2,853 | 2,880 | 2,734 | 91.8 |
| Asian Indian[b] | 2,756 | 2,408 | 2,299 | 1,822 | 66.1 |
| Vietnamese | 2,209 | 1,749 | 3,294 | 1,664 | 75.3 |

[a]Includes China, Taiwan, Hong Kong, and Singapore.
[b]Includes India, Bangladesh, Pakistan, Sri Lanka, and Nepal.

These four classifications of Asian ethnicity were compared in order to examine whether differences emerge in household and individual characteristics. Table 3-3 presents the distributions of selected household and individual characteristics, namely, age, marital status, migration, and type of households for six major Asian ethnic groups, defined in four different ways (i.e., race, ancestry, place of birth, and all three combined). The data show close similarities in the distributions for each variable among the four measures used. For example, the proportion Japanese living in married-couple households varies from 71.8 percent to 72.6 percent, depending on the definition used. No substantial discrepancies are observed for other groups or for other measures observed.

In this chapter, race was used as a measure of Asian ethnicity. This was convenient, since the census questionnaire listed six Asian groups among possible answers plus the category "other" for Asian responses. As discussed in previous research which relied upon this measure (Gardner et. al., 1985), such classification by race may present some problems. Census data based on racial self-identification may be less valid if attitudes about race changes and census procedures do not allow a person to be counted as belonging to a mixed race. The census provides no information on how many individuals reported they were of mixed race. Nevertheless, this appears to be a straightforward way of determining who is Asian.

The analysis will examine Asian ethnic differentials in living arrangement patterns. To meet this objective, comparisons will be made of household patterns by life cycle stage and migration status for the six largest Asian ethnic groups. Variations in residential arrangements among these groups will be identified and factors determining differences in household patterns of these individual immigrants will be analyzed.

Table 3-3

**PERCENTAGE DISTRIBUTION OF SOME SELECTED VARIABLES BY RACE, ANCESTRY, PLACE OF BIRTH, AND ALL THREE VARIABLES COMBINED**

| Variables | Race Only | Ancestry Only | Place of Birth Only | All Three Variables Combined |
|---|---|---|---|---|
| *Percent Living in Married-Couple Households* | | | | |
| Japanese | 71.8 | 72.0 | 72.6 | 72.1 |
| Chinese | 76.9 | 77.2 | 78.9 | 78.9 |
| Filipino | 80.4 | 81.0 | 80.7 | 81.1 |
| Korean | 84.8 | 85.0 | 84.7 | 85.1 |
| Asian Indian | 83.5 | 85.6 | 84.8 | 86.1 |
| Vietnamese | 73.3 | 73.1 | 71.7 | 72.7 |
| *Percent Population Below Age 25* | | | | |
| Japanese | 20.1 | 19.7 | 20.1 | 19.6 |
| Chinese | 26.3 | 27.4 | 23.0 | 23.8 |
| Filipino | 26.0 | 26.0 | 25.5 | 25.5 |
| Korean | 39.5 | 39.0 | 39.6 | 39.2 |
| Asian Indian | 29.5 | 28.8 | 26.3 | 25.0 |
| Vietnamese | 54.3 | 52.9 | 55.6 | 53.1 |
| *Percent Immigrants Arriving During 1975–1980* | | | | |
| Japanese | 33.6 | 34.3 | 34.1 | 34.1 |
| Chinese | 37.6 | 40.9 | 34.9 | 34.9 |
| Filipino | 34.1 | 33.1 | 33.9 | 33.1 |
| Korean | 52.3 | 52.3 | 52.4 | 52.7 |
| Asian Indian | 46.0 | 47.4 | 46.5 | 45.7 |
| Vietnamese | 92.0 | 90.9 | 91.6 | 90.7 |

## Household Types

Family households are subdivided into three categories according to types of head, namely, married-couple, male head without spouse present, and female head without husband present. Nonfamily households are either one person living alone or non-related persons sharing the housing unit together.

Table 3-4 displays the percentage distribution of individual immigrants by household type for six Asian ethnic groups. The majority of each group reside in family households headed by a married couple. Comparisons among six Asian racial groups show that Koreans and Asian Indians have the highest proportions of individuals living in married-couple headed households (86.1% and 84.6%, respectively), while Japanese and Vietnamese exhibit the lowest percentages (74.7% and 74.1%), respectively. Those of Chinese and Filipino ethnicity occupy the intermediate position.

The Japanese have a relatively low proportion of individuals residing in married-couple headed households but a high percentage live in nonfamily households (15.8%). Chinese immigrants also have a relatively high proportion in nonfamily households (10.3%) followed by Asian-Indians (9%). A different pattern is found for Vietnamese. Substantially larger proportions of Vietnamese are reported as living in households without spouse (10.4% for family household with male householder, no wife present and 10.1% for family household with female householder, no husband present). Similar to Korean immigrants, nonfamily living is uncommon for Vietnamese. Only five percent of Vietnamese and Korean immigrants reside in nonfamily households. These findings are consistent with prior research documenting that the vast majority of Vietnamese refugees came to the United States in family groups (Kelly, 1977) and suggest that these families remain together in the United States. Nevertheless, major ethnic differences in living arrangements characterize Asian immigrants to the United States.

**Table 3-4**

**LIVING ARRANGEMENTS OF ASIAN IMMIGRANTS BY HOUSEHOLD TYPE, 1980**

| Household Type | Japanese | Chinese | Filipino | Korean | Asian Indian | Vietnamese |
|---|---|---|---|---|---|---|
| Married-couple family household | 74.7 | 80.0 | 82.2 | 86.1 | 84.6 | 74.4 |
| Family household with male householder, no wife present | 1.8 | 3.9 | 3.3 | 2.4 | 3.2 | 10.4 |
| Family household with female householder, no husband present | 7.7 | 5.9 | 7.7 | 6.5 | 3.3 | 10.1 |
| Nonfamily household[a] | 15.8 | 10.3 | 6.8 | 5.0 | 9.0 | 5.1 |
| Total | 100.0 | 100.0 | 100.0 | 100.0 | 100.0 | 100.0 |
| N | 2,008 | 4,989 | 5,044 | 2,933 | 2,720 | 2,177 |

[a]This term refers to a person living alone or a group of unrelated persons sharing the same housing unit as partners.

## Household Size and Composition

Using the household as a unit of analysis, Table 3-5 shows the

## Table 3-5

## HOUSEHOLD SIZE AND COMPOSITION OF ASIAN IMMIGRANTS, 1980

| Household Indicator | Japanese | Chinese | Filipino | Korean | Asian Indian | Vietnamese |
|---|---|---|---|---|---|---|
| Householders by Type (percent) | | | | | | |
| Family householders, male | 49.3 | 74.4 | 76.2 | 76.2 | 78.9 | 75.2 |
| Family householders, female | 14.0 | 5.9 | 8.7 | 9.0 | 2.9 | 12.1 |
| Nonfamily householders | 36.6 | 19.6 | 15.1 | 14.8 | 18.2 | 12.7 |
| Household Members by Relationship to Householder (percent) | | | | | | |
| Householder | 34.4 | 36.7 | 32.8 | 26.2 | 39.4 | 22.4 |
| Spouse | 40.9 | 27.5 | 27.2 | 31.5 | 28.0 | 18.2 |
| Child | 13.2 | 20.2 | 21.4 | 32.9 | 22.3 | 39.8 |
| Other relative | 6.5 | 11.1 | 15.0 | 7.3 | 7.9 | 13.6 |
| Nonrelative | 5.0 | 4.4 | 3.7 | 2.1 | 2.4 | 6.0 |
| Average Persons per Household by Type of Householder | | | | | | |
| All types of households | 2.4 | 3.3 | 3.8 | 3.4 | 3.2 | 4.4 |
| Married-couple family household | 3.2 | 3.8 | 4.4 | 3.9 | 3.7 | 5.1 |
| Family household with male householder, no wife present | 2.6 | 3.1 | 3.3 | 2.8 | 3.1 | 3.8 |
| Family household with female householder, no husband present | 3.0 | 3.3 | 3.5 | 3.1 | 3.3 | 4.1 |
| Nonfamily households | 1.2 | 1.3 | 1.3 | 1.2 | 1.2 | 1.5 |

distribution of households by type for the six Asian ethnic groups. The results are consistent with the earlier findings. The Japanese ethnics have the highest proportion of nonfamily households (36.6%); approximately one-fifth of Chinese private households are nonfamily households. This type of household appears to be the least common among Vietnamese, accounting for 12.7% of all private households.

Another type of private household which has received increased attention are those headed by women. This category of households has been viewed as a measure of family instability. In the United States, the number of female-headed households has been growing very rapidly especially among Blacks (37.7% in 1984). For the foreign born among Asian minorities, the figures, while far below the level of Blacks, vary substantially: The highest levels are for the Japanese (14%) and for the Vietnamese (12%). In contrast, this type of household is very rare for Asian-Indians, accounting for about three percent of all private households. Korean, Filipino, and Chinese are intermediate, in that less than 10% have this type of household.

Substantial differences in average household size may also be observed among the six groups in this table. Japanese immigrant households are smallest on average (2.4 persons per household). Households of Asian Indians and Chinese are 3.2 and 3.3 persons, respectively and Korean and Filipino households are somewhat larger, containing 3.4 persons and 3.8 persons, on average. Vietnamese households are the largest at 4.4 persons per household. Ethnic differentials in average household size persist even when controlling for type of household head.

In addition to average household size, the household composition of Asian ethnics is examined using data on relationship to household head. Diverse patterns emerge among these six groups. In Japanese households, a small proportion are children (13%) compared with almost 40 percent of the Vietnamese. Family extension as evidenced by the incorporation of other relatives and non-relatives into households is more prevalent among Chinese, Vietnamese, and Filipino than among other Asian immigrants. The proportion who are other relatives in households ranges from 15% of the Filipino to 7% of the Japanese; the proportion who are non-relatives of the household head is higher among the Vietnamese and Japanese (6% and 5%, respectively) than Korean (21%) and Asian-Indian (2.4%).

**Nonfamily Living Versus Family Extension**

In order to assess ethnic differentials in the extent of family extension and nonfamily living, we focus on adult immigrants who are 18 years and over and not currently married. These individual immigrants will be called the "unattached." The categories which are used to operationalize living arrangements are: living alone, nonrelative of head, child of head, and other relative of head.

Table 3-6 presents data on living arrangements of the unattached by sex for six Asian born groups. Ethnic differences in residential patterns are clearly evident. About half of the unattached Japanese males live alone, followed by the Asian-Indian ethnics with more than one-third of the unattached residing in one-person households. In sharp contrast, 11% of the Vietnamese live alone and 19% of the Korean and Filipino males live alone. The tendency to live as nonrelative of head is high for Japanese and Vietnamese males (25% and 29%, respectively). Unfortunately, the operationalization did not allow us to distinguish between two types of living arrangements: those residing in households but unrelated to the household head; and those primary individuals living with others.

There are variations in the extent of living as child of head for unattached adults of these six Asian ethnic groups. Japanese immigrants show the smallest proportion of those individuals reported as child of head. This is true for both males and females. For other Asian groups, the share of this category is much larger. For example, more than half of Korean males who have no immediate family tie still reside in the family as child of head. A relatively high proportion may also be observed for females of other ethnic groups, namely, Vietnamese and Filipino (43%).

An alternative choice of of living arrangements for the unattached is to join others and extend their families. The tendency to live as "other relative of head" varies among ethnic groups. Consistent with the earlier findings, Japanese immigrants show a small percentage of the unattached residing in the family as other relative of head. This is especially true for males (7.9%) but not for females (31%). It is clear that family extension is very prevalent among the Filipino ethnics. Approximately one-third of Filipino males who have no nuclear tie join others to extend their families. The percentage is even higher for females (42.5%). Relatively high levels of family extension are also observed for Vietnamese, especially among females (43%). Surprisingly, Chinese and Koreans exhibit a much lower level of coresidence as compared with the Filipino group. In general, female Asian immigrants are more likely than males to live as an "other relative of head" but other gender differences are not uniform for all Asian ethnic groups. For example, Asian males tend to live alone more than Asian females, except for Korean immigrants; unattached Asian-Indians and Vietnamese women are more likely to be the child of the household head than men, but the reverse gender pattern characterizes the other Asian ethnics examined.

**Table 3-6**

**LIVING ARRANGEMENTS OF THE UNATTACHED BY SEX: ASIAN IMMIGRANTS, 1980**

| Living Arrangement | Japanese | Chinese | Filipino | Korean | Asian Indian | Vietnamese |
|---|---|---|---|---|---|---|
| *Males 18 Years and Older* | | | | | | |
| Total | 100.0 | 100.0 | 100.0 | 100.0 | 100.0 | 100.0 |
| Alone | 50.3 | 25.7 | 19.3 | 19.4 | 36.2 | 10.8 |
| Nonrelative of head | 25.1 | 18.3 | 11.8 | 9.4 | 17.0 | 28.7 |
| Child of head | 16.8 | 37.2 | 35.3 | 57.6 | 21.5 | 30.6 |
| Other relative of head | 7.9 | 18.8 | 33.6 | 13.7 | 25.3 | 29.9 |
| N | 191 | 564 | 414 | 139 | 265 | 268 |
| *Females 18 Years and Older* | | | | | | |
| Total | 100.0 | 100.0 | 100.0 | 100.0 | 100.0 | 100.0 |
| Alone | 43.9 | 20.6 | 17.2 | 22.6 | 34.9 | 4.9 |
| Nonrelative of head | 18.1 | 12.8 | 16.8 | 15.3 | 6.0 | 10.3 |
| Child of head | 6.8 | 31.9 | 23.5 | 27.6 | 28.9 | 41.7 |
| Other relative of head | 31.2 | 34.7 | 42.5 | 34.5 | 30.2 | 43.1 |
| N | 237 | 524 | 541 | 261 | 149 | 204 |

NOTE: The unattached individuals are persons in household, 18 years and older, who are neither married, spouse present, nor the head of a family or subfamily with own children.

## Nonfamily Living

The extent of nonfamily living can be measured by combining the proportion (of the unattached immigrants) residing alone or as nonrelative of head. The choice of such residential arrangement is affected by factors such as life cycle (age) and gender. Table 3-7 presents the percent nonfamily among the unattached by age and sex for the six Asian ethnic groups. The data show that there is a relationship between age, sex, and living arrangement choices. In most cases, men are more likely than women to live away from family and nonfamily living increases with age up to age 65 and then declines in the oldest age groups.

When the six ethnic groups are compared, the data reveal major differences in percent nonfamily for both males and females. Japanese immigrants who are unattached exhibit the highest percent of nonfamily living. Three-fourths of the Japanese men and 62% of the Japanese women live alone. At the other end of the continuum, only 30 percent of the Filipino immigrants live alone. The contrasts are even sharper within age groups. Six times as many Japanese as Filipino young men live alone and ten times as many Japanese women as Asian-Indian women live alone among those age 18-24. In order to eliminate the effects of age on the overall proportion living in this type of family arrangement, percent nonfamily was age-standardized for each sex, using the age distribution of Japanese as the standard population. The results confirm the earlier findings. There are important ethnic differences in the percent of the unattached living in nonfamilies. Japanese immigrants are most likely to live alone or as nonrelative of head (about three out of four males and two out of three females). Asian-Indian immigrants rank second, with about half of unattached men and about half of the unattached women chosing nonfamily living arrangements. It is interesting to note that among Vietnamese, the percent nonfamily for men is much higher than for women overall (47% vs. 17%) and at every age.

Table 3-7

**PERCENT NONFAMILY BY AGE AND SEX: UNATTACHED ASIAN IMMIGRANTS, 1980**

| Age and Sex of the Unattached | Japanese | Chinese | Filipino | Korean | Asian Indian | Vietnamese |
|---|---|---|---|---|---|---|
| Males 18 Years and Older | | | | | | |
| 18-24 | 65.6 | 22.0 | 9.6 | 13.0 | 24.1 | 29.9 |
| 25-44 | 85.3 | 59.3 | 35.0 | 53.2 | 74.6 | 54.6 |
| 45-64 | 86.7 | 90.3 | 53.6 | 100.0 | 85.7 | 75.0 |
| 65+ | 42.9 | 54.4 | 61.0 | 40.0 | 55.6 | 40.0 |
| Total percent nonfamily | 75.4 | 44.0 | 31.1 | 28.8 | 53.2 | 39.5 |
| Age standardized percent nonfamily | 75.4 | 48.3 | 29.5 | 41.8 | 56.4 | 46.5 |
| Females 18 Years and Older | | | | | | |
| 18-24 | 71.8 | 20.4 | 17.1 | 24.7 | 6.3 | 9.6 |
| 25-44 | 84.3 | 49.7 | 54.9 | 75.3 | 67.5 | 24.5 |
| 45-64 | 78.2 | 42.7 | 31.6 | 27.0 | 25.0 | 20.0 |
| 65+ | 35.9 | 29.6 | 18.3 | 16.7 | 72.7 | 13.6 |
| Total percent nonfamily | 62.0 | 33.4 | 34.0 | 37.9 | 40.9 | 15.2 |
| Age standardized percent nonfamily | 62.0 | 35.5 | 29.1 | 33.0 | 49.6 | 16.8 |

NOTE: Percent nonfamily is the proportion (of unattached immigrants) living alone or as nonrelative of head. Age standardized percent family is calculated by using the age distribution of the Japanese as the standard population.

## Family Extension

Instead of living away from family members, another choice for the unattached individuals is to coreside with relatives. The level of family extension can be indicated by percent (of the unattached) residing as other relative of head. This type of living arrangement among immigrants may be affected by several factors such as life cycle, gender, and duration of residence in American society. Gardner et al. (1985) found that the average household size of recent immigrants is large since it contains a large number of other relatives. The inclusion of other relatives in the household may be a strategy which recent arrivals adopt to facilitate the economic transition to the new society. These other relatives may help boost the family income as well as share child care and the costs of rent or mortgage.

We examine the percent in family extension by age, separately for recent and longterm immigrants (Table 3-8). For all groups, there is a consistent and powerful relationship between the extended family living arrangement and duration of residence in the United States. Immigrants arriving between 1975-80 (recent immigrants) are much more likely to live as extended relatives than those who came prior to 1975 (longterm immigrants). There is a tendency for family extension to increase with age, with the unattached elderly more prone than the young to live as extended relatives.

Table 3-8

**PERCENT LIVING IN EXTENDED FAMILIES BY AGE: RECENT AND LONG-TERM UNATTACHED ASIAN IMMIGRANTS, 1980**

| Age and Duration of Residence | Japanese | Chinese | Filipino | Korean | Asian Indian | Vietnamese |
|---|---|---|---|---|---|---|
| Recent Immigrants | | | | | | |
| Total | 3.1 | 32.6 | 55.4 | 34.4 | 35.2 | 35.7 |
| 18-24 | 1.7 | 22.0 | 39.7 | 19.6 | 30.2 | 27.2 |
| 25-44 | — | 27.5 | 46.2 | 16.4 | 25.5 | 37.3 |
| 45-64 | 42.9 | 70.8 | 87.0 | 82.6 | 82.6 | 70.0 |
| 65+ | — | 97.2 | 91.5 | 89.3 | 83.3 | 79.2 |
| Long-Term Immigrants | | | | | | |
| Total | 28.4 | 22.1 | 24.7 | 18.9 | 17.9 | 33.3 |
| 18-24 | 4.2 | 9.6 | 9.3 | 7.2 | 15.6 | — |
| 25-44 | 7.3 | 12.6 | 22.3 | 13.2 | 17.1 | 33.3 |
| 45-64 | 15.9 | 34.1 | 34.8 | 50.0 | 21.1 | 33.3 |
| 65+ | 63.2 | 51.6 | 46.6 | 68.4 | 22.2 | 100.0 |

NOTE: Percent family extension is the proportion (of unattached immigrants) living as other relative of head. Recent immigrants refers to those foreign born who arrived in the United States during 1975-1980. Long-term immigrants refers to those foreign born who arrived in the United States before 1975.

Among recent arrivals, Filipino immigrants exhibit the highest percentage of family extension. Over half of Filipino immigrants with no immediate family tie and arriving between 1975-1980 live as "other relative of head." The corresponding figure for the Japanese is three percent. The remaining ethnic groups show approximately one-third of the unattached have extended family living. The pattern of ethnic differences in family extension is particularly conspicuous among young adults. Among recent immigrants age 18-24, 40 percent of the Filipinos, 30 percent of the Asian-Indians, 20 percent of the Vietnamese, and 2 percent of the Japanese live in family extension. The range is much less among longterm immigrants. At least eight out of ten of the recent immigrants age 65 and over live in family extension.

The pattern for longterm immigrants is different. Japanese are as likely as other Asian ethnics to reside as extended relative. These Japanese immigrants who arrived before 1975 are mainly the elderly. These aged population are prone to live with relatives rather than form independent households.

The evidence presented reveals a consistent and unmistakable variation in residential choices among immigrants of Asian origin. The analysis focused on the residential choice of family extension as opposed to nonfamily living, with an emphasis on the unattached individuals who have no family tie of spouse and/or minor child.

The data demonstrate that the hypothesized factors such as life cycle (as measured by age and marital status) as well as gender have significant relationships to living arrangements. For all Asian ethnics, the tendency for the unattached to live in nonfamily households increases with age and then declines in the older age groups. Moreover, men in general were more prone than women to form one-person households or reside with other nonrelatives.

Residential choices are affected by economic feasibility since it may be more costly to form independent households than to join other relatives to extend their families. In the case of immigrants, duration of residence may indicate economic feasibility. Immigrants who recently arrived in the United States are more prone than their longterm counterparts to have family extension. This phenomenon has been described as a strategy which immigrants adopted to make the economic adjustment to the new society.

The central finding is that there are ethnic differences in living arrangements among Asian immigrants. The data are consistent with the argument that there are cultural preferences for living in extended families that reflect a complex set of family values and kinship norms tied to the cohesiveness of ethnic communities. These values are related to the adjustment process of Asian immigrants in American society, and appear to converge as length of residence increases. Nevertheless, it is clear that research on Asian Americans must include details on ethnic origins and length of exposure to American society. Discussions of family or other values of Asian Americans cannot be treated seriously without considering ethnicity as a variable that may change over time and may vary by national origin.

## REFERENCES

Angel, Ronald and Marta Tienda. 1982. "Determinants of Household Structure: Cultural Pattern or Economic Need?" *American Journal of Sociology* 87(6):1360-1383.

Boyd, Monica. 1974. "The Changing Nature of Central and Southeast Asian Immigration to the United States: 1961-1972." *International Migration Review* 8:507-519.

Carliner, G. 1974. "Determinants of Household Headship." *Journal of Marriage and the Family* 37:28-39.

Gardner, Robert, Bryant Robey and Peter Smith. 1985. "Asian Americans: Growth, Change, and Diversity." *Population Bulletin* 40:1-43.

Huang, Luey Jen. 1981. "The Chinese American Family," in C. Mindel and R. Habenstein, eds., *Ethnic Families in America*. New York: Elsevier Science Publishing Co., Inc.

Jiobu, R.M. and H. Marshall. 1977. "Minority Status and Family Size: A Comparison of Explanations." *Population Studies* 31:509-517.

Johnson, C.L. 1977. "Interdependence, Reciprocity, and Indebtedness: An Analysis of Japanese Kinship Relations." *Journal of Marriage and the Family* 39:351-363.

Keely, C.B. 1971. "Effects of the Immigration Act of 1965 on Selected Population Characteristics of Immigrants to the United States." *Demography* 8:157-169.

Kelly, G.P. 1977. *From Vietnam to America: A Chronicle of Vietnamese Immigration to the United States*. Boulder, Co.: Westview.

Kikumura, Akemi and Harry Kitano. 1981. "The Japanese American Family." In C. Mindel and R. Habenstein, eds., *Ethnic Families in America*. New York: Elsevier Science Publishing Co., Inc.

Kobrin, Frances. 1976. "The Fall in Household Size and the Rise of the Primary Individual in the United States." *Demography* 13:127-138.

Kobrin, F. and C. Goldscheider. 1978. *The Ethnic Factor in Family Structure and Mobility*. Cambridge: Ballinger Publishing Co.

Kobrin, F., and C. Goldscheider. 1982. "Family Extension or Nonfamily Living: Life Cycle, Economic, and Ethnic Factors." *Western Sociological Review* 13(1):103-118.

Massey, Douglas. 1981. "Dimensions of the New Immigration to the United States and the Prospects for Assimilation." *Annual Review of Sociology* 7:57-85.

Periera, Maria. 1985. "The Socioeconomic Adjustment of Portuguese Immigrant Males in Massachusetts and Rhode Island." Unpublished M.A. Thesis. Brown University.

Ross, H. and I. Sawhill, 1975. *Time of Transition: The Growth of Families Headed by Women.* Washington, D.C.: The Urban Institute.

Sweet, James. 1972. "The Living Arrangements of Separated, Widowed and Divorced Mothers." *Demography* 9:143-159.

Sweet, James. 1978. "Indicators of Family and Household Structure of Racial and Ethnic Minorities in the United States." in F. Bean and W. Frisbie (eds.) *The Demography of Racial and Ethnic Groups.* New York: Academic Press.

Tienda, Marta and R. Angel. 1982. "Headship and Household Composition among Blacks, Hispanics and Other Whites." *Social Forces* 61(2):508-531.

U.S. Department of Justice. 1961-77. *Immigration and Naturalization Service Annual Report.* Washington, D.C.

Wong, Morrison. 1985. "Post-1965 Immigrants: Demographic and socioeconomic Profile." in L. Maldonado and J. Moore (eds.) *Urban Ethnicity in the United States: New Immigrants and Old Minorities.* California: Sage Publications.

Wong, Morrison and Charles Hirschman. 1983. "The New Asian Immigrants." in W. McCready (ed.) *Culture, Ethnicity and Identity: Current Issues in Research.* New York: Academic Press.

# 4

# Nonfamily Households and Housing Among Young Adults

PATRICIA B. CHRISTIAN

Over the past several decades, the United States has experienced a more rapid increase in the number of households than in population, with a concomitant decrease in average household size and a proliferation of a variety of nontraditional household types. Some of these nontraditional household types are one-person households (increasing from 10.3 percent of all households in 1950 to 22.5 percent in 1980) and households composed of unrelated individuals. Primary individuals, the heads of households composed of unrelated individuals and people living alone, are concentrated in two age ranges--young people aged 20 to 34, especially males, and women aged 65 and over.

This chapter focuses on nonfamily living arrangements in the contexts of opportunities and constraints facing young men and women. We shall investigate the determinants of the rise in nonfamily households, testing whether it is due at least in part to normative changes in the family (Pampel, 1983) or simply to increases in economic opportunity that have allowed the realization of a constant demand for solitary or nonfamily living (Michael et al., 1980; Smith et al. 1984). An important consideration in the analysis will be the extent to which the availability and affordability of housing have an additional effect on patterns of living arrangements in 1980, beyond changes in the incomes of individuals and the preferences of families.

Young adults face several living arrangement options. They may remain in their family of origin, as "child of head", either married and part of a subfamily, or more commonly, as an unmarried person. The young adult may marry and set up his or her own independent household in the context of a new family. A final choice, and one increasingly selected, is to leave the family of origin to live alone or with nonrelatives. We envision these decisions as two separate steps. First, young adults choose when to marry and set up their own households. Those who are not married can then choose between living with relatives and living on their own, alone or with roommates.

How are these decisions made? On the one hand, family living may be a financial strategy, whereby family members benefit from pooled resources or gain access to resources brought in by other family members. On the other hand, it may be a cultural phenomenon, related to norms about appropriate family relations and behavior. Unraveling these two possibilities has become increasingly important, because the process of leaving home in young adulthood has become more complex now than in the past. No longer is leaving home primarily due to marriage, formerly the most important influence on when young people left home. Now, "other factors are allowing or impelling young people to leave home without forming a new family" (Goldscheider and LeBourdais, 1986, p. 5).

## Background: Nonfamily Living

Through most of history, and around the world, children have lived with their parents at least until marriage and, depending on the household formation system of the area, occasionally well after marriage. When unmarried children were not living with their parents, they were usually living with other relatives or were servants in another family household (Berkner, 1973; Hareven, 1982; Hajnal, 1982). This pattern has changed for much of the developed world, especially since World War II. Young men and women of all economic levels and racial and ethnic groups can be found living alone or with friends and housemates (see Young, 1984 on Australia; Kobrin, 1976 on the United States; Nilsson, 1985 on Sweden; and Baranwal and Ram, 1985, for a comparative overview). Greater affluence in these countries is partially responsible for this trend, as are new norms, aspirations and expectations.

Roussel (1983) finds that the growth in one-person households in more developed countries is due both to an increased preference for living alone and to a loosening of economic constraints against solitary living. His analysis suggests that the growth in one-person households "reflects an increase in the number of temporary situations in an individual's life when he or she is moving from one multi-person household to another, rather than a permanent increase in stable, solitary life situations" (p. 1015). Agreeing that economic and normative changes are important in the increase in one-person households, Hareven notes that "the practice of boarding and lodging has been replaced since the 1920s by solitary living" (1982:76). Hence, a new form of "temporary situation", solitary living, has replaced another, boarding and lodging.

Glick and Lin (1986) propose a demographic interpretation of nonfamily living among young adults. Noting that in the 1980s, there was an increase in the number of young people living with their parents, they suggest that the lower birth rates of the late 1960s and early 1970s, by keeping family size smaller, have made it easier for young adults to remain in, or return to, their parents' homes. The baby boom generation, they assert, was almost literally "crowded out" of their parents' homes. They support their argument with census and Current Population Survey data from 1940 to 1984, showing that more of those age 18 to 29 lived with their parents in 1984 (37%) than in 1970 (34%). Because they did not control for changes in age at marriage, however, their analysis is less than complete.

Using the same data and controlling for age at marriage, Heer, et al., (1985) come to somewhat different conclusions. While the percent of those age 18 to 24 living with parents increased between 1970 and 1983, the percentage living with their own family of procreation (i.e., married) decreased significantly in the same time period. A breakdown of the components of the differences in the proportion of young people living in their parents' households reveals that the decline in the proportion of those ages 18-34 in households with their own families "actually would have produced a slightly *greater* proportion living in their parents' households in 1983 than in 1970." The actual increase was 6.7 percent, while the change expected due to shifts in family status amounted to 7.4 percent.

## Housing and Income

Few studies of the propensity to form nonfamily households have addressed the issue of housing; none have done so adequately. More affordable and/or available housing, like rising income, allows individuals to realize their desire to live alone. Studies have found a positive relationship between income and living alone (Carliner, 1975; Michael et al., 1980) implying that those who are most likely to live alone are those who can best afford it. Between 1913 and 1947 the price of housing was falling relative to other goods. After 1947 it remained remarkably stable until the 1970s (Carliner, 1975), when the costs of owning a home increased dramatically, due mostly to increased energy costs. While the actual purchase price of a house remained fairly stable (in constant dollars), the costs of homeownership, especially fuel oil, gas and electricity, increased greatly.

In addition, the average contract interest rate increased significantly between 1975 and 1980 (from 8.7 percent to 12.3 percent). In an international analysis of headship rates and demand for housing, Smith et al. (1984) found that in the four countries considered, the United States, Canada, Great Britain, and France, the nonfamily household headship rate varied directly with real per capita disposable income and inversely with the real cost of housing services. Beyond the monetary costs of housing, another constraint faced by would-be nonfamily individuals is availability. For example, the availability of public housing had a significant influence on the headship rate for the elderly in Canada, Great Britain, and the United States (Smith et al., 1984).

Chew (1983) found that income, education, and housing supply affect rates of living alone among elderly men in opposite ways compared with elderly women. Higher rents and lower rental vacancy rates decrease the likelihood elderly women live in nonfamily households, but increase it for elderly males. He hypothesizes that since men are more able to choose between marriage and living alone than elderly women (since there are so many fewer men than women at these ages), male income and education are "spent" toward achieving marriage, and are therefore negatively correlated with living alone. On the other hand, since women's choice is primarily between living alone and living with nonspouse kin, female income and education are "spent" toward living alone. The availability and cost of rental housing become key factors in the ability to live away from relatives. At the other end of the adult life course, rent had no effect on the percent of young female primary individuals and had a positive effect on the percent of young male, non-student, primary individuals (Chew, 1983).

## Hypotheses

There have been few studies that have systematically analyzed the effects of housing costs and availability on the number of nonfamily households. The existing studies (Chew, 1983; Carliner, 1975; and Smith et al., 1984) have produced ambiguous and contradictory findings. Building on these studies, together with related analyses of income and household formation, we test the following hypotheses about the factors associated with nonfamily households for young adults:

> 1. Higher housing costs for renters and homeowners, other things being equal, are expected to discourage nonfamily living among young adults. Higher costs may also discourage marriage, potentially increasing the proportion nonfamily among those who would otherwise marry and set up their own family household. A plentiful housing supply for rent or purchase, other things being equal, is expected to encourage nonfamily living among young people. It may also, however, encourage marriage, and thus reduce the proportion of nonfamily households. Taking these effects into account, it is hypothesized that:
>
> > a) High housing costs and low availability decrease the proportion of married young adults in a population, holding constant other factors such as income and education.
> >
> > b) High housing costs and low availability decrease the proportion of young adults living in nonfamily households.
>
> 2. Income is hypothesized to have contradictory effects depending on marital status and gender:
>
> > a) High male income will decrease the proportion of nonfamily young people by increasing the proportion of married young

adults; however, after controlling for marriage, high male income will increase the proportion of nonfamily males.

b) High female income will decrease the proportion married; after controlling for marriage, high female income will increase the proportion of nonfamily females.

## Data and Methods

To test these hypotheses, we focus on the metropolitan area as the unit of analysis. Ordinary least squares regression was applied to the 149 largest SMSAs (over 250,000 population) in the contiguous United States in 1980. The resulting equations predict the proportions of nonfamily households among those ages 25 to 29. The sources of data used are U.S. Census Bureau publications listed in the references to this chapter.

SMSAs are appropriate units of analysis for a number of reasons. On the one hand, the patterns of living arrangements for the 149 largest SMSAs are very similar to those found for the country as a whole, so that results of analyses at this level should apply to the general population. On the other hand, focusing our attention at this level allows for a much more detailed analysis than a country-wide analysis would permit. Metropolitan areas coincide more closely with labor and housing markets than do either states or counties. They are more homogeneous than states, which may contain vastly different areas ranging from rural agricultural areas to heavily industrialized ones. SMSAs tend to be organized around one or two types of industry or service, and are all more or less urban in character. A metropolitan focus allows us to take into account the influences of community level factors. Krivo and Mutchler (1980) point out that community structures influence the household formation decisions of the elderly segment of the population; the same is likely to be true of the younger age groups as well. Looking at SMSAs rather than states renders the results of analysis more interpretable and meaningful. Finally, from a policy perspective, metropolitan areas need information on how the living arrangements of their populations respond to structural conditions within the area, such as unemployment, housing prices and availability, and industrial composition. Housing can be controlled by city and town governments through zoning regulations and building permits, as well as through direct subsidies of housing for special needs groups.

In order to analyze the determinants of living arrangements choices in young adulthood, we have chosen to focus on those between the ages of 25 and 29. In this age range, young adults are still making nest-leaving/marital/career choices in significant numbers, but few are still students or in the military, whose status and living arrangements would confound the analysis.

## Dependent Variables

Four types of dependent variables were used in this analysis: 1) the proportion of young adults living alone; 2) the proportion living with roommates; 3) the proportion experiencing nonfamily living arrangements (1 and 2 combined); and 4) the proportion married. For most analyses, the first three proportions were based on the unmarried population in the SMSA. However, in the final analysis we examine the factors influencing nonfamily living among all young adults, married and unmarried.

Young people living in group quarters, such as military barracks, dormitories, prisons, and hospitals, have been excluded from the dependent variable.[1] By far the majority of adults in this age range live in households rather than group quarters (97.7 percent of males and 99.4 percent of females aged 25-34 were classified by the Census as living in households in 1980). One remaining difficulty with examining the proportion living with roommates reflects the fact that the Census counts as "living with nonrelatives" only those reporting themselves householder (head of house) and living with nonrelatives, resulting in an underestimate of the number of roommates. Roommates who are not householders have been "lost" for the purposes of this and similar analyses using published census data. However, the number of heads of such households and the numbers living in them should be closely related.

Overall, 34 percent of all unmarried young adults living in households live away from their parents. However, there is a wide variation among SMSAs in the percent of young nonfamily individuals. Only 13.8 percent do so in McAllen, Texas, compared with 48.8 percent in Madison, Wisconsin.

## Independent Variables

*The homeowner vacancy rate*, calculated by the Census, is the ratio between the vacant year-round units for sale and the total homeowner inventory (in percentages). Total homeowner inventory is the sum of the owner-occupied units and the vacant year-round units for sale. Vacant units that are seasonal or held off the market are excluded.

*The rental vacancy rate*, like the homeowner vacancy rate, is the

---

[1] Unfortunately, we could not control directly for school enrollment among those at this age. While not important among 25- to 29-year-olds in most SMSAs, a few cities have significant numbers of graduate students. At least five of the ten SMSAs with the highest proportions of nonfamily individuals also have large universities (Minneapolis-St. Paul, Minnesota; Raleigh-Durham, North Carolina; Ann Arbor, Michigan; Austin, Texas; and Madison, Wisconsin).

number of vacant year-round units for rent divided by the sum of the renter-occupied units and the vacant year-round units for rent. The availability of public housing has been used by some researchers as a measure of housing availability (Smith et al., 1984), but it is more likely to be relevant for older people. Rental and homeowner vacancy rates are broader measures of available housing than the public housing vacancy rate.

*Median price of houses for sale* is restricted to single family permanent housing units. Mobile homes, trailers, boats, tents, or vans occupied as a usual residence, and owner-occupied non-condominium units in multi-family buildings are excluded.

*Median gross rent* is the contract rent, that is, the monthly rent agreed to, or contracted for, plus the estimated average monthly cost of utilities and fuels if these are paid for by the renter in addition to rent.

*Selected monthly owner costs* for units with a mortgage include mortgage payments and other debts on the property, real estate taxes, fire and hazard insurance on the property, utilities and fuels.

*Median income:* We distinguish the incomes of males and females, aged 25-29, since we have already noted findings (Chew and Rodriquez, 1986) suggesting that the effects differ by sex. Men, in certain circumstances, use additional income for marriage; women use additional income for independence (Preston and Richards, 1975).

*Unemployment rate:* In SMSAs with high unemployment one would expect to find more individuals "doubling up" with family members and nonrelatives for financial reasons. Poor Black families are especially likely to form extended households, as a form of social insurance and mutual support in facing economic uncertainty (Stack, 1974; Scheirer, 1983).

*Percent Black:* Some researchers have found that Black family structure differs from that of whites (Tienda and Angel, 1982; Chew, 1983; Michael et al., 1980; Goldscheider and Goldscheider, 1987), although other studies found that racial differences in the propensity to live alone and headship rates were due entirely to differences in marital status, motherhood, and income (Pampel, 1983; Carliner, 1975). Hence, the percent of the SMSA population that is Black was entered as a control.

*Population size:* Larger urban areas may have relatively more nonfamily individuals because of a richer institutional infrastructure. Restaurants, laundries, public transportation, and dating services may allow the growth of less traditional households (Chew, 1983).

*Education:* Two measures of education were constructed: the proportion graduated from high school (averaged for both sexes) and the proportion of college graduates (averaged for both sexes). In the analyses for each sex alone, we combined high school and college education for the respective sex.

*In-migration ratio:* The number of in-migrants aged 25-29 divided by the population aged 25-29 in 1980 was used as a measure of in-migration. In-migrants are less likely to have relatives in the area of destination than non-migrants; hence cities with more in-migrants should have more nonfamily young adults.

*Region:* Region has not often been considered in analyses of nonfamily households. However, regional variation may reflect differences in age structure, family size, costs of living, or historical conditions that affect the regions differently. Dummy variables were therefore included for region, distinguishing South, West and Northeast from the mid-West in the regression equations. To the extent that the South has more "conservative" family values and the West more "liberal" ones we may expect to see a negative relationship between South and the proportion nonfamily individuals, and a positive relationship for the West.

## Predicting Nonfamily Living

These independent variables were used to predict the percentage of young adults (aged 25-29) residing in nonfamily living arrangements, the percentage living alone, and the percentage living with other nonrelatives. Comparing these separate results allows us to distinguish between factors that decrease nonfamily living among the unmarried of all kinds and those that simply shift young unmarried adults into more expensive types of nonfamily living (living alone) from those that are less expensive (living with roommates). Table 4-1 presents the results of this analysis. Comparable analyses were performed separately for young men and women, and these results are discussed where they differ from the total patterns (although the data are not presented in tabular form).[2]

---

[2] An examination of outliers from the regression showed five consistently outlying SMSAs: Nassau, New York; Indianapolis, Indiana; and Riverside, California had far fewer nonfamily individuals than predicted by the equations, and Raleigh, North Carolina and Jersey City, New Jersey, had far more. Nassau is essentially a suburb of the New York City SMSA, which may account for its low proportion of nonfamily young adults. Indianapolis may have relatively few nonfamily individuals because many of the local young people are attracted to the university and so are removed from the metropolitan area and income and education levels are above average, due perhaps also to the university, with the result that the regression equations predict an unrealistically high proportion of nonfamily young adults. The Riverside SMSA, 350 square miles reaching from Los Angeles to Nevada, has, like Nassau, a suburban and even rural character. Raleigh's high proportion is easily explained by the presence of several large and well-known universities within the SMSA, and by its location in the South, which has generally low proportions nonfamily, leading the regression equation to predict few nonfamily individuals. Jersey City is somewhat the opposite case: its low educational levels, high unemployment and

**Table 4-1**

**REGRESSION COEFFICIENTS ESTIMATING PROPORTION NONFAMILY, BOTH SEXES, CONTROLLING FOR MARRIAGE**

| Variable | Percent Nonfamily B | Percent with Roommates B | Percent Alone B |
|---|---|---|---|
| Gross rent | −.056** | .019 | −.076** |
| Rental vacancy | .052 | −.174 | .228 |
| Homeowner costs | −.020 | −.008 | −.012 |
| Home price | −.000 | −.000 | −.000 |
| Home vacancy | 1.244 | .434 | .810 |
| Male income | .053* | −.025* | .078** |
| Female income | .159* | .015 | .145** |
| Unemployment rate | −.531* | −.012 | −.519** |
| Population | .048 | .007 | .041 |
| Education | .701** | .355** | .346** |
| Percent black | −.158** | −.070** | −.088* |
| Inmigrant rate | .265** | .093** | .172** |
| Northeast | −6.541** | −1.919** | −4.622** |
| West | .346 | 1.255 | −.909 |
| South | −2.892* | −.241 | −2.650** |
| Constant | −1.991 | −10.706 | −8.716 |
| Adj. $R^2$ | .715 | .758 | .643 |

* $p < .05$.
** $p < .01$.

Northeast location create an expectation of few nonfamily people. However, it is highly urbanized and on New York City's doorstep; many young single people who cannot afford to live in New York live in Hoboken, an easy commute to New York but a different SMSA.

What factors lead to nonfamily living generally, and what forms of nonfamily living are they influencing most? Among the measures of the housing market, only rent has a strong and consistently significant effect on nonfamily living among unmarried young adults. Areas with relatively expensive rental housing reduce the proportions of unmarried adults who will live away from their parents. The effect, however, is most strongly felt on living alone, since clearly some proportion of young people manage to live separately from their parents even in the face of high rentals, shifting toward sharing space with roommates. This suggests that studies that focus only on *living alone* as an indicator of independence from the parental home will overstate the effects of rent, by missing the shift into roommate living. High costs of maintaining an owned home also discourage nonfamily living significantly among young men, but have no influence at all on young women, and hence, are not significant for the total group. Similarly, high vacancy rates encourage nonfamily living among young women, but not among young men. Other indicators of housing costs have no consistent effect in this analysis. (Most have signs in the expected direction, suggesting that the presence of a large group of fairly similar measures may have reduced the ability of any one to reach statistical significance.) Similarly, population size has no effect.

Factors that measure young adults' ability to pay for housing tell very much the same story. Higher incomes and lower rates of unemployment increase nonfamily living, primarily because they increase the percentage who live alone. Male incomes seem to have the same effect as rent, with offsetting effects between living alone and living with roommates. The income effect is much stronger for young women than for young men. This might be the result of the much lower incomes of young women, so that an increase of one thousand dollars per year might make them feel comparatively richer than it would a young man. It is also possible that young men are responding less because they are saving more of their income, and not using it to purchase short-term privacy, reflecting the longer-term economic responsibilities society encourages them to feel for the support of their own families.

The remaining effects are primarily those that strongly influence both living alone and living with roommates, and hence reduce or increase nonfamily living generally. These factors include the rate of in-migration, educational level, proportion Black, and region. Areas with higher proportions of young people who have migrated in from other parts of the country show more nonfamily living, including both living alone and living with roommates. This seems quite reasonable, since new migrants are generally living in areas away from kin, and must live somewhere. Those most able to afford living alone do so, and those who cannot, double up with roommates. Nonfamily living, in this case, represents a reaction to the scarcity of relatives with whom to live.

The other factors, however, cannot be interpreted so directly, and seem to reflect more general differences in preferences for nonfamily living. Those living in areas with higher educational levels are much more likely to live away from family, choosing to live alone or live with roommates rather than live with parents. Areas with a high proportion Black, in contrast, are marked with particularly low levels of nonfamily living, with effects about equally balanced between avoidance of living alone and of living with nonrelatives. These patterns suggest that areas with high proportions Black and low levels of education have a stronger sense of the appropriateness of family living for young, unmarried adults. Both of these patterns are stronger for females than for males (data not presented). This suggests that nonfamily living is a relatively newer phenomenon for young women than for young men, so that even in relatively familistic areas, young men have some freedom from family.

Measures of region can be interpreted in a similar way. The results suggest that nonfamily living is most common in the West and in the Midwest (the reference category). The South shows relatively low levels of nonfamily living, and the Northeast appears to be the most familistic region for young unmarried adults. The form nonfamily living takes in the West is more likely to involve roommates, while in the Midwest, those living away from family are more likely to live alone. This suggests that the high costs of housing in the West continue to influence living arrangements decisions, even controlling for current costs, since those in the West may also be reacting to the *rate* of increase, and there may be other costs not included in the measure of "gross rent," such as deposits, cleaning fees, and other charges.

## Predicting Marriage and Family Living

The results so far indicate that both financial and preference factors are affecting the level of nonfamily living among unmarried adults in their mid- and late-twenties in the United States in 1980. But "family living" typically comes in *two forms* in this age group--living with parents, unmarried, and living with a new family, normally via marriage. Do the processes predicting family versus non-family living among the unmarried resemble those predicting forming a new family? Table 4-2 is organized to allow this comparison. Col. 1 shows the effects of income, housing price, and other variables on the percentage unmarried in this age group. These results measure "familism," focusing only on the rate *new* families are being formed through marriage. Col. 2 is repeated from Table 4-1, showing the effects of these same variables on nonfamily living, given that young adults are unmarried. These results measure "familism" among the unmarried, and hence focus our attention toward the parental family. The final column, Col. 3, combines these two processes, showing the percentage of all young adults living in nonfamily arrangements, so that both high proportions married *and* high proportions living with parents will reduce the proportion living alone or with nonrelatives, giving a total measure of "familism."

The results indicate that many of the factors thought to reduce

## Table 4-2

**REGRESSION COEFFICIENTS ESTIMATING PERCENT MARRIED OF ALL 25–29 YEAR OLDS**

| Variable | Percent Married | Percent Nonfamily Among Unmarried | Total Percent Nonfamily |
|---|---|---|---|
| Gross rent | .078** | −.056* | .003 |
| Rental vacancy | −.051 | .052 | −.014 |
| Homeowner costs | −.009 | −.020 | −.010 |
| Home price | .000 | −.000 | .000 |
| Home vacancy | .603 | 1.244 | .676 |
| Male income | −.190** | .053* | −.049** |
| Female income | .166** | .159* | .125** |
| Unemployment rate | .523** | −.531* | .054 |
| Population | .059 | .048 | .041* |
| Education | .433** | .701** | .456** |
| Percent black | .254** | −.158** | .010 |
| Inmigrant rate | −.139* | .265** | .053 |
| Northeast | 1.415 | −6.541** | −2.145** |
| West | .071 | .346 | .430 |
| South | −2.678* | −2.892* | −1.449* |
| Constant | −94.261** | −1.991 | −14.028** |
| Adj. $R^2$ | .722 | .715 | .766 |

* $p < .05$.
** $p < .01$.

familism by increasing nonfamily living among young adults are also *increasing* familism by increasing marriage. Hence, their effects on overall familism are virtually nil. The rental costs of housing and the level of unemployment are examples of such offsetting processes. Low rents increase unmarried young people's ability to leave their family home, but they also increase their ability to get married. Rent thus has no effect on overall familism, shifting young people between marriage and the parental home. Similarly, low levels of unemployment allow young unmarried people residential independence from their parents, but also allow them to marry.

Areas experiencing high levels of in-migration are also not experiencing sharp changes in their overall familism, despite the results that we presented earlier. This comes about because such areas are also areas with high proportions married. It may be that the in-migrants themselves are arriving already married; or perhaps conditions in these areas not already measured by other control variables facilitate marriage among all their young people. Either or both of these processes may be operating. The net result is that such areas are characterized by slightly more family living among adults aged 25-29.

A similar result characterizes areas that have a high proportion Black. Their high level of familism when considering the unmarried is balanced by their low level of marriage, with the result that the proportion Black has no effect on the overall level of familism in an SMSA. The effect of living in an area with a high proportion Black is thus similar to the effect of living in an area with high unemployment or with high costs of rental housing--young people remain with their parents, and are restrained both from marriage and from premarital residential independence.

One interesting result of the analysis is that higher male incomes actually increase overall familism, contrary to the implication of the first analysis. The effect of higher male incomes on increasing the percentage married is considerably stronger than the effect on increasing nonfamily living among the unmarried. Hence, trends that increase male incomes can be expected to strengthen family living in the United States.

On the other hand, many of the factors that reduce familism when we considered only the unmarried also reduce marriage. These factors are disproportionately the measures we characterized earlier as indicating preferences for nonfamily living. Higher education leads to nonfamily living through both routes, decreasing marriage as well as the likelihood young adults live with their parents. Similarly, those living in the South are more familistic on both dimensions, being very likely to marry and unlikely to live away from parents if unmarried. The result that appears for population size can be interpreted in this manner, as well. Although increases in city size do not significantly affect either measure of familism separately, the two effects reinforce each other, with the result that young people in larger cities are more likely to live away from kin.

However, one of the factors characterized as a "preference" measure in the analysis of nonfamily living among the unmarried is an exception, in that it does not have consistent effects on marriage. Those who live in the Northeast are more likely to live with their parents, but are not more likely to be married. However, the Northeast is also a region that is distinctively Catholic, and Catholics have been characterized by long term patterns of late marriage and higher proportions never married. Hence, this result may also be the result of preferences particular to this region of the country.

The final exceptional result is that for female income, which is a resource measure, but does not have the same effects as the other financial measures. Areas with higher female incomes have very high levels of nonfamilism for females in both ways--they have lower proportions married and higher proportions living alone among the unmarried. As such, female income resembles a "preference" indicator. This result is consistent with our original hypothesis, i.e., increasing resources will reduce family living far more for women than for men because of the different roles of men and women in marriage.

## Conclusions

Clearly, the living arrangements decisions of young adults vary substantially, and reflect both differences in financial dimensions as well as tastes and preferences for family versus nonfamily living. How much young people earn, and how expensive housing is for them, affect their access to separate housing, as economic interpretations of the changes in living arrangements predict. However, there are other dimensions that influence separate living, that seem to tap differences in the appropriateness of living with parents among those in their mid- to late-twenties. The South and the Northeast stand out as more traditional areas, as do SMSAs with lower than average educational levels among their young people.

Economic arguments also need to consider carefully the difference between living alone and living with roommates. When rents are high, young adults do not necessarily have to remain in the parental household. Rather than remaining crowded in with siblings and authority figures, they can be crowded in with a group of roommates, and reduce their costs substantially. Hence, the economic approach to nonfamily living is incomplete. Resources can be used to purchase privacy not only from family but also from roommates; and it is not clear whether family members or roommates reduce a young adult's privacy more.

This analysis of nonfamily living has also shown that in order to understand patterns of living arrangements in young adulthood, it is important to consider not only the characteristics of individuals (such as income, education, and migrant status), but include as well areal characteristics, such as the costs of rental housing and the level of unemployment in an area. Studies of living arrangements have typically not been sensitive to these contextual dimensions, in part because their data have focused at the individual level.

Finally, our results focus attention on nonfamily living in comparison with living with a spouse, not only on nonfamily living in comparison with living with parents. They show that the economic interpretations of nonfamily living fail in another way, since the resources that are used to "purchase" privacy from the parental family are also used to "purchase" the independence of *married* adulthood, at least for young men. Only female incomes are being used to "purchase" independence from family living generally, both from living with parents and from living with a spouse.

## REFERENCES

Baranwal, J.P., and Bali Ram. 1985. "Societal Development, Familialism and Solo Living: A Cross-National Study." *Journal of Comparative Family Studies* 16:61-73.

Berkner, Lutz K. 1973. "Recent Research on the History of the Family in Western Europe." *Journal of Marriage and the Family* 35:395-405.

Carliner, Geoffrey. 1975. "Determinants of Household Headship." *Journal of Marriage and the Family* 37:28-38.

Chew, Kenneth S.Y. 1983. Metropolitan Differences in the Level of Nonfamily Households: A Cross-Sectional Look at the U.S. in 1970. Paper presented at the annual meetings of the Population Association of America, Pittsburgh, April 1, 1983.

Chew, Kenneth and Felix I. Rodriquez. 1986. Urban Industry and Nonfamily Households: 1970-1980. Paper presented at the annual meetings of the Population Association of America, San Francisco, April, 1986.

Glick, Paul C. and Sung-Lin Lin. 1986. "More Young Adults are Living with their Parents: Who are They?" *Journal of Marriage and the Family* 48:107-112.

Goldscheider, Calvin and Frances K. Goldscheider. 1987. "Moving Out and Marriage: What do Young Adults Expect?" *American Sociological Review* 52:278-285.

Goldscheider, Frances K. and Julie DaVanzo. 1985. "Living Arrangements and the Transition to Adulthood." *Demography* 22:545-564.

Goldscheider, Frances K. and Celine LeBourdais. 1986. "The Falling Age at Leaving Home, 1920-1979." *Sociology and Social Research* 70:143-145.

Hajnal, John. 1982. "Two Kinds of Preindustrial Household Formation System." *Population and Development Review* 8:449-494.

Hareven, Tamara K. 1982. "American Families in Transition: Historical Perspectives on Change." In *Family in Transition*, Skolnick and Skolnick, (eds.). Little, Brown and Company, Boston. Fourth Edition, pp. 73-91.

Heer, David M., Robert W. Hodge and Marcus Felson. 1985. "The Cluttered Nest: Evidence that Young Adults are more Likely to Live at Home Now than in the Recent Past." *Sociology and Social Research* 69:436-441.

Kobrin, Frances E. 1976. "The Fall in Household Size and the Rise of the Primary Individual in the United States." *Demography* 13:127-138.

Krivo, Lauren J. and Jan E. Mutchler. 1986. Metropolitan Variation in Household Status of the Elderly: A Cross-Sectional Analysis. Paper presented at the annual meetings of the Population Association of America, San Francisco, April, 1986.

Michael, Robert, Victor Fuchs and Sharon Scott. 1980. "Changes in the Propensity to Live Alone: 1950-1976." *Demography* 17:39-56.

Nilsson, Thora. 1985. "Les Menages en Suede, 1960-1980." *Population* 40:223-247.

Pampel, Fred C. 1983. "Changes in the Propensity to Live Alone: Evidence from Consecutive Cross-Sectional Surveys, 1960-1976." *Demography* 20:433-448.

Preston, Samuel H. and Alan Thomas Richards. 1975. "The Influence of Women's Work Opportunities on Marriage Rates." *Demography* 12:209-222.

Roussel, Louis. 1983. "Les Menages d'une Personne: L'evolution Recente." *Population* 38:995-1015.

Scheirer, Mary Ann. 1983. "Household Structure Among Welfare Families: Correlates and Consequences." *Journal of Marriage and the Family* 45:761-771.

Smith, Lawrence B., Kenneth T. Rosen, Anil Markandya, and Peirre-Antoine Ullmo. 1984. "The Demand for Housing, Household Headship Rates, and Household Formations: An International Analysis. *Urban Studies* 21:407-414.

Stack, Carol B. 1974. *All Our Kin: Strategies for Survival in a Black Community*. New York: Harper and Row.

Tienda, Marta and Ronald Angel. 1982. "Headship and Household Composition among Blacks, Hispanics, and Other Whites." *Social Forces* 1982:508-531.

U.S. Bureau of the Census. 1982a. *State and Metropolitan Area Date Book, 1982*. Washington, D.C.: Government Printing Office.

U.S. Bureau of the Census. 1982b. *Statistical Abstract of the United States: 1982-83*. (103rd edition). Washington, D.C.: Government Printing Office.

U.S. Bureau of the Census. 1983a. *1980 Census of Population. Volume 1, Characteristics of the Population. Chapter B, General Population Characteristics, State Volumes, Table 25*. Washington, D.C.: Government Printing Office.

U.S. Bureau of the Census. 1983b. *1980 Census of Population. Volume 1, Characteristics of the Population. Chapter D, Detailed Characteristics of the Population, State Volumes, Tables 205, 206, 234, 237*. Washington, D.C.: Government Printing Office.

U.S. Bureau of the Census. 1983c. *1980 Census of Housing. Volume 1, Characteristics of Housing Units. Chapter A, General Housing Characteristics. United States Summary, Tables 1, 76*. Washington, D.C.: Government Printing Office.

U.S. Bureau of the Census. 1983d. *1980 Census of Housing. Volume 1, Characteristics of Housing Units. Chapter B, Detailed Housing Characteristics. United States Summary, Table 153*, Washington, D.C.: Government Printing Office.

U.S. Bureau of the Census. 1985a. *1980 Census of Population. Volume 2, Subject Reports. Geographic Mobility for Metropolitan Areas, Table 7*. Washington, D.C.: Government Printing Office.

U.S. Bureau of the Census. 1985b. *1980 Census of Population. Volume 2, Subject Reports. Living Arrangements of Children and Adults, Table 4*. Washington, D.C.: Government Printing Office.

Young, Christabel M. 1984. The Effect of Children Returning Home on the Precision of the Timing of the Leaving Home Stage of the Family Life Cycle. Presented at the seminar on "Demography of the later Phases of the Family Life Cycle," Berlin, 3-7 September, 1984. German Association for the Scientific Study of Population and International Union for the Study of Population.

# 5

# Living Arrangements Among the Older Population
## Constraints, Preferences, and Power

CALVIN GOLDSCHEIDER AND MALI B. JONES

**Autonomy and Dependence Among the Elderly**

A series of revolutionary changes over the last several decades have altered the living arrangements patterns of older persons in the United States. Increased life expectancy has resulted in a growing number of persons surviving into the later years of the life cycle, with a disproportionate number of women outliving men at the older ages. Having had lower fertility, these older persons have relatively fewer children around to care for them, or to live with, as they age. Over the course of the life cycle, they and their children have been residentially mobile, resulting in greater geographical separation between the generations. Economic changes and government policies have increased the resources available to older persons, so more can afford continued economic and residential independence from extended family. At the same time, lifestyle and normative changes have reinforced these demographic and economic patterns, with an increasing priority given to privacy, independence, and leisure time activities that are age segregated. Few older persons expect to become dependent on their family, residentially or otherwise, as they grow older.

These and related changes have had major consequences for the shift among the older population toward living in what has been called "minimal" household structures -- either toward living alone among the widowed, divorced, or never married or living in two person households among married couples (Ermisch and Overton, 1985). Concomitantly, there has been a shift away from those forms of family extension where older persons were incorporated within the two-generation nuclear family structure or within other types of extended household co-residence. In 1986, 30 percent of the non-institutionalized population 65 years of age and older in the United States were living alone, 54 percent were living with their spouse, and 16 percent were living with their relatives or friends. Of those not currently married, 65 percent were living alone (Harris, N.D.).

These patterns of living alone are relatively new among the older population in the United States, emerging over the last several decades (see among others Pampel, 1983; Kobrin, 1976; Kobrin 1981; Michael et al, 1980). In the past, family centrality implied the incorporation of older family members within a larger, more complex household; it also resulted in relatively high status for the older person within these households. In more modern communities, with the opportunity structure no longer located in a family context, older persons lose some of their control over resources and no longer possess the power derived from knowledge. Hence, the status of the elderly is reduced in proportion to the rate of change.

One element involved in the autonomy and status of the elderly is whether older persons have more or less power than others in the household. There is likely to be greater symmetry in relationships within households where only older persons live than in households where older and younger persons live together. Relative power within extended households reflects both the economic contribution of the older person to the resources in the household and the social status of older persons within the value system of particular groups.

Important variations at any point in time in the extent of living alone and in the status and power of the elderly parallel the factors associated with the increase over time. Age, health, and the differential availability of households containing family members in which to incorporate older persons affect living arrangements. For example, persons age 60-65 are less likely to live alone than those age 80-85; healthy older persons are more likely than the chronically ill to live independently; never married persons and childless couples average fewer potential family members to join together in a household than those who have been married and couples who had large numbers of children (see for example, Bishop, 1986).

Economic resources should differentiate the ability of older persons to afford the desired privacy and autonomy of living alone. Furthermore, access to resources may buy power and status within the household. There may also be differential preferences for living arrangement patterns among older persons, since not all those who can afford to live alone do so. Ethnic origin has been used as an indicator of preferences and values in the absence of direct data on values and normative preferences. For example, those from traditional communities where family ties are more extensive (e.g., first generation immigrants to the United States from non-European countries) are significantly less likely than those from more modern, less family-oriented societies to live alone, even after controlling for income and demographic factors (Kobrin, 1981). Recent research among the elderly population in the United States has also documented that Hispanic origin groups and Blacks are less likely than non-Hispanic whites to live in independent nuclear households, net of age, sex, marital status, and poverty status (Mutchler and Frisbie, 1987). Ethnic and racial differences in living arrangements and in the norms associated with residential independence has also been documented in studies of young adults and their parents in the United States (Goldscheider and Goldscheider, 1988).

This chapter focuses on the older end of the life course (those aged 50 and over) to investigate the determinants of nonfamily living arrangements and of status within more complex households. The designation of those 50 years of age and older as the "older" population allows us to examine and take into account the processes associated with aging. We shall compare among age groups within this "older" population to identify how the younger-aged differ from the older-aged. Age 50 is a convenient starting point for the analysis of households and living arrangements since nestleaving is well under way by then. We attempt to clarify the demographic and economic factors associated with living arrangements of older persons of different ethnic groups and measure the differential power of the elderly who live in extended households.

The basic structure of living arrangements among the older population in the United States includes living alone, joining or being joined by others to extend families, combining with friends and acquaintances, as well as living with spouse (for the married). In this chapter we ask: What are the constraints and preferences shaping the choice of living arrangements among the older population? We focus on the choices by the married and the non-married (including the never married and once married). We compare those who live in "minimum" households (living alone if non-married and living as a couple if married) with those living in more complex households, thus measuring residential autonomy. For those living in complex households, we examine (a) whether these "others" are age peers or persons below age 50 and (b) whether the older person is designated as the head of the household. We shall also include a measure of relative income, comparing the ratio of income of the elderly to others living in complex households. In this way, we obtain some indicator of the power and status of the elderly within complex households.

Based on previous research (in particular, Kobrin, 1981; Pampel, 1983; Angel and Tienda, 1982; Mutchler and Frisbie, 1987), we have organized the constraints and preferences in these living arrangements categories into three sets of determinants:

(1) The first set deals with the availability and accessibility of households containing relatives. Clearly if there are no relatives available, choices about living arrangements are circumscribed.

(2) Even when relatives are available, the question is whether it is feasible to live alone or to extend a household. The issue of feasibility involves both economic and health dimensions as powerful influences on the choices about alternative living arrangements. Economic and health factors are linked as well to the status and power of the elderly within complex households.

(3) The third set of issues revolves around preferences for particular types of living arrangements. The actual choice about

living arrangements, while limited by the availability of relatives to extend a household and the feasibility of such extension, turns on whether such household extension is valued or desired. And family values should be associated with the power and status of the elderly within households.

These three sets of determinants--availability, feasibility, and desirability--are useful to categorize the range of determinants of living arrangements patterns (Kobrin, 1981; Kobrin and Goldscheider, 1982; for a parallel usage of these categories for an analysis of the determinants of age at marriage, see Dixon, 1971). While demographic availability and economic and health feasibility provide the parameters of choices in living arrangements among the older population, the particular choices that are made are shaped by whether household extension is desirable. Notions of family responsibility may encourage family extension, on the one hand, while considerations of privacy and independence may make household extension less likely. The relative status of the older person within the household and whether household extension involves age segregation or generational integration may be linked to family values and the changing place of the elderly within the community.

**Data**

Few data sources contain refined measures to tap the constraints, preferences, and power associated with the living arrangements of the elderly. Yet, data on the living arrangements of the older population derived from census materials yield important insights into the ways these determinants operate and help direct our focus toward areas where intensive research is likely to be most fruitful. We shall present some first results of a larger project designed to disentangle demographic, economic, health, and ethnic factors in the living arrangements of the older population using 1980 Public Use Microdata Sample A (5% sample). These data allow us to combine individual and household level information so we can study not only older persons but the composition and characteristics of the households where older persons reside.

Our focus is on the population of the state of Rhode Island, with a particular emphasis on the ethnic dimension of living arrangements. We argue that ethnic communities affect the choices older persons make about their living arrangements: whether to live in extended households, with whom to co-reside, and whether to retain the headship role. Ethnic communities may be viewed as one primary source of traditional values, emphasizing the centrality of the family and the extension of households to incorporate, where possible, older persons. We expect that these traditional values involve a wide range of household extension types, so that older persons from traditional ethnic origins will live with age peers as well as with younger persons and will be less likely to live in minimum households.

When living with others in more complex households, we expect that older persons from more traditional ethnic origins will remain the household head in line with the value placed on family centrality. Hence, ethnic variation in living arrangements that does not reflect demographic, economic, and health variation among ethnic populations should provide clues about differential living arrangement preferences. Ethnic communities are most salient at the local rather than at the national level; hence, our focus is on one particular community characterized by ethnic pluralism. Such a focus also has the advantage of comparing groups that have access to similar housing and job markets.

The state of Rhode Island contains a variety of ethnic communities as well as racial groups that vary in living arrangements. There are large foreign born subpopulations among the elderly from diverse places of origin. Some of those from earlier waves of immigration can be identified in this data set, e.g., Irish, Italian, and French Canadian, as well as broader subgroups of persons who identify their origins from "western" and "eastern" European countries. Immigrants from non-European countries can also be compared (e.g., Armenians, Central Americans, and Asians), while some ethnic groups can be subdivided into immigrants from earlier and more recent waves of immigration (e.g., Portuguese). Many of these groups have been characterized by strong family and kinship ties (Kobrin and Goldscheider, 1978; Kobrin and Goldscheider, 1982; Kobrin, 1981; Angel and Tienda, 1982). Older persons from more recent waves of immigration originating from non-European countries (largely from Asian countries and Central America for Rhode Island) are most likely to express these family connections. Thus, a focus on one state allows us to approximate real ethnic communities (as opposed to aggregates of persons at the national level who do not necessarily form communities). The limitations of examining living arrangement patterns in only one state are, therefore, balanced by our ability to examine diverse ethnic communities in greater depth.

The race and ethnic categories included in the analysis are: Black, Irish, French Canadian (including those who identified themselves as French or French Canadian), Italian, Portuguese, Non-European (including Armenian), and a general category labeled European-North American. Blacks were defined by the question on race, while ethnic communities were constructed primarily through the 1980 census ancestry question (first entry), filling in where necessary with country of birth data. The European-North American category combines English, Scottish, German, Swedish, Polish, Russian, and other "west" and other "east" Europeans, together with those who reported themselves "American" or "Canadian". These were collapsed into one category after establishing that there were no systematic differences among these subgroups in their living arrangements. Moreover, their longer exposure to American society made it difficult to argue theoretically that they would be more likely to emphasize family-oriented living arrangements because of the preferences derived from their countries of origin. Therefore, these European groups were joined with the North American categories to represent the overall standard by which one could measure expected patterns of ethnic differences.

The impact of ethnic origins will also be examined by investigating the effect of foreign birth on living arrangements patterns. These comparisons should provide a basis for inferring the direction of ethnic changes over time in living arrangement preferences under similar economic and demographic constraints and for assessing the impact of exposure to American society on living arrangements.

We have only limited measures of the "availability" of relatives to tap the demographic constraints of family extension. Age and marital status will be incorporated into our model, since there is evidence that kin availability decreases with age and that those who were once or are currently married should have more family bonds than the never married. For ever married older women we will examine children everborn as a measure of whether children are available to provide the option for older persons to live in extended households (see R. Avery, et al., 1987, for a similar strategy).

Personal income data are available as a measure of the economic feasibility of living in a minimum household and of the links between income and the status and power of the elderly. We have included the income of the individual along with the individual's other characteristics (e.g., age, disability, and ethnic origins). We have also included a measure of relative income, linking the personal income of the older person to total household income. Data on health status that may constrain living alone or may be linked to the status and power of the older persons in complex households are not directly available from the census. We will use one of the measures of disability that was included in the census (whether the person has any difficulty using public transportation) to provide clues to health constraints. While there are clear limitations to these data to measure the health of the older population, our focus on Rhode Island is again helpful since the state is urban and well served by public transportation. (For an assessment of census data on public transportation see Logue, 1987).

Our focus is on three dependent variables constructed from data on relationships within the household:

(1) The proportion in minimum households, defined as those living alone (if unmarried) or living only with spouse (if married);

(2) Of those not living in minimum households, the proportion living with others who are above age 50;

(3) Of those not living in minimum households, the proportion who are household heads (or spouse of head).

## Living Arrangements of Older Persons

As a first descriptive step, we present for each ethnic group the fraction living in minimum households; of those in more complex households, we present the proportion living only with other elderly; and the proportion who are the household head or spouse of head, by age and marital status (Table 5-1). These data show that overall, about 65 percent of the white population of Rhode Island age 50 and over and from North America or of European origins live in minimum households. This is somewhat higher than among Blacks, or among Italians, French Canadians, and the Irish, and much higher than for Portuguese (48 percent) and those of non-European origins (41 percent).

There are also obvious indications in these data that age and marital status are important considerations in the extent to which older people live in minimum households. For all ethnic groups, the youngest of the older population (age 50-59) are least likely to live in minimum households. In general, the proportion living in minimum households is lower among those age 80 and over than those age 60-79. Older persons who are currently married and once married are different from the never married in the extent of living in minimum households, with the never married less likely overall to live in minimum households.

The extent of living in minimum households, however, varies significantly by ethnic origin within age groups. Among those age 50-59, the proportion in minimum households ranges from 49 percent of the Europe-North Americans to 28 percent of those of non-European origins. Similarly, while about three-fourths of the European origin ethnics age 60-79 are in minimum households, only about half of the non-Europeans and 61 percent of the Portuguese are in these types of households. There is also ethnic variation in the extent of living in minimum households in the oldest age segment, those 80 years of age and older, and within marital status categories.

The data also show considerable variation in the proportion of older persons living in complex households, where there are only age-peers as co-residents. Among those in more complex households, about 30 percent of the whites from Europe-North America, and those of Irish and Italian origins, are in households where the other co-residents are age peers (age 50 and over) compared with 16 percent of the Blacks and about one-fourth of the French Canadians and Portuguese. And there is enormous variation by age and marital status. The age effect on coresidence with age peers is positive: the older the age, the higher the proportion in households where there are only older persons. The never married living in complex households are almost exclusively living with age peers, about twice the level when compared with the once married who, in turn, are more likely than the currently married to be in complex households only with persons over the age of 50. Within age and marital status categories, ethnic variation persists in the proportion co-resident with older persons in complex households.

### Table 5-1

**MEASURES OF LIVING ARRANGEMENTS BY ETHNIC ORIGIN, AGE, AND MARITAL STATUS: RHODE ISLAND POPULATION 50 YEARS OF AGE AND OLDER, 1980**

| Age and Marital Status | Europe North America | Blacks | Italian | Irish | French Canadian | Portuguese | Non-European |
|---|---|---|---|---|---|---|---|
| *Percent in Minimum Households* | | | | | | | |
| Total | 65 | 55 | 53 | 54 | 61 | 48 | 41 |
| Age | | | | | | | |
| 50–59 | 49 | 39 | 35 | 37 | 40 | 34 | 28 |
| 60–79 | 76 | 70 | 67 | 65 | 74 | 61 | 54 |
| 80+ | 68 | 50 | 56 | 65 | 71 | 55 | 52 |
| Marital status | | | | | | | |
| Currently | 65 | 52 | 55 | 52 | 60 | 48 | 40 |
| Never | 59 | 76 | 35 | 53 | 54 | 39 | 40 |
| Formerly | 68 | 53 | 54 | 59 | 64 | 49 | 69 |
| N | 5,787 | 191 | 2,573 | 1,749 | 2,131 | 1,001 | 344 |
| *Percent Coresident with Older Persons in Complex Households* | | | | | | | |
| Total | 31 | 16 | 29 | 31 | 25 | 23 | 28 |
| Age | | | | | | | |
| 50–59 | 18 | 07 | 21 | 17 | 15 | 14 | 13 |
| 60–79 | 37 | 23 | 34 | 39 | 36 | 27 | 43 |
| 80+ | 87 | — | 81 | 82 | 74 | 79 | 75 |
| Marital status | | | | | | | |
| Currently | 14 | 02 | 13 | 13 | 12 | 10 | 17 |
| Never | 96 | — | 97 | 89 | 98 | 83 | 78 |
| Formerly | 50 | 29 | 47 | 85 | 38 | 37 | 34 |
| *Percent Heads or Spouse of Heads in Complex Households* | | | | | | | |
| Total | 81 | 90 | 81 | 80 | 83 | 80 | 76 |
| Age | | | | | | | |
| 50–59 | 93 | 94 | 88 | 94 | 94 | 90 | 87 |
| 60–79 | 73 | 92 | 75 | 66 | 72 | 70 | 62 |
| 80+ | 36 | — | 44 | 43 | 33 | 45 | 50 |
| Marital status | | | | | | | |
| Currently | 99 | 99 | 99 | 99 | 98 | 97 | 93 |
| Never | 36 | — | 28 | 36 | 41 | 31 | 28 |
| Formerly | 51 | 79 | 50 | 53 | 58 | 54 | 56 |
| N | 1,998 | 87 | 1,201 | 803 | 835 | 521 | 202 |

The proportion of the older population who are "heads" of households or spouses of heads in more complex households also varies by age and marital status, but less so by ethnic origin. Almost all those age 50-59 are household heads and there is an inverse relationship between age and headship: old persons over the age of 80 are least likely to be household heads. Virtually all the currently married are household heads and the once married are more likely to be household heads than the never married. Except for Blacks, about 80 percent of the older population living in complex households are household heads or spouses of heads.

Taken together, these descriptive data show considerable variation among ethnic groups in these forms of living arrangements, within the demographic constraints of age and marital status. To disentangle the factors associated with ethnic variation while including the effects of gender and resources, we need to examine these patterns in a multivariate format. To this end, we present in Table 5-2 logistic regression coefficients predicting (1) the likelihood of living in a minimum household, (2) the likelihood of being co-resident with older persons in a complex household, and (3) the likelihood of being head or spouse of head in a complex household. We present these coefficients separately for the married and non-married. Included as predictors are age, income, disability, ethnicity, and foreign born status; for the non-married we add as well details on marital status categories (never married, widowed, and divorced) and gender.

The analysis is organized in terms of the three themes noted earlier: (1) availability, (2) resources, and (3) preferences. We focus first on issues of availability by examining the interplay of age and marital status (Table 5-2).

## Availability

The data show clearly the importance of demographic and life cycle constraints on living arrangement choices. The younger age segment is significantly less likely than those age 60-79 (the reference category) to live in minimum households, whether married or not. They are less likely to live with age peers when they are in more complex households. When not living alone or only living with their spouse, they are more likely than those age 60-79 to be living with younger persons. In most cases that means their children. It is not surprising, therefore, that those age 50-69 are more likely than those age 60-79 to be the household head, whether married or not.

In sharp contrast, those age 80 and over are significantly more likely than those age 60-79 to live only with their spouse when married but less likely to live alone when unmarried. Reflecting the life cycle effects of aging, the "old-old" are more likely to be living with age peers when they live in complex households. They are also more likely to be a dependent member of complex households (i.e., they are less likely than those age

### Table 5-2
### MODELS OF LIVING ARRANGEMENTS FOR THE OLDER POPULATION OF RHODE ISLAND, 1980

| | Logistic Regression Coefficients | | | | | |
|---|---|---|---|---|---|---|
| | Minimum Household | | Old with Old | | Headship | |
| | Married | Unmarried | Married | Unmarried | Married | Unmarried |
| Intercept | 5.733* | 5.599* | 4.367* | 5.022* | 6.058* | 4.681* |
| Age | | | | | | |
| 50–59 | −.755* | −.376* | −.289* | −.398* | .598* | .388* |
| 80+ | .198* | −.105* | 1.031* | 1.004* | −.672* | −.175* |
| Marital status | | | | | | |
| Never | — | −.223* | — | 1.806* | — | −.588* |
| Divorced | — | .082† | — | .331* | — | −.148† |
| Female | — | −.140* | — | −.134† | — | .249* |
| Income (1000s) | −.010* | .009* | .000 | −.020* | .040* | .040* |
| Disability | .030 | −.213* | .196† | .083 | −.455* | −.242* |
| Ethnic group | | | | | | |
| Blacks | −.275* | −.148 | −.813* | −.543* | .126 | .702* |
| Irish | −.279* | −.164* | −.079 | −.109 | .151 | −.023 |
| French-Canadians | −.116* | −.197* | −.141† | −.118 | .111 | .108 |
| Italians | −.248* | −.322* | −.092 | .027 | .168 | −.085 |
| Portuguese | −.332* | −.380* | −.236* | −.285* | .052 | .043 |
| Non-Europeans | −.563* | −.407* | .099 | −.457* | −.401* | .129 |
| Foreign born | −.015 | .002 | −.034 | .005 | −.278* | −.124† |
| Chi-square | 9,072.53 | 4,739.43 | 3,804.92 | 2,106.81 | 4,881.05 | 1,926.25 |
| (DF) | (12) | (15) | (12) | (15) | (12) | (15) |
| N | 9,072 | 4,743 | 3,769 | 1,883 | 3,769 | 1,883 |

\* $p < .05$.
† $.10 > p < .05$.

60-79 to be the household head).

In part, these age effects reflect the changing life cycle patterns associated with aging: the decline in the presence of children in the household with age; increasing dependence of the aged on others because of health and resource constraints; and the declining power of the older person within the household and, hence, the emergence of others as head in extended households. The data show that the cost of moving in with others increases with age in terms of the loss of power within the household.

An examination of previous marital status patterns among the elderly who are not currently married reveals that the never married are less likely than the widowed (the reference category) to live alone; when living with others, the never married are much more likely to live with age peers and less likely to be the head of the household. The divorced are somewhat more likely than the widowed to live alone and display the same patterns as the never married in living with age peers and being the household head. The patterns for the divorced, while statistically significant, do not contrast as sharply with the widowed as do the patterns of the never married.

There are gender differences in these living arrangements patterns, in particular, women are less likely than men to live alone. When living in complex households, women are less likely than men to live with age peers (i.e., they are more likely to be in households with persons less than age 50, probably with their children) and are more likely to be the household head. Thus, older unmarried women are less likely than men to live by themselves; but when living with others they are more likely to be the head, incorporating others within their households rather than being incorporated within the households of others.

A more direct indicator of demographic availability is the number of children everborn to women. Data in Table 5-3 show the importance of

**Table 5-3**

**THE EFFECT OF NUMBER OF CHILDREN EVER BORN ON LIVING ARRANGEMENTS OF THE OLDER POPULATION: LOGISTIC COEFFICIENTS**

|  | Minimum Household | | Old with Old | | Headship | |
|---|---|---|---|---|---|---|
|  | Married | Unmarried | Married | Unmarried | Married | Unmarried |
| Number of children ever-born | −.191* | −.093* | −.134* | −.124* | .074* | .070* |

\* $p < .05$.
NOTE: Same variables as in Table 5-2.

children everborn for living arrangements choices among the older population. These data are for women only and include all the other variables in the model as in Table 5-2; the detailed model, however, is not presented in tabular form. Except where noted, the other effects are similar. The number of children everborn is clearly related negatively to living in minimum households and to living with age peers among those in more complex households. Moreover, the probability of headship increases as the number of children everborn increases.

**Feasibility**

The next set of influences on the living arrangements of older persons focuses on the feasibility of living alone. There are clear indications from the data that there are resource and health constraints on the living arrangements of the older population. Higher personal income increases the probability of living alone among the non-married, but decreases the probability of living in a minimum household among the married. Data not presented in tabular form show that this finding is particular to men: higher personal income significantly increases the likelihood that women live in minimum households, whether they are married or not. Income also purchases power, as evidenced by the positive relationship with headship among those in complex households. Increased income also buys "out" of living with older co-residents: When older unmarried persons live in more complex households, they are less likely to live with age peers if they have more money. Viewed in another way, the data are consistent with the general argument that poorer older persons are more likely to extend a household; richer households are more likely to become extended.

Confirming these findings are data, not presented in tabular form, on the impact of the relative income of older persons on their living arrangements within complex households. For both the married and the unmarried, the higher the ratio of the income of the older person to total household income, the lower the probability of living with age peers. And as with measures of individual income, there is a clear and strong negative relationship between the relative income of older persons and household headship: For both the married and the non-married, the larger the ratio of the older person's income to total household income, the more likely the older person will be the household head. Thus, higher relative income of older persons within complex households allows them to avoid living with age peers and increases the "power" of older persons within these households as indicated by headship.

Our measure of disability reflects the difficulty, noted earlier, of using public transportation. It is crude measure of the health constraints on living arrangements. But the patterns are consistent with the view that an important factor associated with the choices involved in living arrangements of the elderly is the functional health status of older persons. The data show a negative effect of health constraints on living alone among the non-married. However, this effect does not characterize the married, suggesting that the spouse is likely to care for those less than fully mobile in minimum households. Those expressing difficulty using public transportation are very unlikely to be the household head. So dependency in one area of life (health) is linked to dependency within the household.

## Preferences

The third set of factors examines the relative probabilities of living in minimum households, living with age peers, and being the household head among ethnic subgroups. We treat ethnic origin as an indicator of preferences for family and non-family living and for the status and power of the older person within complex households. The reference category is the white population from European-North American origins.

The data show significant effects of ethnic origin on living in minimum households among both the married and non-married. All the white ethnic groups identified are significantly less likely than those of European-North American origins to live alone (or with spouse, if married). The more traditional of the ethnic populations (Portuguese and non-Europeans) are also very unlikely to live with age-peers if non-married; this pattern also characterizes Blacks.

Ethnic origin, however, appears to have little effect on headship in complex households, except for unmarried Blacks (who are more likely to be the household head), and the married from non-European origins (who are very unlikely to be a household head). The major effects on headship stem from demographic-life cycle factors and resource and health constraints rather than preferences, at least as reflected in our ethnic measure.

Interestingly, foreign born status does not seem to change the probability of living in minimum households or living with age peers. However, it has an effect on headship: for those living in more complex households, being foreign born reduces the probability of headship. Thus, household extension among the older foreign born population means joining a household as a dependent rather than having others join the household of the elderly person. Reverence for the elderly, often described for older first generation Americans, does not characterize the headship patterns of the foreign born living in complex households.

As an extension of these findings, we examined whether the effect of foreign born status differed among ethnic groups. We found that while foreign born status generally did not significantly affect the proportion living in minimum households, this was not the case for all ethnic groups. Data not presented in tabular form show that married foreign born Portuguese and foreign born non-Europeans are significantly less likely to live in minimum households than are the native born of these groups. Thus, while Portuguese and non-Europeans in general are less likely to live in minimum households, the first generation, foreign born among them are even less likely to be living in minimum households. This pattern does not characterize the other ethnic groups considered, suggesting that for them the lower probability of living in minimum households is an ethnic effect and not particularly characteristic of the foreign born. For the non-married, the ethnics considered are less likely to live alone than those from

North American and other European origins. But the Irish and the French Canadian foreign born are significantly more likely to live alone if non-married. In part, the foreign born older population of these ethnic groups may be facing greater constraints for household extension, given the demographic availability of relatives. More directly, these data clearly suggest that for the native born of these and other ethnic groups, ethnic networks and preferences for family extension operate to discourage living alone. The values and preferences of the ethnic community seem to be the more powerful factor, rather the "traditional" values associated with the first generation, foreign born.

## Discussion

Whether older persons live alone, with whom they share their households, and what the status of the elderly is within these households are emerging issues for sociological analysis and policy. The data we have analyzed demonstrate the importance of demographic, life cycle, economic, and health factors in shaping the living arrangements of older persons. More importantly, we have documented the significance of membership in ethnic communities in determining these living arrangement choices. The ethnic factor remains powerful after the effects of other variables have been controlled. Thus, even when income is sufficient and relatives are available, ethnic origin shapes the choices older persons make in terms of household extension. The ethnic effect is not particularly characteristic of the foreign born and for most extends into subsequent native born generations. Thus, the effects of ethnicity on living arrangements are not the simple transfer of "old world" or "traditional values" but reflects the importance of both ethnic networks and family values that result in the greater probability that ethnic communities will extend their households to incorporate older persons.

In contrast to the effects of ethnic origin on living in minimum households, ethnicity seems to have little effect on headship and an inconsistent pattern for whether the household extension is age segregated. Issues of power and status may require other measures than available in the census. Perhaps, being in a complex household is the relevant status issue for ethnic groups, whether the elderly are the head of the household and irrespective with whom they live.

We interpret the effects of ethnic origin on living arrangements as revealing preferences and ethnic networks. In particular, these values stress the importance of family and the power of ethnic networks to incorporate isolated older persons within complex households. We have no direct measures of these values and preferences but the data presented clearly are consistent with such a view.

There are related issues that can be clarified by further analysis of census data. In particular, census data can be organized to exploit the combined household and individual files so as to describe the composition of complex households in greater detail. We should be able to uncover the relative similarity of persons in the household not only in terms of age but also in terms of relationships and ethnic origin.

We have shown that ethnic groups form networks of relationships in American communities that extend their impact on older persons and their living arrangements patterns. While this has been noted in the past, it has been associated with disadvantages of race and Hispanic origin. But ethnicity extends beyond Blacks and Hispanics and persists even when income factors are controlled. Indeed, the patterns noted for Irish and Italian origin groups clearly reflect the involvement of the third and perhaps the fourth generation in the living arrangements of the elderly.

Census data are not fully adequate for measuring demographic availability. Our inferences have therefore been indirect from data on age, and marital status, and the number of children born to women. Similarly, census data cannot clarify the preferences we have inferred from ethnic group membership. Alternative methodological strategies are needed to obtain data that not only tap the effects of ethnic intensity but also measure values and preferences directly. Census data, however, are most useful to document general patterns that require further analysis.

There are two general implications of this analysis that extend beyond issues of aging per se. The first relates to the continuity of the ethnic factor over the generations. Although we continue to document the persistence of ethnicity as a factor in American life, we have not yet clarified the factors that sustain ethnic continuity. How are values and preferences reinforced over time and conveyed between generations? Are some values and interests more likely to be transmitted than others? Are there ethnic groups that are more successful in transmitting those values over time?

Secondly, the incorporation of the older population into more complex households affects the nature of family relationships. Contacts between the generations as well as family conflict continue to be shaped by the living arrangement choices older persons make. These choices not only affect the lives of older persons but are likely to have a profound impact on the lives of their children and other relatives. Issues of privacy, autonomy, age segregation, and independence contrast with the interdependence of family members, knowledge of, and respect for, those at other life cycle stages, and the general mutuality associated with family relationships. In this sense, the examination of the living arrangements of older persons is linked to broader sociological concerns about ethnic continuity and family changes.

## REFERENCES

Avery, R., A. Speare, and L. Lawton. 1987. "Social Support, Disability, and Independent Living of Elderly in the United States." Paper presented at the ISA Inter-Congress Meeting of the Research Committee on Aging, University of Manitoba, Winnipeg, Manitoba.

Angel, R. and M. Tienda. 1982. "Determinants of Extended Household Structure: Cultural Pattern or Economic Need?" *American Journal of Sociology* 87:1360-1383.

Bishop, Christine. 1986. "Living Arrangement Choices of Elderly Singles: Effects of Income and Disability." *Health Care Financing Review* 7:65-73.

Dixon, Ruth. 1971. "Explaining Cross-Cultural Variations in Age at Marriage and Proportions Never Marrying." *Population Studies* 25:215-233.

Ermisch J. and E. Overton, 1985. "Minimal Household Units: A New Approach to the Analysis of Household Formation." *Population Studies* 39:33-54.

Goldscheider, C. and F. Goldscheider. 1988. "Ethnicity, Religiosity, and Leaving Home: The Structural and Cultural Bases of Traditional Family Values." *Sociological Forum* 3:525-547.

Harris, L. and Associates. N.D. *Problems Facing Elderly Americans Living Alone*. Study # 854010, Mimeo.

Kobrin, Frances. 1976. "The Fall in Household Size and the Rise of the Primary Individual in the United States. *Demography* 13:127-138.

Kobrin, Frances. 1981. "Family Extension and the Elderly: Economic, Demographic, and Life Cycle Factors." *Journal of Gerontology*. 3:370-377.

Kobrin, F. and C. Goldscheider. 1978. *The Ethnic Factor in Family Structure and Mobility*. Cambridge: Ballinger Publishing Co.

Kobrin, F. and C. Goldscheider. 1982. "Family Extension or Nonfamily Living: Life Cycle, Economic, and Ethnic Factors." *Western Sociological Review* 13:103-118.

Logue, Barbara. 1987. "Public Transportation Disability and the Elderly: An Assessment Based on 1980 Census Data." *Population: Research and Policy Review* 6: 177-194.

Michael, Robert, Victor Fuchs and Sharon Scott. 1980. "Changes in the Propensity to Live Alone: 1950-1976." *Demography* 17:39-53.

Mutchler, Jan and W. Frisbie. 1987. "Household Structure Among the Elderly: Race/Ethnic Differentials." *National Journal of Sociology* 1:3-23.

Pampel, Fred. 1983. "Changes in the Propensity to Live Alone: Evidence from Consecutive Cross-Sectional Surveys, 1960-1976." *Demography* 20:433-447.

# 6

# Are Mormon Families Different?
## Household Structure and Family Patterns

ANNE CASTLETON AND FRANCES K. GOLDSCHEIDER

Patterns of family life in the United States are changing. The "traditional" American family--with a male head defined by his role as sole or major breadwinner and a female defined by her roles as wife, mother, and housekeeper--is yielding to less traditional family forms. Increasingly, families are headed by only one parent, usually a female. Families with two breadwinners and less clearly differentiated roles in the home are also becoming common. And more people are living outside of families altogether as young people increasingly leave home before marriage and older adults continue on alone after widowhood or divorce.

There is much debate about the source of these changes. It is generally accepted that increasing affluence is contributing to changes in family and household patterns. Considerable debate also focuses on the extent to which these changes reflect changing attitudes toward family roles (Michael, et al., 1980; Burch, 1983; Jacobsen and Pampel, 1987), perhaps reflecting increases in individualism, generally, and a redefinition in women's roles, in particular.

In this context, the state of Utah presents an interesting case study, since its history combines both an emphasis on individualism and a religious tradition that strongly reinforces traditional roles for women. Based on its location in the heart of the western region, Utah might be expected to participate in the lifestyle trends that originated in and are still strongest in the west, such as high divorce rates and female independence. But Utah was settled by a group of dedicated religious pioneers, whose descendants still dominate the religious and cultural life of Utah and make up about 70% of the population (Church Almanac, 1987, Glenmary, 1982). Most traditional religious groups strongly reinforce family life, and particularly emphasize the centrality of the role of wife and mother for women, limiting their independence and autonomy. This paper discusses the "western" and traditional religious influences and links them to various demographic indicators of family life in Utah. For comparison, we examine similar values for California -- the quintessential western state -- and Rhode Island, another state that reports an even higher percentage of religious affiliation than Utah, but has a majority Catholic population (Glenmary, 1982).

We define two types of behavior: individualistic and family-oriented behavior. In a woman's life, individualistic behavior ordinarily means fewer children, later age at marriage, higher rates of divorce, and higher rates of female household headship. Individualistic behavior is consonant with the western lifestyle.

In contrast, family-oriented behavior has been historically typical of women and is still socially normative in fundamental, traditional religions. Family-oriented behavior is manifest in: younger age at marriage (signifying that the women's lifework will be circumscribed by work within family and home), more childbearing, lower divorce rates, and lower female household headship rates, both before marriage when young women might live in the parental home, and after divorce or widowhood.

**Religion and Family Patterns**

It has frequently been noted that there is a link between affiliation with religions that hold to traditional sex roles and demographic variables like age at first marriage, proportions ever married and ever divorced, and the number of children ever born (Scanzoni, 1975; Thornton and Camburn, 1986). Traditional religions hold that women's purpose in the world is circumscribed by the roles of wife and mother and that women belong in the home. This has generally characterized Catholicism and Mormonism.

The Catholic religion strongly favors traditional sex roles. John Scanzoni states, in reviewing the literature on fertility: "...(since) Catholic women may be more likely to see motherhood and related traditional behaviors in sacred terms, fulfillment of these kinds of behaviors may provide a sense of reward and satisfaction that they do not see as attainable in any other way... (Hence) women who view their role more traditionally are more likely to have more children" (Scanzoni, 1975:8-10). The Catholic church reinforces its support of traditional sex roles with its birth control and divorce policies. Birth control is still officially anathema in the Church and divorce constitutes the breaking of a sacrament. Those who cannot annul their marriages officially commit adultery by remarrying. However, there has been considerable change in some family-related behavior among Catholics, particularly in family size and contraceptive usage (Goldscheider and Mosher, 1988), which may carry over to other family behaviors as well.

Rhode Island is a state with 77.3% of its people claiming religious affiliation (Glenmary, 1982); most of these are Catholic. In comparing our selected demographic variables in Rhode Island and Utah, we can examine the cases of two states with high traditional religious affiliation.

Although notions of family life and marriage have been central to

Mormonism from its inception, the specific forms of marriage and family structure have undergone significant changes. Once part of the avant-garde in innovative marital and family living patterns, contemporary Mormons are firmly ensconced in the camp of family traditionalists. Polygyny was officially banned in 1890, and by 1904, official Mormon sanctions were levied against those who still participated (Quinn, 1985).

The first few decades of the twentieth century mark what Mormon historians call the Great Accommodation. Mormonism has become a uniquely conservative American religion. Mormons are known for their pecuniary acumen, their health code, and some of their political stances. The church's response to the sexual revolution of the 1960s and 1970s was to become even more firmly committed to traditional views on family life, marriage, and sexual purity.

The church, while espousing the concept of equal rights, has opposed efforts to make gender equality legally binding. In the late 1970s, the church joined Phyllis Schlafly in opposing the ERA as a threat to the family and was embarrassed by the activities of Sonia Johnson and other "Mormons for ERA," who exposed secret church-sponsored funding of anti-ERA activities.

Within the church, women have lost organizational autonomy. Late in the 1960s, in response to phenomenal growth, Church leaders developed a plan to organize and streamline church administration (Gottlieb & Wiley, 1984). While this plan, called "Correlation", was organizationally effective, it stripped the three women's auxiliaries of their autonomy. Especially hard hit was the Relief Society, perhaps the oldest continuing women's organization in the nation (est. 1842) and the Church's only organization for adult women. The Relief Society lost its financial independence, its organizational organ *The Relief Society Magazine*, and control over its building, its policy decisions, and the content of its lesson manuals.

The most powerful leaders of the church, all male, are elderly, making them, in general, less amenable to change and more traditionally focused. Currently, church leaders tend to be selected from the swelling ranks of successful Mormon businessmen. Some serve for life. As a result, the median age of the 79 male General Authorities is 64.1 years; the leaders of this group, the 12 apostles, average 67.8 years. In the top level, the three-member first Presidency, the average age is 73.3 (Church Almanac, 1987).

The effect of geriatric leadership on a burgeoning bureaucracy is conservatizing. When family and lifestyle are in question, they tend to look to the past for precedents. In a televised address in February of 1987, Ezra Taft Benson (age 88), the current Church President, called on mothers to stay or return home from work and for young couples not to delay childbearing. This address created much controversy in the church but was viewed by many orthodox Mormons as the will of God.

The recent political foment over women and family issues and the stance taken by Mormon church leaders suggests that the Mormon church is moving even further toward the traditional, fundamentalist position on these issues than they were in the 1950s. Though this could be a response to rapid behavioral change, it could also prevent the incursion of new egalitarian ideas. This suggests that Mormons and thus Utah will show patterns similar to those of the members of traditional, fundamental religions. In contrast, it is likely that Catholics, particularly in the United States, are moving in the direction of greater individualism and more freedom in family matters.

**Individualism and Family Patterns**

It is also the case that Utah is a western state with a frontier heritage. Several studies support the notion that regional attitudinal differences exist that are linked to individualism. In a series of in-depth interviews taken in 1943, the Roper-Survey sampled the attitudes of young women between the ages of 20 and 35. The analysis of these data uncovered some peculiarly western patterns. Western women were more likely to support egalitarian sexual standards and less likely to demand virginity in either sex. This western view on sexual morality became the national norm after World War II (Campbell, 1978).

"Western" attitudes move towards greater personal freedom and individuality. One would expect that these attitudes, if enacted behaviorally, would have a destabilizing effect on the traditional nuclear family. Those with lower expectations for chastity would be more likely to break up an unhappy marriage and delay first marriages. Regional data also show high divorce rates in the west.

Historically, there is precedent for western women's attitudes. The women who settled the west were women with a sense of adventure and the willingness to take risks (Faragher, 1979). Those who came west with their husbands and families faced great hardships and those who survived were strong, determined, not easily discouraged, and often used to being independent and resourceful.

The initial state successes for women's suffrage occurred almost exclusively in the west. Wyoming was the first state to allow women to vote in statewide elections in 1870 (Flexner, 1959) and Utah was the first state where women actually voted in city and municipal elections. Colorado, Washington, Oregon, and California followed quickly. Historians argue that in places and circumstances where the community is new and firm traditions have yet to be established, innovative women and other oppressed groups have greater economic, social, and educational opportunities. This was certainly true in the west.

Utah, in particular, is an interesting historical case. First settled by Mormon pioneers in 1847, Utah was in all but name a theocracy. Polygyny was practiced openly from Utah's earliest days. Though this marital anomaly would seem to lead to subservience among participating Mormon women, upon examination there was the potential for an opposite effect. The net result of having one-half, one-third, or one-fifth of a husband compared with a normal monogamous union was that polygynous women were forced to be resourceful and independent, especially when a separate residence was established for each wife. Many supported themselves and their children financially, while others managed good-sized households with no man present much of the time (Arrington, 1971). In addition to the experience of independence based on polygyny, many married Mormon men were sent by church leaders on two to five year proselytizing missions abroad, on colonizing expeditions within the Great Basin area, and some to the East Coast and Europe to be educated in various skills and professions needed to develop Utah (particularly in art, organ building, and medicine).

The lack of men present in Mormon households resulted in the development among Mormon women of many skills unusual for the day. Mormon women cooperated collectively on commercial enterprises like wheat growing and silk farming. Polygyny enabled a number of women to leave their husbands and children in the care of their sister-wives and travel East to obtain medical degrees. By 1890, Utah had the largest enclave of women doctors in the nation (Arrington, 1971). Women published their own newspapers, such as the *Women's Exponent*, which was edited by wives and daughters of prominent church leaders and dedicated to promoting suffrage and the improvement of women's condition. Mormon women supported suffrage and women's causes at the same time they supported the Mormon church leaders.

While Mormon women supported their husbands and church leaders both financially and religiously, they also had the encouragement and support of the church for developing autonomy, independence, and career skills. They participated in the nineteenth century western pattern of individuality, independence, and innovation.

## Hypotheses, Methods, and Data

We are using data for the state of Utah as a surrogate for Mormonism. Mormons constituted 70 percent of Utah's population in 1983 (Church Almanac, 1983) and the long-standing cultural traditions and highly organized local congregations of the church wield an influence greater than the population figures suggest (Heaton, 1986, Chap. 14). Salt Lake City proper is 66.1 percent Mormon (County and City Data Book, 1983). The further one travels from Salt Lake City, within the state, the higher the proportion of Mormons. In rural counties, the population averages 87 percent Mormon (County and City Data Book, 1983).

We test two major hypotheses: First, given our arguments about the relationship between religion, individualism and familism, together with likely changes among Catholics, we hypothesize that:

> States with high levels of traditional religious affiliation, such as Rhode Island, should exhibit family patterns for women more consistent with intense family involvement and stratified gender

roles, while states with a tradition of individualism, such as California, should show the reverse, although differences should be declining over time.

Utah presents a mixture of these two dimensions in its past history, and could reasonably fall into either the western individualistic pattern or the traditional religious family-oriented pattern. However, recent changes in religious theology and practice would seem to be diluting any remaining individualistic and feminist strands. Hence, we hypothesize that:

> Utah will be intermediate between Rhode Island and California in its family patterns; over time, we expect Utah to become more like Rhode Island and less like California.

We will test these hypotheses by examining recent census data on four different dimensions of the centrality of family in women's lives. The first family dimension to be examined is the extent of marital and family roles, measured by the proportion of women ever married by age 20-24 and age 40-44, and by the number of children ever born by age 20-24 and age 45-49.[1] These measures are indicators of the centrality of marital and parental roles in women's life course agenda: the proportion evermarried by age 20-24 taps the immediacy with which women enter family roles upon entering adulthood; the proportion evermarried by age 40-44 is a measure of the extent of marriage, an indicator of long-term alternatives to family roles. Similarly, the number of children ever born indicates the extent of a woman's commitment to parenting, both early in the marital relationship (for those age 20-24) and throughout the childbearing period (i.e., by age 45-49). Data are directly available on the proportion evermarried for 1960, 1970, and 1980, and can be calculated from the information given for 1950. Data on children ever born are only available for 1960, 1970, and 1980. This truncates the period of observation for this variable. However, our data include the period of greatest recent fertility decline, which began in 1957.

The second dimension of the centrality of family in women's lives focuses attention on the quality of the marital relationship, as indicated by the proportion ever divorced by age 49 and percent currently divorced, age 20-49. These measures of divorce should be considered in conjunction with one another. The proportion ever divorced provides an estimate of the balance between structural commitment to family and relationship quality as bases for remaining married. Those with more romantic expectations from marriage are more likely to dissolve unsatisfactory marriages to look

---

[1] It was not always possible to produce exactly comparable age categories, since the categories presented for a given piece of information varied by indicator and by year.

for greater warmth and companionship in a later marriage than those whose commitment is to marriage as an institution. The proportion currently divorced is increased both by high levels of divorce and low levels of remarriage; it allows us to infer the presence of nonmarital alternatives to an unsatisfactory marriage. Low levels on these measures suggests that the quality of the marital relationship is less an important concern in women's commitment to family roles. Data on the proportion currently divorced are available in each of the censuses from 1950 to 1980, but it is only possible to calculate the proportion ever divorced in 1970 and 1980.

The third dimension of family life that we shall examine is headship rates for unmarried women, ages 20-24. Household headship among unmarried women indicates women's relative independence by focusing attention on their access to a home of their own. Residential independence from parents is an indicator of adulthood in the youngest adult years. In families characterized by traditional sex roles, young women entering adulthood but not yet married are more likely to remain in the parental home than establish their own residence for the period between the completion of their education and their marriages (Goldscheider and Goldscheider, 1988). These data are available for all four time points.

Our final dimension of the role of family in women's lives focuses our attention on the extent to which marriage and parenthood serve to limit women's access to nonfamily roles and opportunities compared with their effects on men. Census data on marital, parental, and household status provide no direct information on who holds primary responsibility for the tasks associated with these roles, and the assumption is commonly made that women take most responsibility for caring for family, for their spouse, for their children, and for kin in general. However, one piece of data is available to allow some inference about the extent to which married women are relegated to lower status positions within marriage. We use for this purpose the married headship rate. It only became possible to measure this aspect of the marital relationship in 1980, and most evidence suggests that couples who consider their relationship relatively egalitarian will nevertheless report their husbands as the head of the household. Nevertheless, a small proportion of married couples report the wife as the head, and we will examine these data for California, Utah, and Rhode Island, as well.

## Family Patterns of Religious Groups

Figure 6-1 displays the geographic and temporal patterns of evermarriage. Overall, Utah and California most resemble each other, with high levels of evermarriage, and (through 1970) pronounced early marriage, at least compared with Rhode Island. Women in Rhode Island marry later (about 55 percent had married by ages 20-24 in 1950 compared with more than 70 percent for California and Utah at the same time) and are less likely to have married by age 40-44 throughout the

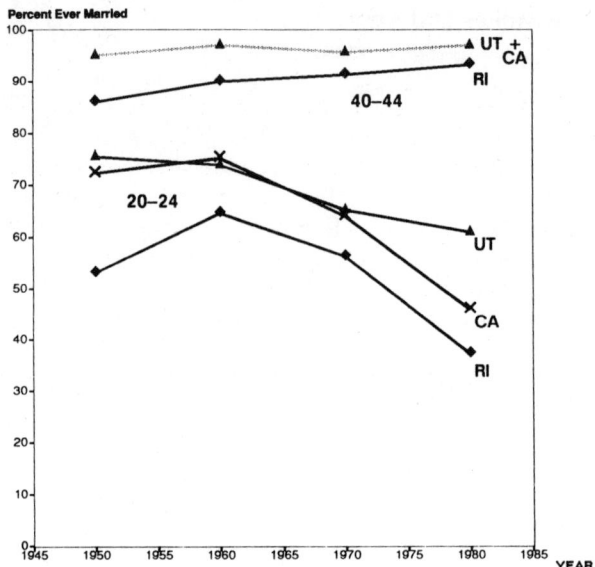

**Fig. 6-1—Percent Ever Married, Women Aged 20–24 and 40–44: 1950–1980**

SOURCES: In U.S. Bureau of Census, *Census of Population,* for specific years (listed in References), see Table 57(1960), Table 105(1960), and Table 152(1970). And in *U.S. Census of Population: 1980,* see Table 205.

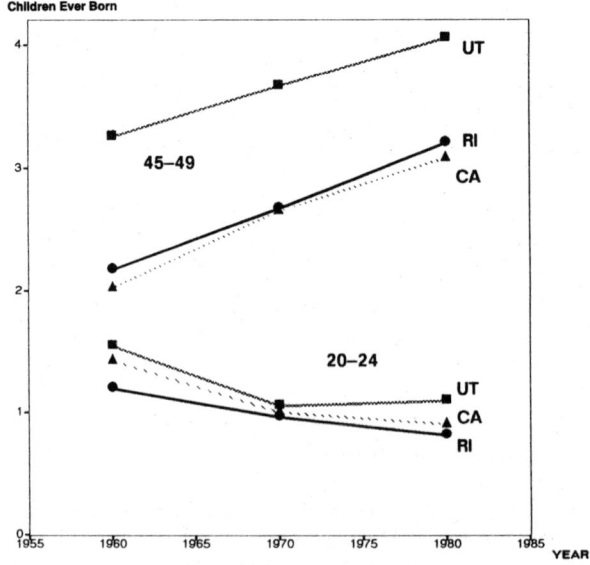

**Fig. 6-2—Children Ever Born for Women Aged 20–24 and 45–49: 1960–1980**

SOURCES: In U.S. Bureau of Census, *Census of Population,* for specific years (listed in References), see Table 113(1960), and Table 161(1970). And in *U.S. Census of Population: 1980,* see Table 211.

period (85 percent to 90 percent evermarrying compared with approximately 95 percent for both Utah and California). Hence, if marriage is an indicator of traditional family behavior, then Rhode Island, despite its high proportion Catholic, is less "traditional" and Utah resembles California in being more "traditional." Actually, the Rhode Island pattern is a longstanding Irish phenomenon that has characterized the state for most of the last century (Kobrin and Goldscheider, 1978). Other ethnic communities show more "normal" marriage behavior, both in terms of marriage timing and in terms of proportions marrying, although Catholics in the United States normally marry later than Protestants. These overall patterns show that Mormons more resemble Protestants than Catholics in terms of the extent of marriage.

However, it is clear that the youngest cohorts are delaying marriage in all three states, with California showing the most pronounced decline in the proportions marrying young, and with Utah showing the least. To the extent that delays in marriage provide young women time to develop alternatives to marital and family roles, Utah is becoming increasingly an outlyer on this dimension, continuing to recruit most of its young women into early marriage.

Utah also appears to be at one extreme on parenthood, as indicated in Figure 6-2. Women in Rhode Island and California have completed childbearing throughout the period with essentially similar family sizes (increasing over time from about 2.1 to 2.8 children ever born, reflecting each later cohort's greater participation in the baby boom) while at each date women in Utah had borne nearly one child more than women in the other states. Women in Utah also seem to be less likely to delay childbearing within marriage, a difference that has increased over the period. In 1950, Utah more closely resembled California, having about 1.4 children born by women aged 20-24, with Rhode Island at a lower level, given its later age at marriage. But by 1980, Rhode Island and California shared a similar low level of early marital childbearing, with less than one child each, while Utah, after dropping considerably between 1960 and 1970, had recovered some of its early childbearing momentum by 1980.

By these indicators, marriage and childbearing are more central in the lives of Utah's women than women in either California or Rhode Island, displaying patterns consistent with strong religious familism with no sign of western individualism. In contrast, both Rhode Island and California, despite their vast differences in traditional religious affiliation and individualistic histories, resemble each other relatively closely.

The story becomes a little more complicated, however, when we turn to marital stability. Figure 6-3 shows the percentage ever divorced by age 45-49 among evermarried women. On this indicator, Utah looks genuinely intermediate between traditional Rhode Island, which has the lowest proportion divorced (less than 10 percent in 1950) and California, which is clearly pioneering on this dimension (with nearly 28 percent of women aged 45-49 who had evermarried having divorced at some point). All three states have participated fairly equally in the rapid increase in divorce over

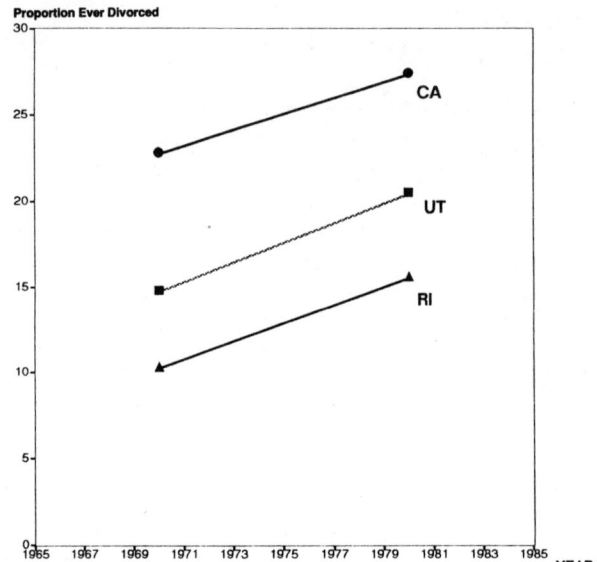

**Fig. 6-3—Proportion of Ever Married Women Ever Divorced by Age 49: 1970–1980**

SOURCES: In U.S. Bureau of Census, *Census of Population* (1970), see Table 152; and in *U.S. Census of Population: 1980,* see Table 205.

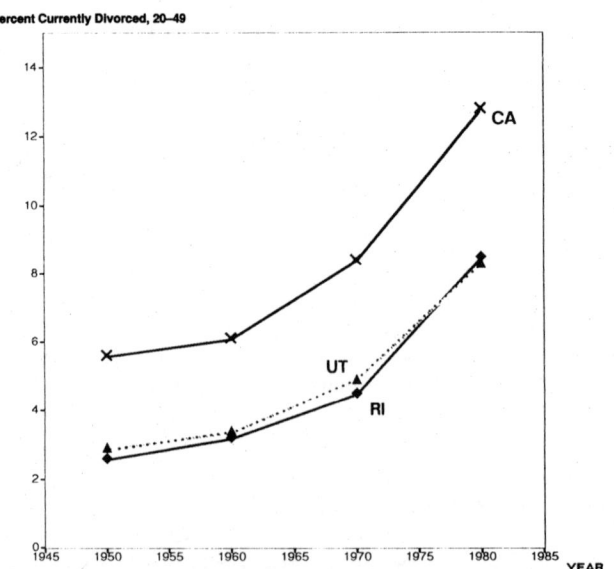

**Fig. 6-4—Percent of Women Currently Divorced, Aged 20–49: 1950–1980**

SOURCES: In U.S. Bureau of Census, *Census of Population,* for specific years (listed in References), see Table 57(1950), Table 105(1960), and Table 152(1970). And in *U.S. Census of Population: 1980,* see Table 205.

the period shown (1960-1980). The particularly low levels of everdivorce found in Rhode Island may reflect the theological differences between Catholicism, on the one hand, which does not allow divorce, and Mormonism and Protestantism, on the other, which do. This interpretation is reinforced by Figure 6-4, which shows that divorcing women in Utah are more likely to remarry than comparable women in Rhode Island, so that both states show distinctly low proportions currently divorced at a given date.

California, in contrast, has more than double the proportion currently divorced of either of the other states. On this indicator, then, both Utah and Rhode Island show high commitments to marriage, although through somewhat different routes, reflecting theological differences. In contrast, the women of California, despite their high level of evermarriage, differ from women in these other two states. Only in California are there increasing proportions of women living outside of marriage, as a result either of extremely high levels of marital dissolution, of lower rates of remarriage, or of both.

While marriage and parenthood are important dimensions of familism, they are not the only ones. Figure 6-5 turns our focus to a quite different dimension, that of independence from parents in early adulthood, prior to marriage. Do the same patterns of family involvement shown for marriage and parenthood characterize this dimension, as well?

Like divorce and fertility, residential independence among young unmarrieds is a rapidly changing dimension of familism. Whereas in 1950, only about 10% of unmarried women aged 20-24 were household heads, by 1980 these three states show levels between 25% and 30%. Utah women have participated actively in this trend, much more so than they have in the retreat from marriage and childbearing. On this dimension, Mormon women have been nearly as independent as those in California, with women in Rhode Island always showing a distinctly lower level of residential independence. In fact, in data not shown, Utah women by 1980 exceeded California women in household headship at almost all ages.

Finally, we test the assumption that family roles are necessarily less independent for women than for men, and examine household headship rates for married women. This information is only available for 1980, the first year in which it was possible for a married woman to be recorded as head of household when her husband was living in the household. Clearly, few did so in any state. Figure 6-6 shows that in no age group for any state did even five percent of marriages make this statement. Nevertheless, the differences among the states are consistent with a portrait of greatest inequality within marriage for Mormon women and most equality for women in California. The Mormon pattern is reinforced by distinguishing between rural and urban Utah populations, since rural Utah is almost entirely traditionally Mormon. In these areas, it was rare for even one percent of married women to be counted as head of their household.

## Discussion

These results indicate that communities that vary in their religious traditionalism and western individualism also vary in demographic behavior linked to the roles of women. The patterns indicate a clear difference, however, between Utah (Mormons) and Rhode Island (Catholics) in the ways their religious traditionalism links to marital family roles--wife and mother--on the one hand, compared with other family roles--in particular, daughter--on the other. Further, there was a considerable difference between the two communities in their response to the rapid changes in family roles of the last two decades.

California in many ways presents the most extreme patterns, but not always in terms of current definitions of individualism. Currently the picture is a coherent one, in which all indicators are consistent with a relatively strong rejection of traditional family roles for women. California women appear to exit the daughter role early in adulthood, establishing independent households outside of marriage. They also exit the wife role easily, and many delay both marriage and remarriage. Their marital roles seem the most egalitarian, with relatively low fertility and the highest household headship rates among married women. However, this picture is the result of very rapid change in the last two decades. In the 1950s, California was characterized by extremely early marriage and high rates of ever marriage.

Rhode Island women, in contrast, appear to be relatively traditional on all dimensions of female family roles, although their religious traditionalism seems to cling more to family ties outside of marriage than to marriage. Rhode Island women defer marriage, but not necessarily to be independent adults, since they are most likely to remain in the parental home for an extended period. Data not presented show that unmarried women of all ages in Rhode Island have relatively low household headship rates, being included as extending members in the households of their parents, children and other relatives. Within marriage, however, their religious traditionalism is only marked in their extremely low levels of divorce; otherwise they exhibit moderate fertility and marital headship. Moreover, like Californians, it is clear that Rhode Island women have been participating actively in the changes of the last two decades, reducing further their levels of marriage and fertility and increasing their headship rates in young adulthood.

Both these states, then, show patterns consistent with our hypotheses, differing from each other in their levels but following the same trends. The results for Utah are also consistent with our general hypotheses. First, it clearly presents a considerably more mixed picture, indicating that, at least until the recent past, Utah really did combine in interesting ways the influence both of its religious and western heritages. Second, it is also clear that the western influence seems to be fading, while the power of religious traditionalism may actually be strengthening.

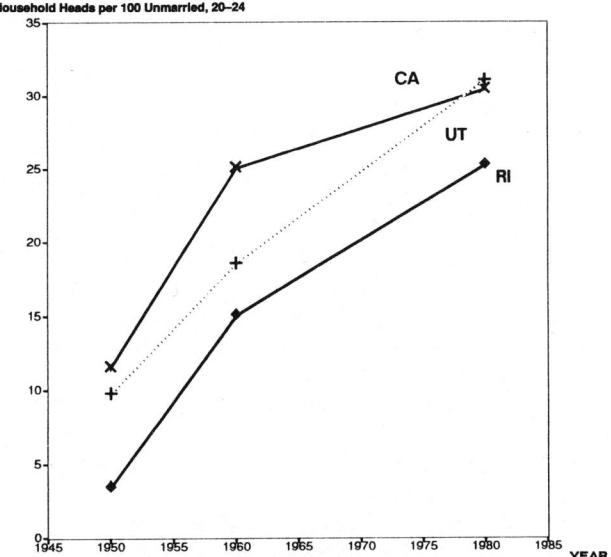

**Fig. 6-5—Headship Rates for Unmarried Women
Aged 20–24: 1950–1980**

SOURCES: In U.S. Bureau of Census, *Census of Population,* for specific years (listed in References), see Table 58(1950), Table 106(1960), and Table 153(1970). And in *U.S. Census of Population: 1980,* see Table 206.

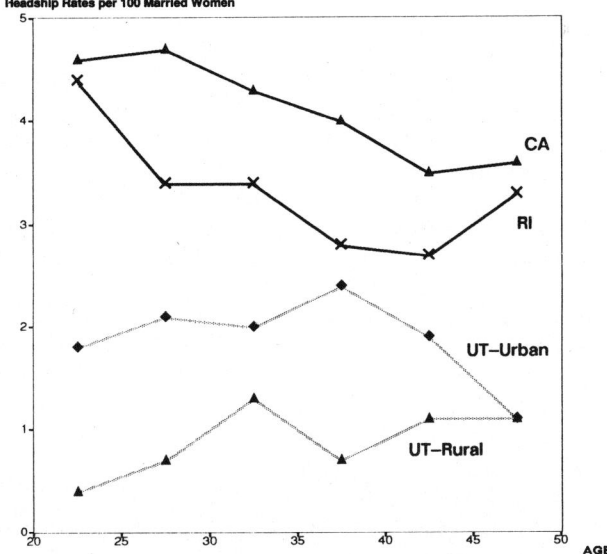

**Fig. 6-6—Headship Rates for Married Women, 1980**

SOURCES: In *U.S. Census of Population: 1980,* see Table 206.

The western tradition seems to translate for the women of Utah into considerable independence, both from the continuing ties of the parental home in early adulthood, and from those of an unsatisfactory marriage. These are indicated by their high rates of household headship among unmarried women as well as their high rates of ever divorce. Within marriage, on the other hand, Utah women seem to have embraced the most traditional definitions of the wife and mother roles. Their patterns of early marriage, high evermarriage, extremely high fertility, and low headship within marriage create an extreme composite of women's adult roles vis a vis marriage and parenthood, in which the roles of spouse and mother are intense and extensive, with strong gender segregation.

Further, only Utah seems to be resisting most of the nonfamily trends of the last two decades. Their marriage rates have declined relatively little and therefore have become much more distinct, compared with trends in Rhode Island and California. Having children early in marriage actually shows some recovery in Utah, unlike the pattern of consistent decline in the other two states. Utah seems to be participating less in the move toward equality in the roles of men and women within marriage, providing women some family role hiatus prior to marriage, reducing the differential responsibilities associated with parenthood through reducing parenthood, or increasing equality of power within marriage. The only dimension on which the women of Utah seem to be responding to family change much like the rest of the country is in the increase in unmarried household headship. This spark of the western tradition seems still to be alive, for the few women who remain unmarried.

In sum, the association of religious traditionalism and family patterns is clearly evident in these states, as are the effects of western individualism. However, the specific patterns differ between Catholic Rhode Island and Mormon Utah, consistent both with differences in doctrine and in current religious interpretations. It would also be interesting to see the ways other religious traditions leave their impress on family patterns, such as the relatively closed communities of the Amish or of Hasidic Jews, as well as the many other religious groups that people these states. However, this analysis of Catholicism and Mormonism was only possible because of the great religious homogeneity of Utah and of Rhode Island, since the census does not provide information on religion. To explore differences among other groups will require data that actually measure religion and its intensity, and that provide large enough samples to explore patterns of variation in relatively small groups. Nevertheless, census data are useful in demonstrating that religion continues to be an important influence on family processes that be studied in depth and in detail.

## REFERENCES

Arrington, L.J. 1971. "Blessed Damozels: Women in Mormon History." *Dialogue* 6:22-31.

Arrington, L.J. and D. Bitton. 1979. *The Mormon Experience: A History of the Latter-day Saints.* New York: Knopf.

Campbell, D. 1978. "Was the West Different? Values and Attitudes of Young Women in 1943." *Pacific Historical Review* 47: 453-463.

*Church Almanac, 1983.* Salt Lake City: *Desert News.*

Faragher, J.M. 1987. *Women and Men on the Overland Trail.* New Haven: Yale University Press.

Flexner, E. 1959. *Century of Struggle: The Women's Rights Movement in the United States.* Cambridge: Belknap Press of Harvard.

Glenmary Research Center. 1981. *Churches and Church Membership in the United States 1980.* Atlanta, Ga.

Glenn, N.D. and J.L. Simmons. 1967. "Are Regional Cultural Differences Diminishing?" *Public Opinion Quarterly* 46:172-180.

Goldscheider, C. and F. Goldscheider. 1988. "Ethnicity, Religiosity, and Leaving Home: The Structural and Cultural Bases of Traditional Family Values." *Sociological Forum* 3: 525-547.

Goldscheider, C. and W. Mosher. 1988. "Religious Affiliation and Contraceptive Usage: Changing American Patterns." *Studies in Family Planning* 19: 48-57.

Gottlieb, R. and P. Wiley. 1984. *America's Saints: The Rise of Mormon Power.* New York: Putnam.

Heaton, T. 1986. "The Demography of Mormons" in *Utah in Demographic Perspective.* SLC: Signature Books.

Kobrin F. and C. Goldscheider. 1978 *The Ethnic Factor in Family Structure and Mobility.* Cambridge, Mass.: Ballinger Publishing Co.

Quinn, M. 1985. "LDS Church Authority and New Plural Marriage, 1890-1904." *Dialogue* 18:9-105.

Scanzoni, J.H. *Sex Roles, Life Styles, and Childbearing: Changing Patterns in Marriage and the Family.* N.Y.: Free Press, 1975.

Stump, R. 1984. "Regional Divergence in Religious Affiliation in the US." *Sociological Analysis* 45:283-299.

Thornton, A. and D. Camburn. 1986. "Religious Commitment and Adolescent Sexual Behavior and Attitudes." Unpublished paper, Survey Research Center, University of Michigan.

U.S. Bureau of Census. 1952. *Census of Population: 1950. Vol. II Characteristics of the Population: Part 5, California.* U.S. Government Printing Office.

U.S. Bureau of Census. 1952. *Census of Population: 1950. Vol. II Characteristics of the Population: Part 39, Rhode Island.* U.S. Government Printing Office.

U.S. Bureau of Census. 1952. *Census of Population: 1950. Vol. II Characteristics of the Population: Part 44, Utah.* U.S. Government Printing Office.

U.S. Bureau of Census. 1963. *Census of Population: 1960. Vol. I Characteristics of the Population: Part 6, California.* U.S. Dept. of Commerce. U.S. Government Printing Office.

U.S. Bureau of Census. 1963. *Census of Population: 1960. Vol. I Characteristics of the Population: Part 41, Rhode Island.* U.S. Dept. of Commerce. U.S. Government Printing Office.

U.S. Bureau of Census. 1963. *Census of Population: 1960. Vol. I Characteristics of the Population: Part 46, Utah.* U.S. Dept. of Commerce. U.S. Government Printing Office.

U.S. Bureau of Census. 1973. *Census of Population: 1970. Vol. I, Characteristics of the Population: Part 6, California, Section 2.* U.S. Government Printing Office, Washington DC.

U.S. Bureau of Census. 1973. *Census of Population: 1970. Vol. I, Characteristics of the Population: Part 41, Rhode Island.* U.S. Government Printing Office, Washington, DC.

U.S. Bureau of Census. 1973. *Census of Population: 1970. Vol. I, Characteristics of the Population: Part 46, Utah.* U.S. Government Printing Office, Washington, DC.

U.S. Bureau of Census. 1983. *County and City Data Book 1983.* Washington, DC: U.S. Government Printing Office.

U.S. Census of Population: 1980. 1983. Detailed Population Characteristics: Part 6, Section 1, California. U.S. Government Printing Office.

U.S. Census of Population. 1983. Detailed Population Characteristics: Part 41, Rhode Island. U.S. Government Printing Office.

U.S. Census of Population. 1983. Detailed Population Characteristics: Part 4, Utah. U.S. Government Printing Office.

# PART II

# 7

# Children Leaving Home and the Household Economy

## FRANCES K. GOLDSCHEIDER

**The Transition to Adulthood**

The process whereby people reduce their connections to the parental family and assume roles more separate from them is marked by a series of transitions: finishing school, beginning work, leaving the parental home, marrying, having children. These may occur very close together or more widely spread over the life course, and many sequences are possible. Substantial research has been done on changing patterns for most of these transitions: we know about the extension of education and the resulting postponement of labor force participation; about age at marriage and changing age patterns of fertility. We are also beginning to learn more about sequences; about the effects of early marriage on educational achievement, of prolonged education on fertility, and we have seen evidence of the compression of these transitions into a narrower span of time (Modell, 1976). However, we know less about the role of leaving home in relation to any of these other processes. It is clear that most leave home before they marry: the two-couple household has been rare throughout U.S. history (Laslett, 1973). And increasingly young single parents are heading separate households (Ross and Sawhill, 1976). But before the formation of a new family through marriage or parenthood, there is a complex of transitions of school, work, and residence about which we know surprisingly little.

There are three basic patterns which characterize this process in contemporary America. One is what could be called the "clean break" sequence, in which maturing children remain at home until they finish school, and leave home almost immediately, fully independent financially. The second is the pattern with which academics are most familiar, in which maturing children leave home while still continuing their education, usually with financial help from their parents. The third pattern is the reverse, in which school ends with no residential change. The children remain at home, often contributing financially to the parental household. In Rhode

Island in the 1970s, as we shall show in the analysis to follow, one-fifth left when they finished school, a quarter continued school after leaving home, and slightly more than half remained in the parental home for at least some time after completing their education.

This variability suggests that we have not yet reached a high level of uniformity in early life cycle transitions. More importantly, the form which this sequence takes warrants study because it relates directly to theories of intergenerational family change. One way to interpret our new knowledge on the history of childhood (Aries, 1962), and the changing role of children in the family, is to see the modern family as primarily a "consumer" of children, in the economists' terms, deriving emotional rewards and spending money on them with no expectation of financial return. In contrast, the traditional family used children as an economic resource (Caldwell, 1982). We are just beginning to realize the magnitude of the consequences of that transition, but it resulted in a dramatic decline in fertility and also a new intergenerational authority pattern that could best be described as "companionate parenthood."

Seen in this theoretical framework, the traditional sequence relating school and residence changes is for children to remain at home until they marry, using the time after school is completed to work, contributing in cash or kind to the well being of the parental family and saving or stitching for the family to come with what time and resources are left over. Although children have become adults, finished with their preparations (i.e., school), and functioning economically as adults, they yet remain at home and contribute to their parental family, sharing in the life, and to some extent the authority structure, of that group. They accept residential and social dependence despite their financial independence.

In contrast, the modern sequence of transitions is characterized by a pattern where children separate from the residential family, its rules and requirements, and its ability to observe their behavior, before they are finished school, before they are self-supporting, receiving parental contributions to their continued education as an investment towards their own, not their parents' financial security. The flow of resources is reversed between the generations, and the children experience greater independence of the family despite their greater financial dependence. The historical record is somewhat oversimplified by this schematic rendering of family change, since it ignores apprenticeship and domestic service, both of which require that children leave home before becoming financially independent. It seems likely, however, that the older adults in such settings, as in 19th century factories and even 20th century colleges, served somewhat in loco parentis, i.e., as parental surrogates.

To test the extent to which such a transition is in process requires data on changes over time in the relationship between educational change and nestleaving patterns. In place of change data, this chapter will examine cross-section patterns in home and school sequences. As an indicator of change over time we shall examine selected ethnic groups. Previous research on family patterns has shown that Catholic families, particularly

Catholic ethnic groups from southern Europe, have persisted in many traditional family forms, including low incidence of divorce, patriarchal and sex specialized division of labor, and higher fertility (Greeley, 1974; Mindel and Habenstein, 1976; Goldscheider and Goldscheider, 1988). They have also been less likely to take advantage of the new opportunities offered by high education as a route to social mobility (Kobrin and Goldscheider, 1978). Other groups have shown more modern patterns in a variety of ways. It seems reasonable to expect, then, that ethnic differences in school and nestleaving patterns will appear among religious and nationally-defined ethnic groups, consistent with other differences which have already been shown.

**Data**

The analysis uses data drawn from a panel of 3,345 households interviewed in Rhode Island between 1967 and 1969 and reinterviewed in 1979. Information was collected on the major life cycle transitions of all children over 16, whether or not they were still present in the household. In the follow-up study, 2,156 households were successfully reinterviewed, yielding information on 2,861 of their children aged 16 to 35 in 1979.

Although the parents were part of a random sample of households, the children are less representative, since children from larger families have a greater probability of inclusion. In addition, as a result of panel attrition, the children are somewhat younger, on average, than a representative distribution of the 16 to 35 year old children of that sample would yield; since older panel members (who are disproportionately the parents of older children) were more likely to have died or to have refused to participate in the interview. We are also less able to observe the nestleaving patterns of those who leave home at an older age, since more of them would still have been living with their parents at the time of the reinterview. Since age patterns are the focus of the analysis, however, this should not be problematic. Finally, the group of children remaining was less likely to have been involved in Viet Nam war-related mobilization.

On the other hand, this is the first data collected in the United States that focused directly on demographic patterns of leaving home. Although the dataset is restricted to the state of Rhode Island, analyses that have used these data have produced important results that have added to our understanding of national patterns observed in other work (Goldscheider and LeBourdais, 1986).

The focus on Rhode Island also adds interest to an analysis of ethnicity. In general, family differences for these ethnic groups have been shown to be similar in other studies. Further, it is an ethnically diverse state, and thus produces richer data than national surveys. In addition, the size and strength of many of the ethnic groups have allowed greater continuity of ethnically distinctive patterns than would be possible for more fragmented groups.

## Nestleaving and Schoolleaving

The first question in an analysis of the relationship between nestleaving and schoolleaving patterns is, what are the separate patterns? A preliminary basis for describing nestleaving (the less well-understood of the two processes) can be gained from Figure 7-1, which shows the proportion of children still living with the survey respondent by sex and age in 1979.[1] The decline with age is very rapid. A sharp drop occurs between age 18 and 19, followed by a slower rate of departure to age 22. The proportion at home agains falls rapidly for several years, until it reaches about 10 percent about age 27, after which point declines are much slower. Not surprisingly, the greatest declines seem to be associated with the normal ages for finishing high school and college. At each age daughters are more likely to have left home than sons, but the differences are slight. Fifty percent of the daughters have left by age 19 and a half; 50 percent of the sons by age 20.

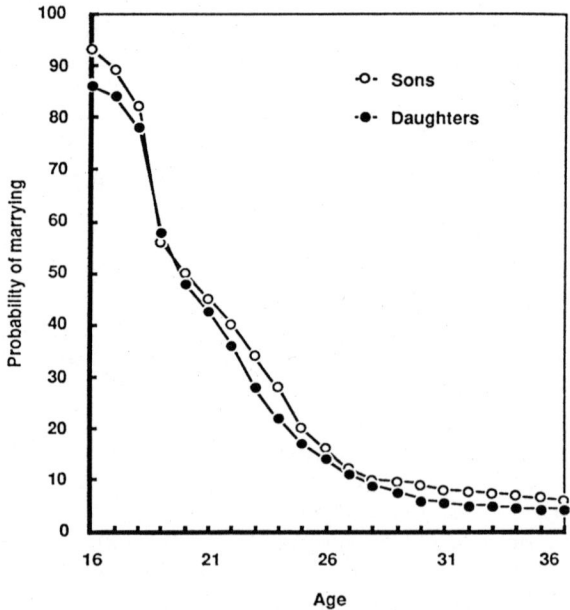

Figure 7-1--Percentage of respondents' children living with them by age and sex of child, 1979

---

[1] Some portion of the children of divorced or remarried respondents, particularly among the youngest group, was living with the other parent or an other relative.

This, however, does not tell when they left. By using the longitudinal data on reported age of leaving home, more detailed comparisons are possible. Table 7-1 presents age at leaving home for the 1,156 children who were living at home at age 16 and had left by age 36, grouped into three broad ages at departure: early (age 17 to 18); modal (age 19 to 22); and late (age 23 to 35). Differences can be examined by sex and ethnicity, including the three major religious groups and the four largest Catholic ethnic groups in Rhode Island.

Table 7-1

**AGE OF LEAVING HOME BY ETHNICITY AND SEX**

|  | Total | Protestant | Jewish | Catholic | Catholic Ethnic Groups | | | |
|---|---|---|---|---|---|---|---|---|
|  |  |  |  |  | French Canadian | Irish | Italian | Portuguese |
| All nestleavers |  |  |  |  |  |  |  |  |
| Both sexes | 1,156 | 339 | 21 | 796 | 105 | 134 | 187 | 69 |
| Male | 595 | 173 | 12 | 410 | 101 | 68 | 95 | 39 |
| Female | 561 | 166 | 9 | 386 | 104 | 66 | 92 | 30 |
| Early (17–18) |  |  |  |  |  |  |  |  |
| Both sexes | 22.8 | 26.8 | 57.1 | 20.2 | 20.5 | 20.1 | 20.3 | 17.4 |
| Male | 22.1 | 27.7 | 75.0 | 18.0 | 19.6 | 16.2 | 20.0 | 15.4 |
| Female | 24.9 | 25.9 | 33.3 | 22.5 | 21.2 | 24.2 | 20.7 | 20.0 |
| Modal (19–22) |  |  |  |  |  |  |  |  |
| Both sexes | 49.1 | 44.2 | 28.6 | 51.8 | 55.6 | 52.2 | 48.1 | 58.0 |
| Male | 45.5 | 40.5 | 16.7 | 48.8 | 47.5 | 50.0 | 48.4 | 53.0 |
| Female | 52.3 | 48.2 | 44.4 | 54.9 | 63.5 | 54.5 | 47.8 | 63.3 |
| Late (23–35) |  |  |  |  |  |  |  |  |
| Both sexes | 28.0 | 28.9 | 14.3 | 28.0 | 23.9 | 27.6 | 31.6 | 24.6 |
| Male | 32.5 | 31.8 | 8.3 | 33.2 | 32.7 | 33.8 | 31.6 | 30.8 |
| Female | 22.8 | 25.9 | 22.2 | 22.5 | 15.4 | 21.2 | 31.5 | 16.7 |

SOURCE: Rhode Island Survey, 1979.

Overall, half of those who left were age 19 to 22 when they left home, with slightly more leaving late (28 percent) than early (23 percent). Sex differences appear more clearly than was the case in Figure 7-1. Girls are slightly more likely to leave early, but the big difference is in the proportions leaving late. Nearly a third of all sons stayed home after age 22 compared with 23 percent of daughters.

Turning to ethnic differences, a sharp contrast is immediately clear between the Jews and everybody else. The number of Jews is small, but the differences are very large. More than half the Jewish children left at age 17 or 18. Protestants were more likely to leave early than Catholics, but the differences between these two groups in leaving early--27 percent as compared to 20 percent--were much smaller. There was no difference between the two large religious groups in leaving late. Overall, then, Catholic families retain their children the longest, while Jewish children leave the nest almost immediately after high school.

Additional differences appear among these three groups when

considering sons and daughters separately. For Protestants it is sons who are most likely to leave early, whereas Catholic daughters are more likely to leave earlier than sons. (Jews resemble Protestants in this respect, but the numbers are too small to be reliable.) Catholic sons are the most likely to leave late, but Protestant sons also follow the same pattern, and remain after their sisters. Sex differences, however, are much less sharp for Protestant children than for Catholic children.

Among the Catholic ethnic groups only two groups stand out in any way from the overall Catholic pattern. The Portuguese are markedly less likely to leave early, particularly Portuguese sons, and Italians are distinctly more likely to remain to a later age. Italian daughters are the most unusual. Unlike other Catholics, young women in Italian families remain in the home as long as their brothers, and are about twice as likely to leave later as the daughters of French Canadians and Portuguese.

One possible interpretation of these differences is that age at leaving home is mostly a reflection of children's differential enrollment in higher education: those who go to college leave early; those who do not remain behind. To examine this issue, data in Table 7-2 show ethnic differences in high school completion and college attendance, separately for men and women.

Table 7-2

**EDUCATIONAL ATTAINMENT BY ETHNICITY AND SEX**

|  | Total | Protestant | Jewish | Catholic | Catholic Ethnic Groups ||||
|---|---|---|---|---|---|---|---|---|
|  |  |  |  |  | French Canadian | Irish | Italian | Portuguese |
| At least some college |  |  |  |  |  |  |  |  |
| Both sexes | 37.4 | 42.2 | 91.3 | 33.9 | 31.9 | 48.9 | 36.7 | 23.1 |
| Male | 37.3 | 40.1 | 92.3 | 34.7 | 32.4 | 51.5 | 36.0 | 18.6 |
| Female | 37.5 | 44.3 | 90.0 | 33.0 | 31.5 | 46.2 | 37.5 | 28.6 |
| High school graduate |  |  |  |  |  |  |  |  |
| Both sexes | 47.4 | 43.8 | 8.7 | 49.8 | 54.0 | 44.4 | 46.4 | 43.6 |
| Male | 45.8 | 41.8 | 7.7 | 48.1 | 53.3 | 41.2 | 44.0 | 51.2 |
| Female | 49.0 | 45.9 | 10.0 | 51.5 | 54.6 | 47.7 | 49.0 | 34.3 |
| Less than high school |  |  |  |  |  |  |  |  |
| Both sexes | 15.2 | 14.0 | 0.0 | 16.4 | 14.1 | 6.8 | 16.8 | 33.3 |
| Male | 16.9 | 18.1 | 0.0 | 17.1 | 14.3 | 7.4 | 20.0 | 30.2 |
| Female | 13.5 | 9.8 | 0.0 | 15.5 | 13.9 | 6.2 | 13.5 | 37.1 |

The relationship between early nestleaving and college attendance seems quite strong, since ethnic differences in college attendance frequently parallel the differences in early nestleaving. As before, the Jews are outstanding in the proportions attending college, with a level of more than 90 percent. Protestants are more likely to have sent children to college than Catholics, and the Portuguese were the least college-bound. There are, however, exceptions in the ethnic pattern. The Irish are highly educated, with more attending college than Protestants despite their lower level of early nestleaving. The gap is particularly great for Irish males. This sex difference illustrates another difficulty with the education hypothesis: whereas generally it is women who are most likely to leave early, in general in this population it is males who are more likely to attend college. The Protestants are an exception, with 44 percent of girls attending college compared with 40 percent of the boys.

The weakness of higher education as a simple answer to the pattern of differences in nest leaving is clearly shown by the difference between the levels of early nest leaving and college attendance. Overall, 50 percent more went to college than left home by age 19. The gap is small for Portuguese sons and daughters, where very few either attend college or leave home early, and largest for Irish sons, who are nearly three times as likely to attend college as to leave home at an early age. Clearly many remain at home while attending college, and the proportions vary substantially. In addition, college attendance adds nothing to our understanding of variations in remaining at home at later ages.

A more systematic way to demonstrate these interrelationships is to relate school and nestleaving directly by creating a sequence typology consistent with modern and traditional types: the modern nestleaver finishes education after leaving home; the traditional family retains its children for some period after education is complete. Since these data are only precise to one-year intervals, there is an intermediate category of those who finish school and leave home in the same year. Table 7-3 illustrates these sequence types for the religious and the Catholic ethnic groups by sex.

**Table 7-3**

**SEQUENCE OF LEAVING HOME AND FINISHING SCHOOL BY ETHNICITY AND SEX**

|  |  |  |  |  | Catholic Ethnic Groups | | | |
|---|---|---|---|---|---|---|---|---|
|  | Total | Protestant | Jewish | Catholic | French Canadian | Irish | Italian | Portuguese |
| Leave home, then finish school | | | | | | | | |
| Both sexes | 24.8 | 24.4 | 75.0 | 22.9 | 22.8 | 24.4 | 22.3 | 21.8 |
| Male | 27.0 | 26.4 | 71.4 | 25.3 | 20.8 | 33.8 | 25.7 | 20.9 |
| Female | 22.6 | 22.4 | 80.0 | 20.4 | 24.8 | 14.9 | 18.8 | 22.9 |
| Leave home and finish school in same year | | | | | | | | |
| Both sexes | 19.6 | 22.5 | 16.7 | 18.2 | 20.5 | 27.4 | 16.2 | 15.4 |
| Male | 17.7 | 21.4 | 21.4 | 15.9 | 20.8 | 22.1 | 11.9 | 9.3 |
| Female | 21.5 | 23.5 | 10.0 | 20.7 | 20.2 | 32.8 | 20.8 | 22.9 |
| Finish school, then leave home | | | | | | | | |
| Both sexes | 55.6 | 53.2 | 8.3 | 58.9 | 56.7 | 48.1 | 61.4 | 62.8 |
| Male | 55.3 | 52.2 | 7.1 | 58.9 | 58.5 | 44.1 | 62.4 | 69.8 |
| Female | 55.8 | 54.1 | 10.0 | 58.9 | 55.0 | 52.2 | 60.4 | 54.3 |

In general, these patterns look very similar to those which have already appeared. Jewish children, who leave home early and achieve high levels of education, are overwhelmingly found in the modern nestleaving category. Protestant-Catholic differences are negligible in proportions who leave home before finishing school, and differences among the Catholic ethnic groups overall are slight. Sex differences, however, are larger than in the earlier tables. The modern pattern is usually more associated with sons than daughters and is true of both Catholics and Protestants. Among the Catholic ethnic groups, the pattern by sex characterizes the Italians and particularly the Irish. Irish daughters are less likely than daughters in any other group to leave home before completing school, and Irish sons are most likely (after Jews) to follow the modern form.

There is a greater range of variation in proportions following a more traditional pattern of remaining in the parental home after finishing school. Religious variation is consistent with previous tables, with somewhat more Catholics following the traditional path relative to Protestants and distinctively few Jews. Fifty-nine percent of Catholic children, 53 percent of Protestant children, and less than 10 percent of Jewish children followed a traditional sequence of school and home leaving. The Catholic ethnic groups show a much wider range than the Protestant/Catholic difference, with low levels for the Irish, and very high levels among the two southern European groups, the Italians and the Portuguese. Generally sex differences are weak, except that it is only the Irish sons, rather than daughters, who are distinctively non-traditional, and Portuguese sons, not daughters, who are the most traditional.

In sum, the data show that Jews are on the far modern extreme, combining high educational attainment with an early residential break between the generations. Protestant-Catholic differences are small, although this may be more characteristic of Rhode Island than elsewhere, since a high proportion of Protestants have intermarried with Catholics. Among the Catholic ethnic groups there is a general tendency toward postponed family separation despite substantial intergroup variation in educational levels.

**Resource Flows Between the Generations**

Implicit in this discussion has been that school and home leaving sequences are associated with differential resource flows between the generations. The traditional form allows for economically able children to contribute money and/or services to the household. Continuing education after leaving home, the modern form, requires that children be somehow subsidized at a time when their earning capacities are reduced by continuing in school. However, it is also possible that children could remain at home and use household resources without contributing to them; in fact an extreme form of the modern parent-child relationship implies that parents support their children indefinitely. In addition, financial aid and part time work allow many students away from home to be essentially self-supporting.

To examine the connections to intergenerational resource flows, information was collected in this survey on the direction of income flows between the generations. Respondents were asked both whether the child contributed anything to the income of the household at any time while s/he was living at home, and whether they themselves had provided any support to the child at any time after leaving the household. These results are presented in Table 7-4. While over half reported neither type of contribution, almost none (less than one percent) indicated that income flows had gone both ways (data not presented in tabular form). Generally, money, if it were passed at all, went one way or the other. The few cases of two-way exchange were included with those contributing to children, since that was the more unusual pattern.

Even with the inclusion of the two-way group, parental contribution to children after they left home was quite rare, with only one-eighth of all children receiving such aid. On the other hand, more than one third of the children contributed financially to their parents while still living at home. The most common pattern, however, characterizing just over half of the children in the sample, was that neither contributed financially in these ways. This was particularly the case for daughters, who were less likely either to contribute or receive money than were sons, although overall differences were not large.

Table 7-4

**RESOURCE FLOWS BETWEEN PARENTS AND CHILDREN BY ETHNICITY AND SEX**

| | | | | | Catholic Ethnic Groups | | | |
| --- | --- | --- | --- | --- | --- | --- | --- | --- |
| | Total | Protestant | Jewish | Catholic | French Canadian | Irish | Italian | Portuguese |
| Parents contribute to children after the children leave home | | | | | | | | |
| Both sexes | 12.0 | 12.4 | 50.0 | 10.8 | 9.0 | 14.5 | 7.8 | 3.8 |
| Male | 13.1 | 11.0 | — | 12.7 | 11.9 | 16.4 | 9.2 | 4.7 |
| Female | 10.9 | 13.7 | — | 8.9 | 6.5 | 12.5 | 6.4 | 2.9 |
| Neither contribute | | | | | | | | |
| Both sexes | 53.1 | 56.6 | 41.7 | 51.3 | 51.4 | 51.9 | 55.2 | 47.4 |
| Male | 50.7 | 56.6 | — | 47.9 | 50.0 | 44.8 | 52.0 | 41.9 |
| Female | 55.6 | 56.6 | — | 54.9 | 52.8 | 59.4 | 58.5 | 54.3 |
| Children contribute to parental household while still at home | | | | | | | | |
| Both sexes | 34.9 | 31.0 | 8.3 | 37.8 | 39.5 | 33.6 | 37.0 | 48.7 |
| Male | 36.2 | 32.4 | — | 39.4 | 38.2 | 38.8 | 38.8 | 53.5 |
| Female | 33.5 | 29.7 | — | 36.2 | 40.7 | 28.1 | 35.1 | 42.9 |

Taking childrens' contributions as the more traditional family form and continued parental support as more modern, the three religious groups sort out the same way on this dimension as they did on home- and school-leaving patterns. Jews rarely receive money from children at home, and are far more likely to support children who have left. In contrast, Catholic-Protestant differences are small, with Catholics consistently more traditional. Among the Catholic ethnic groups, the Irish are more likely to follow a modern pattern than are other Catholic ethnic groups, even moreso than Protestants; they also have more children who contribute to the household. Protestants have the weakest financial ties between the generations, rarely either collecting from, or contributing to, their children. Protestant were also unique in supporting their daughters more than their sons. The Irish pattern, on the other hand, suggests both tighter and more flexible connections. The only other distinctive ethnic pattern is that of the Portuguese, who mirror the Jews by almost never showing a modern pattern of parents aiding children, and show the highest level of childrens' contributions, with nearly half the Portuguese children contributing to their family's income while still living at home.

Some of these differences, however, arise from differences in school- and home-leaving sequences. If few remain at home after leaving school, the extent of their support will be low even if all who remain home contributed to the household. Similarly, differences in post-departure school financing are obscured. Tables 7-5 and 7-6 address this problem directly, Table 7-5 presents the proportions contributing to the parental household among those remaining at home after finishing school and Table 7-6 shows the proportions receiving parental aid among those continuing school after they leave home.

Overall, nearly half of the children remaining at home make some financial contribution. Despite the greater Catholic than Protestant sex differences that appeared in the earlier data, the same proportion of Catholic sons and daughters take some financial responsibility for the household (50 percent). In contrast, Protestant sons contribute nearly as frequently as Catholics (45 percent), but only 36 percent of Protestant daughters were making some financial contribution to the household while they remained at home. Too few Jews remained home to calculate meaningful percentages.

**Table 7-5**

**PERCENT CONTRIBUTING TO HOUSEHOLD INCOME AMONG THOSE WHO REMAIN AT HOME AFTER FINISHING SCHOOL BY ETHNICITY AND SEX**

|  | Male | Female |
|---|---|---|
| Protestant | 45.3 | 36.4 |
| Catholic | 49.6 | 49.6 |
| French Canadian | 49.2 | 59.3 |
| Irish | 46.7 | 38.2 |
| Italian | 44.0 | 41.4 |
| Portuguese | 70.0 | 63.2 |

## Table 7-6

### PERCENT RECEIVING AID FROM PARENTS AMONG THOSE LEAVING HOME BEFORE FINISHING SCHOOL

|  | Male | Female |
|---|---|---|
| Protestant | 22.9 | 40.0 |
| Jewish | 80.0 | 50.0 |
| Catholic | 29.2 | 28.9 |
| French Canadian | 27.3 | 18.5 |
| Irish | 36.4 | 50.0 |
| Italian | 20.8 | 29.4 |

The Irish among the Catholic ethnic groups are the least likely to contribute, resembling Protestants in level and pattern of sex differences. Fewer than half of Italian children contribute as well. French Canadian children, particularly daughters, are distinctly more likely to have contributed to their families while at home and finished with school. Most striking are the Portuguese. Earlier we documented that Portuguese children are more likely than others to remain at home after completing their education. This pattern is reinforced by an extremely high level of contribution by those children: fully two-thirds diverted some portion of their earnings to the family. This high level of contribution, coupled with low education and late nestleaving, suggests that Portuguese children are widely used as a family resource, and that pressure to leave school and begin contributing may well account for their very high drop out rate from high school. The lower levels of contribution among other groups suggests, on the other hand, that families are more frequently being used as a resource for the children rather than the reverse, and that staying home after finishing school represents an opportunity to live less expensively before going out to live independently.

It is possible that children are making valuable contributions in kind which are not revealed by these data, such as child care. However, the pattern of sex differences does not strongly suggest such a phenomenon. Daughters in Irish families, which have quite high fertility, stay home long yet contribute little financially, suggesting that the family's need for them may be greater in child care than money; however Protestants have lower fertility but a similar pattern of contribution, suggesting that continuing coresidence is not simply a reflection of this form of traditional intergenerational exchange.

Data in Table 7-6, on the other hand, show clearly that the modern pattern of parents contributing to childrens' education after they leave home is not as widespread as might have been expected. These are self-reports of parents, not of children, who would seem to have no reason to underreport, yet these data indicate that two-thirds of children who continued schooling after leaving home did so without parental aid. Jewish parents are again exceptions to this pattern, providing support to the continued education of about two-thirds of their children. Only the Irish reach much above the common level, supporting 36 percent of sons and 50 percent of daughters.

Part of the explanation for differences in parental contribution to children undoubtedly lies in differences in levels of parental resources. While considering fully the complexities of social class is beyond the scope of this analysis, data not presented indicate that the few Jewish parents at the lowest income levels are more likely to send children away to school and support them there than are any other religious or Catholic ethnic group at the highest income level. The general (non-Jewish) pattern for this population, then, seems to be that children who left home before finishing school in Rhode Island in the 1970s found other resources to finance their education. Families were unlikely to finance them if they left the home.

Thus, although earlier data on education and nestleaving suggested that the pursuit of higher education would be associated with leaving home early, as in the case of the Jews, data on parental contribution makes this seem extremely unlikely. In this sample, families contribute to their children's higher educational attainments primarily by providing continued support to the children in the home, not away, with the result that higher education requires a later, not an earlier departure from the parental home. Data presented in Table 7-7, showing nestleaving ages for those who attended college, indicates that this is in fact the case. Comparing the data in Table 7-7 with Table 7-1, it becomes clear that only Jewish children and Irish sons leave earlier if they go to college, whereas for the children of other ethnic and religious groups, those who attended college were less likely to leave early and particularly likely to leave late. Well over 40 percent of both Italian sons and daughters who attended college remained at home until at least age 23.

**Table 7-7**

**AGE OF LEAVING HOME FOR COLLEGE ATTENDEES BY ETHNICITY AND SEX**

|  | Total | Protestant | Jewish | Catholic | Catholic Ethnic Groups | | |
|---|---|---|---|---|---|---|---|
|  |  |  |  |  | French Canadian | Irish | Italian |
| Early (17–18) |  |  |  |  |  |  |  |
| Both sexes | 19.6 | 20.9 | 61.1 | 15.1 | 12.1 | 13.8 | 13.0 |
| Male | 21.7 | 21.9 | 80.0 | 17.4 | 15.6 | 17.1 | 12.1 |
| Female | 17.5 | 20.0 | — | 12.7 | 8.8 | 10.0 | 13.9 |
| Modal (19–22) |  |  |  |  |  |  |  |
| Both sexes | 44.2 | 44.4 | 22.2 | 45.7 | 54.5 | 53.8 | 43.5 |
| Male | 37.0 | 41.1 | 10.0 | 36.8 | 40.6 | 45.7 | 45.5 |
| Female | 51.5 | 47.5 | — | 55.2 | 67.6 | 63.3 | 41.7 |
| Late (23–35) |  |  |  |  |  |  |  |
| Both sexes | 36.2 | 34.6 | 16.7 | 39.2 | 33.3 | 32.3 | 43.5 |
| Male | 41.3 | 37.0 | 10.0 | 45.8 | 43.8 | 37.1 | 42.4 |
| Female | 31.0 | 32.5 | — | 32.1 | 23.5 | 26.7 | 44.4 |

## Discussion

This examination of school- and home-leaving patterns shows that variation in the nestleaving process and in its relationship to schooling are important indicators of change in the relationships between the parental and young adult generations. In addition, though this is not the focus of this analysis, such variations probably have important consequences for children's mobility, geographic and social.

Two groups can be identified as extreme types on a modern-traditional axis. At the modern extreme are Jewish families, who send their children to college, and send them early and far, providing extensive subsidies to maintain them. This is a case where children contribute little directly to the household, and the parental generation sacrifices extensively to them. At the other extreme are the Portuguese, whose children not only receive little subsidy for higher education, but leave school early and remain at home, contributing extensively to the household economy. Parents sacrifice little for the children, and the children may sacrifice some of their educational aspirations to meet what are probably felt as family obligations. Among other Catholic ethnic groups, all of which seem to share a common pattern of late nestleaving, a strategy seems to have emerged which maintains a late nestleaving pattern, and, incidentally, retains the children in the community, without sacrificing higher education. This pattern is most characteristic of the Irish and Italians, who have achieved much higher levels of education than either French Canadians or Portuguese, while retaining a late nestleaving pattern. This is in contrast to Protestants, whose intermediate level of education (behind the Jews and the Irish) seems to be associated with a more intermediate nestleaving pattern as well--not as dramatically young as the Jews, but younger than the Irish, despite the higher levels of education of the Irish.

Important questions remain. The issue of the long run consequences for childrens' economic mobility is an obvious and important one. More immediately, however, the effects of other transitions must be explored. One factor in late nestleaving is a higher Catholic age at marriage, although the direction of causality is not immediately clear. It may be that Catholic men and women marry later *because* they have greater obligations to the parental household.

An important task at the structural level is to relate leaving home to new household formation. National data indicate that a major factor in the recent increases in the rate of household formation is an increased propensity of young adults to begin lives residentially independent from their parents before marriage. Measuring the period between leaving home and marriage and exploring the factors related to this interval will provide some clues to this rise in household formation. In addition, an important question is the extent to which such household formation is associated with the recent delays in marriage which have been occurring among young adults. It seems quite reasonable that family patterns, like currents in the ocean, are more complex than we ordinarily think, and that apparently small changes have far reaching consequences.

## REFERENCES

Aries, Philippe. 1962. *Centuries of Childhood.* New York: Knopf.

Caldwell, J. 1982. *Theories of Fertility Change.* New York: Academic Press.

Goldscheider, C. and F. Goldscheider. 1988. "Ethnicity, Religiosity, and Leaving Home: The Structural and Cultural Bases of Traditional Family Values." *Sociological Forum* 3:525-547.

Goldscheider, F. and LeBourdais, C., 1986. "The Decline in Age at Leaving Home, 1920-1979." *Sociology and Social Research* 72:143-145.

Greeley, A. 1974. *Ethnicity in the United States.* New York: John Wiley.

Kobrin, F. and C. Goldscheider. 1978. *The Ethnic Factor in Family Structure and Mobility.* Cambridge, Mass.: Ballinger Publishing Company.

Laslett, B. 1973. "The Family as a Public and Private Institution: An Historical Perspective." *Journal of Marriage and the Family* 35:480-492.

Mindel, C. and R. Habenstein (eds.). 1976. *Ethnic Families in America: Patterns and Variations.* New York: Elsevier Scientific Publishing Company.

Modell, J., et al. 1976. "Social Change and Transitions to Early Adulthood in Historical Perspective." *Journal of Family History* 1:7-32.

Ross, H. and I. Sawhill. 1975. *Time of Transition: The Growth of Families Headed by Women.* Washington, D.C.: The Urban Institute.

# 8

# Family Transfers and Household Living Arrangements Among the Elderly

CAROL SHUCHMAN

The gradual transfer of financial responsibility for the elderly from the family to the public sector is not yet complete in American society. There are significant ambiguities in sources of support for the elderly. While we tend to assume that the public sector has relieved children from supporting their parents in old age, this is not always the case. In fact, public measures often do not provide sufficient economic support.

Historically, kin served as the exclusive resource for economic assistance and security for relatives. They provided the assistance now covered by the public sector. Mutual aid and exchange relations among kin insured survival in old age. In the past, kin were the source of social security (Hareven, 1981). Regardless of whether the elderly were part of the household, mutual kin obligations put great pressure on children to support aging parents and relatives. In the twentieth century, however, family functions have been increasingly replaced by the public sector and the central role that families play in support of the elderly has been reduced. In addition, the rise in individual incomes and a desire for privacy have led an increasing number of adults, particularly older unmarried women, to live alone (Kobrin, 1976). Moreover, there is a qualitative difference between a situation in which the family is the exclusive agent of support for the aged and that in which the kin supports are variable and take place within the framework of support from other institutions (Hareven, 1981).

This research explores the economic relationships of the elderly with their families and, in particular, examines how private economic transfers between family members are influenced by an older person's living arrangements. We will present data on all income sources available to the elderly, with special attention to the interaction between public transfer income and family transfers.

## Income Sources, Family Transfers, and Living Arrangements

The income of the elderly has a direct bearing on the level and stability of their welfare. This general relationship has been well-documented (Bixby, 1970; Soldo, 1980), but actual measures of the economic well-being of older adults have tended to be incomplete and inaccurate (Moon and Smolensky, 1977). Definitions of money income or economic status which exclude many public in-kind transfers, lump-sum payments, the value of non-market productive activities, and private transfers between family members are particularly problematic for research on the elderly. Substantial proportions of the income of the elderly are derived from these sources (Grad and Foster, 1979; Moon, 1976) and their exclusion results in a distorted view of the economic well-being of families and households where elderly reside. Consequently, we are often unable to make unbiased comparisons across age groups (Moon, 1981). Although economists, sociologists, and policy analysts have attempted to derive more accurate measures of net worth and economic well-being by using broader definitions of total current income (Moon and Smolensky, 1976; Taussig, 1973), little of this research has focused on the elderly, and even less has concentrated on the private economic transfers between family members.

Family transfers represent a small but nonetheless significant form of income for the elderly. Approximately eighty percent of the total money income of the average older American derives from three sources: social security, earnings, and assets. Earnings, however, apply mainly to those who are not yet retired or to those who live with a working spouse, and the effects of assets are rarely apparent except among the wealthy (Pampel, 1981; Schultz, 1980).[1] In-kind transfer income amounts to nearly ten percent of the average elderly person's own economic resources, while the remaining ten percent of total income comes from family financial aid and assistance, known as transfers (Moon, 1974). Although family transfers have been estimated to contribute a relatively small amount of income for the total population (Baerwaldt and Morgan, 1973), many elderly people depend heavily on this source of support.

The extent to which older persons depend on family transfers seems to vary dramatically by the living arrangement of the elderly person. Economic transfers between family members who live in the same household (intra-household transfers) have been estimated to be much greater than those between households (inter-household transfers) (Baerwaldt and Morgan, 1973; Morgan, 1978). However, older persons living with relatives are usually in greater need than independent older persons (Viscusi and Zeckhauser, 1974).

---

[1] The exception is home ownership since a substantial number of elderly own their own homes; however, homes can rarely be tapped for expenses (Friedman and Sjogren, 1981).

Using varying definitions of income--including the value of housework, childcare and the benefits of residing with relations--researchers have tried to estimate the extent of intra-household family transfers (Morgan, 1978; Weisbrod and Hanson, 1968). But little of this research has focused on the elderly. Probably less than thirty percent of all elderly persons receive intra-household transfers, although the size of the transfers for those who receive them is often substantial (Moon, 1974). Morgan, et al. (1962), using a definition of economic welfare that included non-money components, found that for the elderly who lived with family, nearly two-thirds of their resources came from the family, while only one-third of their resources came from the public sector. The reverse is true for elderly who live alone: more than two-thirds of their resources are received from outside sources (Baerwaldt and Morgan, 1973). It is clear that for elderly persons who do not live alone, government income maintenance programs account for only a fraction of their total resources; the family is their main source of support.

Inter-household economic transfers, which represent income received by the elderly from family with whom they do not live, are more difficult to ascertain. While estimates of the value of housework or the value of residing with relatives can be made, actual transfers of income between households are not as easily discernible. Government policy generally discourages economic aid from relatives by penalizing the elderly recipient through higher taxes and loss of benefits and penalizing the family donors by not recognizing such transfers as deductions. Consequently, older Americans are unlikely to divulge accurate estimates of this income to government data sources. Survey data have provided more complete estimations, but again the focus has mostly been on general households rather than specifically on the elderly. Based on survey results, Lopata (1978) noted that nearly ten percent of a sample of older widows received economic aid from their children. Baerwaldt and Morgan (1973) estimated that nearly thirteen percent of elderly households received income from family members. Hence, while the independent nuclear family or single person household may be the norm in American society (Smith, 1981), kinship assistance networks operate on an economic basis for a substantial minority of American households (Shanas and Streib, 1965).

## Family Transfers and Public Transfers

Public transfer programs are important factors that may influence both household living arrangements and family transfers. Government income maintenance, in-kind and welfare programs, may provide between thirty to one hundred percent of an elderly person's income and these programs affect over ninety percent of the aged population. These programs were initially designed to relieve desperate economic situations for those who could no longer work and who had no resources upon which to rely (Kreps, 1977; Spitler, 1981).

Unfortunately, there are discrepancies between the ideals and the realities of the system. Low income is much more prevalent among women and the functionally impaired than it is among the male population, since their pension benefits reflect their low earnings, irregular work histories and the failure of most private pension systems to provide survivor benefits (Mallon, 1980). Women make up fifty-nine percent of those over the age of sixty five; their problems are of special concern. Over 26 percent of these older women rely on social security as their sole means of support (Marsh, 1981; Lingg, 1982); only 20 percent of them receive private pensions, whether as workers' widows or as a result of their own work record (Mallon, 1980).

In addition, many supplemental income and welfare programs are restricted to particular subgroups or by means-testing to certain incomes. Unrealistically low threshold levels of income and assets, as well as great disparities among the programs in which constitutes "poverty," compound the problems of older women. Clearly, a change in household situation may be one response of an older person to financial stress. Moving into a household with relatives will affect the sources of income for the elderly, but this situation remains a default rather than a preference for the elderly poor (Soldo, 1981). Preference seems to be for an independent household apart from relatives (Kobrin, 1976). In an effort, then, to enable a functioning, capable aged individual to live independently, relatives may opt to supplement public transfers. It is unclear whether such arrangements are made so that the elderly are not forced, by necessity, to move in with family. Yet when the elderly face severe financial problems, children are often willing to provide needed help (Bane, 1976), but less willing--unless there is no other choice--to place their relatives in institutions (Brody, 1977; Troll, 1971).

The end result is similar: family income transfers, both intra-household and inter-household, may often interact with the public transfer system to more closely approximate an adequate income level. Whether between households or within extended families, relatives may supplement the income or in-kind resources received from social security, supplemental security income and food stamps (Moon, 1981). However, the interaction between living arrangements and public income, as well as the flexibility of family transfers with regard to the interaction, requires further clarification. There is insufficient evidence showing how family transfers contribute to total money income for the elderly or how the elderly rely on these transfers for economic well-being.

The interaction between living arrangements and transfer income is especially relevant. An increasing proportion of adults, particularly older women, have chosen or preferred to live alone in the post-World War II period. The large literature documenting this phenomenon links the rise of income with a rise in the demand for privacy and autonomy and consequently, a greater propensity for individuals to live alone (Carliner, 1975; Kobrin, 1976, 1981; Michael, Fuchs and Scott, 1980). Steiner and Dorfman (1957), who examined the living arrangements of aged couples and individuals, found that people were much more likely to be sharing a household at lower, than at higher, levels of income. Similarly, Beresford and Rivlin (1966) found that there was a positive relationship between income and the likelihood of maintaining a household separate from relatives among older unmarried women. Indeed, research has consistently shown this to be the case for elderly individuals (Murray, 1971; Tissue, 1979; Tissue and McCoy, 1981), bearing out the theme of preference for autonomy and independence among American adults.

However, in these studies a rather simplistic approach is usually taken in dealing with income. Income has been defined through census categories, which exclude many types of in-kind and non-money income.[2] While the use of total money income (census definition) may be a valid indicator for the general population, an income measure that includes government transfers and family cash transfers would be a better indicator for those over age sixty-five. It would provide a clearer notion of the economic factor for examining the elderly.

Though many researchers have observed the need for more explicit income measures, their work has been hindered by problems in acquiring accurate data. Michael, Fuchs and Scott (1980:48-49) added several more comprehensive income measures in an effort to get strong results for determining the propensity to live alone, but still concluded that there is "difficulty in adequately measuring the income of elderly widows."

This is not to argue that previous findings on the relationship between living arrangements and income would change with additional research. Rather, exploring the effects and inter-relations of more income sources, (especially those which are particularly relevant to the elderly) might clarify exactly how income relates to living arrangements and whether, in fact, some types of income are determined by living arrangements instead of the reverse. Consider, for example, the conclusion that the financial situation of the elderly depends on the *sources* of their income (Soldo, 1980). We know that the majority of the elderly rely on a mixture of several types of income (social security, pensions, savings, assets and transfers). It is also clear that the allocation of some types of public welfare income (for example, SSI) depends on the income of the household in which the elderly person resides, while other types (such as social security) are received by all those over age sixty-five regardless of living arrangements. By distinguishing between the public income sources that are affected by living arrangements and those that have no connection to living arrangements, it may be possible to clarify the circumstances in which relatives might attempt to aid the elderly through the transfer of resources.

This research examines the income sources and living arrangements of

---

[2] Steiner and Dorfman (1957) attempted to incorporate the concept of net worth into their definition of economic welfare by adding to total current income the results of any dissaving.

the elderly. It differs from previous work in operationalizing types of income so that they more clearly reflect their relationship to living arrangements. It also investigates the effect of this interaction on income transfers between family members.

## Data and Methods

The focus on public income and family transfer income precludes the use of many data sets. Since family economic transfers generally serve as a supplement to government and private sources and there are numerous legal and economic disadvantages to accurate reporting, the elderly are unlikely to provide information on family transfer income to government data sources. Therefore, while the Longitudinal Retirement History Survey, the Census, the Current Population Survey and the Matched CPS-IRS-SSA data sets are excellent sources for the majority of income, family structure and household living arrangement data, they are inadequate for this research (Herriot and Spiers, 1975; Moon, 1981).

Survey data provide more complete estimations of the income of the elderly. With a general emphasis on income and all its components and information on approximately 20,000 individuals, the Panel Study of Income Dynamics (PSID) is uniquely suited for this research. There is extensive information on income sources and amounts, and questions have been added since 1976 to examine family in-kind and cash transfers (Morgan, 1978). As such, it can provide guidelines for measures of economic welfare for any particular group. In addition, the PSID has data on household structure and familial relationships that will allow clarification of the relationships between economic transfers and living arrangements of the elderly. We will be using the PSID for 1980.

The population under study consists of all those individuals over age 60 who are not currently married. There are several reasons for restricting the population in this way. While most individuals receive social security at age sixty-five, some receive it at age sixty-two (widows). Using age sixty insures that we have the vast majority. Of those over age 65, 59 percent are women and the proportion rises to 64 percent for those over age 75. In addition, widows predominate (52 percent of women over age 65; 69 percent over age 75) and over half of women over age 75 live alone (Congresswomen's Caucus, 1981). These figures give clear indications of the situation of the elderly, but there are stronger reasons for concentrating on the majority. The literature on families and households, in both the contemporary United States and historically, concludes that married couples rarely live within extended households (Tilly and Cohen, 1982) and even more rarely do they receive family income transfers (Moon, 1977). They are more likely to be receiving income from earnings and pensions and to have greater assets, which identifies them more strongly with the general population than with the elderly in particular. Considering the goal of this research--to explore how various income sources interact with various living arrangements--it is clear that married couples would add little to our understanding of these processes.

*Total Income* represents the total money income of the elderly individual. It is the sum of all taxable income (labor and assets) and all transfer income. It does not, however, include the value of food stamps, housework, imputed rent or the value of a house, if the individual owns his/her own residence. As such, it closely resembles a census measure of income and provides a good comparison with national data.

*Public Income* represents all income that stems from sources restricted by government policies to particular individuals or to households in certain income brackets. It will be measured as the sum of all restricted government transfers (i.e., supplemental security income, AFC/AFDC, and heating cost subsidies) and the estimates of any government in-kind transfers (i.e., food stamps).

*Living Arrangements* will be treated as a dichotomous variable: living alone or living with others.

*Family Transfers* will be measured as the sum of actual cash transfers from relatives, the value of housework and the value of imputed annual rent. Since people living alone do a minimum of housework, we will add the difference between the mean value of housework for those living alone and those who live with others to the family transfers of individuals living with household heads. (The hours of housework performed by the individual have been valued at a market cost of $5.00 an hour.)[3] For any individual who neither owns nor rents the residence in which he/she lives, we will add the value of the imputed rent. The vast majority of those who neither own or rent define their housing as a gift (primarily from relatives).

*Net Worth* represents the wealth of the individual. Moon (1977) computed a measure of net worth that incorporated all assets, all debts, home equity, the rate of return on the assets and the expected lifetime of the household's members. This measure yields the portion of net worth allocated to consumption for the year in question, assuming that there is a yearly depletion of wealth for the elderly. However, recent research refutes the life cycle hypothesis (i.e., that the young save and the old dissave). The evidence shows that, indeed, the elderly seem to save significantly more than the non-elderly (Danziger et al., 1982). Consequently, the measure of net worth utilized in this model will include all assets (i.e., interest, rent and dividends) and home equity if the individual owns the house he or she lives in.

*Private Income* consists of all wage and salary income, any other retirement pay, pensions, annuities, unemployment compensation,

---

[3] There is an extensive literature on the value of housework which distinguishes between opportunity cost wages and market cost wages (Baerwaldt and Morgan, 1973). We are using the latter to determine the relative values of this variable.

workman's compensation and social security. The inclusion of social security in this variable needs some explanation. Social security as a transfer payment is available to almost all those over age 65 and to some at younger ages. It is a secure and guaranteed form of income whose amount is based upon personal characteristics rather than household living arrangements. Since it should not relate to living arrangements, we have included it within this category.

The *Socio-Demographic Characteristics* of the individual include age, sex, race, and whether or not the individual has children. Age has been divided into three categories reflecting need and resource differences among the elderly (Soldo, 1980): under age 65, 65 through 74, and 75 and above. It is particularly important to recognize income differences among the elderly (Duffy et al., 1980; Schultz, 1980). It is possible that the "old-old" (those over age 75), especially older women with fewer resources and more financial difficulties, would receive greater amounts of family transfers and/or they might live in an extended household. Race will be treated as a dichotomous variable.

**Living Arrangements and Income**

Nearly three-fifths of the unmarried elderly live alone (Table 8-1).

**Table 8-1**

**PERCENT LIVING ALONE BY AGE, SEX, AND RACE**

|  | Percent Living Alone | Total Number of Cases |
|---|---|---|
| Total | 58.4 | 878 |
| Age |  |  |
| 60–64 | 54.4 | 248 |
| 65–74 | 62.5 | 355 |
| 75 and over | 56.7 | 275 |
| Sex |  |  |
| Male | 56.3 | 197 |
| Female | 59.0 | 681 |
| Race |  |  |
| White | 65.6 | 563 |
| Black | 45.7 | 315 |

SOURCE: Panel Study of Income Dynamics, 1980.

Data not presented indicate that of those who live with others, nearly half are heads of households. However, it is possible that the designation of head is honorary, in deference to age, and an adult child is contributing the majority of the resources, rather than the elderly head. Elderly living with other adults, but not the household head, are most likely to be either parents or other relatives, most of whom are undoubtedly parents-in-law. They are rarely unrelated people or siblings, a fact which lends support to the argument that nuclear households diversify in only a few directions (Laslett and Wall, 1972).

Data in Table 8-1 also indicate that the "young-old" (those between 65 and 74 years old) are the most likely to be living independently and that the "old-old" are more apt to live with others. The higher costs associated with older age may make it more difficult for a functioning and capable elderly person to live independently. A slightly higher proportion of women live alone. However, the sharp contrasts by race represent the major difference between the two living arrangement groups. They confirm previous findings that Blacks are less apt to maintain households alone and more apt to live with other adults (Chevan and Korson, 1972; Moon, 1981; Soldo, 1981). Our data show that more than half of the Black elderly in this sample live with other adults as compared to only a third of the white elderly. With these observations about the sample's socio-demographic characteristics, we can examine income sources and amounts to determine how these differ by living arrangement for the elderly.

Data on total income and income sources by sex and by living arrangements are presented in Table 8-2. The first measure presented is total money income. This measure does not include various in-kind sources which directly affect the elderly (although it does include income from assets); it nonetheless provides a general notion of the financial situation.

The difference between those living alone and those living with others in total money income is substantial. Those who live alone, with an average income of $7,373, have an income more than twice that of those living with others, whose average income is only $3,537. The elderly living alone are also, however, much more likely to have some income, since nearly all report at least some, while nearly 30 percent of the elderly living with others report no income of any kind. Comparing only those with any income reduces the differences between the two groups, although the difference remains quite large (more than $2,400 per year). Evidently, those living with others are quite heterogeneous with regard to income, with some essentially destitute, while others contribute a disproportionate amount to the total income of the group.

The incomes of males and females living alone differ sharply, reflecting both men's greater incomes and the greater likelihood that men are the beneficiaries of private pensions, an income source less likely to be available to older women (Mallon, 1980). However, there is almost no difference in the average incomes of males and females living with others, a much more unusual observation. This substantiates the findings of Shanas (1980) and others that, regardless of sex, individuals tend to live with others out of need. The similarity in incomes of men and women living

## Table 8-2

### LIVING ARRANGEMENTS AND MEAN INCOME BY SEX AND BY CATEGORY OF INCOME

| Category | Living Alone | Living with Others |
|---|---|---|
| **Both sexes** | | |
| Total money income | 7,373 | 3,537 |
| (Percent with none) | (0.6) | (29.3) |
| Total for those with any income | 7,418 | 5,003 |
| **Males** | | |
| Total money income | 8,382 | 3,620 |
| (Percent with none) | (2.7) | (33.7) |
| Total for those with any income | 8,615 | 5,461 |
| **Females** | | |
| Total money income | 7,097 | 3,507 |
| (Percent with none) | (0.0) | (28.0) |
| Total for those with any income | 7,097 | 4,872 |
| **Both sexes** | | |
| Total private income | 4,906 | 3,208 |
| (Percent with none) | (4.9) | (34.8) |
| Total for those with private income | 5,159 | 4,876 |
| **Both sexes** | | |
| Total net worth | 18,774 | 6,139 |
| (Percent with none) | (26.1) | (80.3) |
| Total for those with any net worth | 29,380 | 31,163 |
| **Both sexes** | | |
| Total public income | 440 | 512 |
| (Percent with none) | (63.2) | (68.2) |
| Total for those with any public income | 1,196 | 1,609 |
| **Both sexes** | | |
| Total family transfers | 261 | 52 |
| (Percent with none) | (86.6) | (67.7) |
| Total for those with any family transfers | 1,951 | 161 |

SOURCE: Panel Study of Income Dynamics, 1980.

with others, however, is the result of the somewhat greater likelihood that men living with others will have no income (34 percent compared with 28 percent), since among those reporting income, males still receive 10 percent more than females. This suggests that males living with others are a somewhat more heterogeneous group than comparable females, with many more being the main earner in the family than is the case with women.

Each of the four financial sources (as defined above)--private income, net worth, public income, and family transfer income--by living arrangements are also presented in Table 8-2. We will note where appropriate if gender patterns differ from those shown for total income.

Private income is made up of earnings, pensions, and social security. There is much less difference between those living alone and those living with others on this measure of income, since those living with others report nearly as much private income as total income, while those living alone report much less private income compared with their total income. The difference by living arrangements is nevertheless substantial, since those living alone have a private income of $4,906, nearly half again as much as those living with others ($3,179). Again, however, it reflects the greater heterogeneity among those living with others, since 34.2 percent of this group report receiving no private income of any kind. This is possible, since this population includes individuals under the age 65, and social security coverage is not universal. Evidently, many of these individuals also have no earnings, and hence report having no private income.

If the differences between those living alone and those living with others are smaller for private income than for total income, those living alone must have other sources of income. The third panel, which reports on total net worth, suggests that at least some of their greater income must come from assets. Those living alone report a net worth more than three times ($21,418) that of those living with others ($6,139). Those living alone are also far more likely to report a positive net worth, since only 27 percent report no assets, compared with four-fifths (80.3 percent) of those living with others.

On the other hand, among those with assets in the group who are living with others, the value actually exceeds by nearly $2,000 the level of assets of those living alone. This reinforces the view that the elderly living with others are a highly diverse group. In some cases, the elderly are the dependents of others in the household; in other cases, it is the other family members who are dependent on the elderly person. This pattern suggests that those with high levels of assets (normally an owned home) in fact have larger homes than those living alone, and are likely to be heads of these households. It is also possible that the elderly with these larger homes may be induced to invite others in to share accommodations as a way to reduce daily expenses.

Part of the answer to the greater difference in total income between those living alone and those living with others, then, appears to stem from differences in net worth (particularly home ownership). Does public assistance also play a role in supporting residential independence? The evidence from the fourth panel of Table 8-2 is that, whatever role public assistance has played among the very youngest adults (Ellwood and Bane, 1985), it does not appear to be implicated in the living arrangements of the elderly. Although a substantial proportion of those living alone report income from some combination of SSI or food stamps (36 percent), nearly as high a share of those living with others (32 percent) also receive income from these sources. Neither group reports much public transfer income, both averaging around $500. Surprisingly, although SSI stipulates that individuals sharing living quarters receive only two-thirds the level of an individual living alone,[4] the mean amount is higher for those sharing living arrangements.

Even with the supplement to income provided by public assistance programs, which these data suggest is fairly small, many elderly may find it very difficult to make ends meet. Robert Ball, past Commissioner of the Social Security Administration, has bluntly asserted that many who receive Supplemental Security Income do not get enough from the program to reach the poverty level (Bell, 1978). The poverty line in 1980 for one person over the age of 65 was $3,939. Nearly 32 percent of our sample who lived alone were at, or below, the poverty line, using the census definition of income. The percentage was closer to 50 percent for those living with other adults.[5]

How important are family transfers to make up this deficit? Data in the bottom panel of Table 8-2 suggest that even for the elderly, the magnitude of average family transfers is quite low. Those living alone reported an average family transfer of $261; those living with others barely came out ahead in the exchange of household services for imputed rent, averaging barely $50. For the one out of seven elderly living alone who received family transfers, however, their magnitude was quite substantial--nearly $2,000 per year. In many cases, families were making up the difference in the incomes of their elderly relatives, allowing them to maintain an independent residence.

There were no gender differences either in the likelihood of receiving family transfer income or in the amount received for those living alone. However, this was not the case for those living with others (data not presented). Males who were living with others were much less likely than

---

[4] Total household income rather than personal income determines eligibility for programs such as Supplemental Security Income and food stamps.

[5] Nationally, of unmarried persons over age 65 who live alone, a total of 31 percent are below the poverty line (24 percent of the males and 32 percent of the females). Among those who live with others, 51 percent are below the poverty line (37 percent of the males and 54 percent of the females) (Grad, 1983).

comparable females to receive family transfers, which is consistent with the fact that 61 percent of men living with others own their own home. But males reporting the receipt of transfers received 50 percent more than women. Although levels of imputed rent were low for both sexes, females contributed far more housework hours than men, offsetting a substantial portion of their room expenses.

Table 8-3

**MEAN VALUES OF FAMILY TRANSFERS BY LIVING ARRANGEMENT, SEX, AND RECEIPT OF PUBLIC INCOME**

|  | Total | Male | Female |
|---|---|---|---|
| Alone | | | |
| Grand mean* | $1,951 | $2,043 | $1,925 |
| % nonzero | 13.4 | 13.5 | 13.4 |
| (N) | (513) | (111) | (402) |
| Mean without public income* | 2,217 | 2,365 | 2,170 |
| % nonzero | 59.4 | 66.7 | 57.4 |
| (N w/Ft) | (69) | (15) | (54) |
| Mean with public income* | 1,561 | 1,398 | 1,596 |
| % nonzero | 40.6 | 33.3 | 42.6 |
| (N w/Ft) | (69) | (15) | (54) |
| With Others | | | |
| Grand mean* | $161 | $223 | $146 |
| % nonzero | 32.3 | 25.6 | 34.3 |
| (N) | (365) | (86) | (279) |
| Mean without public income* | 115 | 271 | 77 |
| % nonzero | 65.2 | 68.2 | 64.6 |
| (N w/Ft) | (118) | (22) | (96) |
| Mean with public income* | 264 | 102 | 299 |
| % nonzero | 28.8 | 27.3 | 29.2 |
| (N w/Ft) | (118) | (22) | (96) |

*Means are for nonzero income.

Our original perception of family transfers was as a supplement to public income and as a means to allow an elderly person the "luxury" of a separate residence. Those elderly who live alone receive a much greater amount of family transfer income than those who share a residence, but it is necessary to compare those who do and do not receive public income in order to establish the nature of family transfers.

Table 8-3 shows that mean family transfers for the elderly who do not receive public income and who live alone are substantially higher than for their counterparts who receive public income. Among those living alone, family transfers seem to be used in two ways. They raise income to an adequate level for individuals ineligible for public income benefits and they supplement public income benefits for those who receive them. However, the situation is not so clear among those aged sharing living arrangements. Women who share living arrangements and are without public income are more apt to be household heads and, consequently, have very low levels of family transfers. Those women within extended households with public income are more likely to be relatives of the head receiving higher amounts of income from family members.

## Discussion

We have operationalized the income sources of the elderly in terms of their relationship to household living arrangements. A source such as social security is a guaranteed form of income, with few restrictions that might affect the living arrangement of an elderly person. Thus, we have included it within private income. Earnings and social security are theoretically balanced. The inclusion of social security in a measure of income unrelated to living arrangements should tend to stabilize this measure by age. Indeed, while the average for private income drops appreciably at age 65, the decrease is accounted for by the difference between social security and earnings. However, our results show that private income is linked directly to living arrangements: those who are lacking this form of income are more apt to be living in an extended household.

Eligibility for SSI and food stamps, by contrast, is determined by total household income, which in turn may affect the living situation of an elderly person. Therefore, we have kept these and similar sources separate as public income. Net worth includes home ownership, which in retrospect might prove more useful as a separate variable. Many of the elderly own their own homes, which inflates the value of net worth and gives the impression that they have large amounts of assets. Home ownership, while it relates to household headship and living arrangement, is not included in the countable income which determines eligibility for public welfare assistance (SSA, 1982). Non-liquid assets (such as a house) cannot be drawn upon to pay expenses. However, they interact with living arrangements insofar as owning a home is apt to mean residence in that home. A measure of net worth that excluded home ownership might indicate more directly the relationship to living arrangements.

The measure of family transfers needs refinement, but provides more than adequate results in its present form. The interaction between family transfers and public income provides substantial evidence that relatives do indeed supplement public assistance. Families both replace and support the benefits of public income, especially when the aged person lives alone. Aid from relatives provides the necessary component that interacts with public income sources to allow the elderly the option of an independent existence.

The empirical results presented are preliminary. What emerges, however, is the importance of a broad range of financial considerations in the study of the living arrangement patterns of the elderly. Families as well as public sector institutions play a critical role in affecting the living arrangements options available to the elderly. Other factors, such as the changing health of the elderly and their preferences, need to be included along with direct evidence on family networks, in our research on the living arrangements of the other population.

## REFERENCES

Baerwaldt, Nancy A. and James N. Morgan. 1973. "Trends in Inter-Family Transfers." In *Surveys of Consumers, 1971-72*, eds., Lewis Mandell et al. Ann Arbor: Institute for Survey Research.

Ball, Robert M. 1978. "Income Security for the Elderly." *National Journal* 10-28-78.

Bane, M.J. 1976. *Here to Stay: American Families in the Twentieth Century*. New York: Basic Books.

Beresford, J.C. and A.M. Rivlin. 1966. "Privacy, Poverty and Old Age." *Demography* Vol. 3.

Bixby, Lenore E. 1970. "Income of People Aged 65 and Older: Overview from 1968 Survey of the Aged." *Social Security Bulletin* (April): 3-34.

Brody, Elaine. 1977. *Long Term Care for Older People*. New York: Human Sciences Press.

Carliner, Geoffrey. 1975. "Determinants of Household Headship." *Journal of Marriage and the Family* Volume 37.

Chevan, A. and J.H. Korson. 1972. "The Widowed Who Live Alone: An Examination of Social and Demographic Factors." *Social Forces* Vol. 51.

Congresswomen's Caucus. 1981. "Older Women: The Economics of Aging" Women's Studies Program. George Washington University.

Danziger, S., J. van der Gaag, E. Smolensky and M. Taussig. 1982. "The Life Cycle Hypothesis and the Consumption Behavior." Institute for Research on Poverty. Discussion Paper No. 697-82. University of Wisconsin-Madison.

Duffy, Martin et al. 1980. *Inflation and the Elderly*. Data Resources Inc. Boston, MA.

Ellwood, David T. and Mary Jo Bain. 1985. "The Impact of AFDC on Family Structure and Living Arrangements." In Roland G. Ehrenberg, ed., *Research and Labor Economics* Vol. 7.

Friedman, Joseph and Jane Sjogren. 1981. "Assets of the Elderly as they Retire." *Social Security Bulletin* (January) Vol. 44(1).

Grad, Susan. 1983. "Income of the Population 55 and Over, 1980." Social Security Administration.

Grad, Susan and Karen Foster. 1979. "Income of the Population 55 and Older, 1976." *Social Security Bulletin* (July) Vol. 42(7).

Hareven, Tamara. 1981. "Historical Changes in the Timing of Family Transitions: Their Impact on Generational Relations." In *Aging: Stability and Change in the Family* eds., R.W. Fogel, E. Hatfield et al. New York: Academic Press.

Herriot, Roger and Emmett F. Spiers. 1975. "Measuring the Impact on Income Statistics of Reporting Differences between the Current Population Survey and Administrative Sources." In *Proceeding of the Social Statistics Section*, American Statistical Association.

Kobrin, Frances. 1976. "The Primary Individual and the Family: Changes in Living Arrangements in the United States Since 1940." *Journal of Marriage and the Family* Vol. 38:233-249.

Kobrin, Frances. 1981. "Family Extension and the Elderly: Economic, Demographic and Family Cycle Factors." *Journal of Gerontology* Vol. 36:370-377.

Kreps, Juanita. 1977. "Intergenerational Transfers and the Bureaucracy," in *Family Bureaucracy and the Elderly*, eds., E. Shanas and M. Sussman. Durham, N.C.: Duke University Press.

Laslett, Peter and Richard Wall. 1972. *Household and Family in Past Time*. Cambridge, England: Cambridge University Press.

Lingg, Babara A. 1982. "Social Security Benefits of Female Retired Workers and Two-Worker Couples." *Social Security Bulletin* (February) Vol. 45(2).

Lopata, Helena Z. 1978. "Contributions of Extended Families to the Support Systems of Metropolitan Area Widows: Limitations of the Modified Kin Network." *Journal of Marriage and the Family* 40:355-364.

Mallon, Linda. 1980. "Economics and the Older Woman." *Aging* November-December.

Marsh, Robert. 1981. "The Income and Resources of the Elderly in 1978." *Social Security Bulletin* (December) Vol. 44(12).

Michael, Robert, V. Fuchs and Sharon R. Scott. 1980. "Changes in the Propensity to Live Alone: 1950-1976." *Demography* (February) Vol. 17(1).

Moon, Marilyn L. 1976. "The Economic Welfare of the Aged and Income Security Programs." *Review of Income and Wealth* Vol. 22(3):253-269.

Moon, Marilyn L. 1977. *The Measurement of Economic Welfare: Its Application to the Aged Poor*. New York: Academic Press.

Moon, Marilyn L. 1981. "Intrafamily Transfers and the Elderly," Final Report, Administration on Aging: Washington, D.C.

Moon, Marilyn L. and Eugene Smolensky. 1976. "Income, Economic Status and Policy Toward the Aged." Institute for Research on Poverty. Discussion Paper No. 350-76. University of Wisconsin-Madison.

Moon, Marilyn L. and Eugene Smolensky. 1977. *Improving Measures of Economic Well-Being*. New York: Academic Press.

Morgan, James S. 1978. "Intra-Family Transfers Revisited: The Support of Dependents Inside the Family." In *Five Thousand Families-Patterns of Economic Progress*, Vol. VI, eds., G. Duncan and J. Morgan. Ann Arbor: ISR.

Morgan, James, M. David, W. Cohen and H. Brazer. 1962. *Income and Welfare in the United States*. New York: McGraw-Hill.

Murray, Janet. 1971. "Living Arrangements of People Aged 65 and Older: Findings from the 1968 Survey of the Aged." *Social Security Bulletin* (September).

Pampel, Fred C. 1981. *Social Change and the Aged: Recent Trends in the United States*. Lexington, MA: Lexington Books.

Schulz, James H. 1980. *The Economics of Aging*. Second Edition. New York: Wadsworth Publishing Co., Inc.

Shanas, Ethel. 1980. "Living in Families: Cross-national Research on the Family Life of Old People." In *Families and Older Persons*, eds., George Maddox et al. Durham, N.C.: Duke University Press.

Shanas, Ethel and Gordon Streib. 1965. *Social Structure and the Family: Generational Relations*. New Jersey: Prentice-Hall, Inc.

Smith, Daniel Scott. 1981. "Historical Change in the Household Structure of the Elderly in Economically Developed Societies." In *Aging: Stability and Change in the Family*, eds., R.W. Fogel, E. Hatfield et al. New York: Academic Press.

Social Security Administration. 1982. *Annual Statistical Supplement 1980*. U.S. Department of Health and Human Services.

Soldo, Beth J. 1980. *America's Elderly in the Eighties*. Population Reference Bureau. (November).

Soldo, Beth J. 1981. "The Living Arrangements of the Elderly in the Near Future." In *Aging: Social Change*, eds., S.B. Kiesler, J.N. Morgan and V.K. Oppenheimer. New York: Academic Press.

Spitler, B.J. Curry. 1981. "Policies Affecting Older Americans" in *Aging: Prospects and Issues*. Eds., Richard Davis, Ethel Percy, Andrus Gerontological Center: USC Press.

Steiner, Peter O. and Robert Dorfman. 1957. *The Economic Status of the Aged*. Berkeley: University of California Press.

Taussig, Michael. 1973. *Alternative Measures of the Distribution of Economic Welfare*. New Jersey: Industrial Relations Section, Princeton University.

Tilly, Louise and Miriam Cohen. 1982. "Does Family Have a History?" *Social Science History* (Spring), Vol. 6(2).

Tissue, Thomas. 1979. "Low Income Widows and Other Aged Singles." *Social Security Bulletin* Vol. 42(12).

Tissue, Thomas and J.L. McCoy. 1981. "Income and Living Arrangements Among Poor Aged Singles." *Social Security Bulletin* Vol. 44(4).

Troll, L.E. 1971. "The Family In Later Life: A Decade Review." *Journal of Marriage and the Family* Vol. 33.

Viscusi, W. Kip and Richard Zeckhauser. 1974. "Welfare of the Elderly." Kennedy School of Government. Discussion Paper 25D. Boston: Harvard University.

Weisbrod, Burton and W. Lee Hanson. 1968. "An Income-Net Worth Approach to Measuring Economic Welfare." *American Economic Review* Vol. 8:1315-1329.

# PART III

# 9

# Household Structure and Living Alone in Israel

FRANCES K. GOLDSCHEIDER AND ZARA FISHER

A central theme in the study of the modernization of societies has been the transformation of the family. In relatively traditional societies, family and kin were the central institution integrating economic, political, religious, and other dimensions of social life, maintaining them through the generations. In more modern societies, by contrast, powerful institutions have developed that are increasingly separate from family ties and that maintain themselves over time. For example, the increased importance of achievement in occupational placement and of elections in public affairs has weakened the influence of family relationships in economic and political processes.

The general framework of family transformation has been useful in understanding many concrete changes in family structure and family processes, such as the decline in fertility and the decreasing role of parents in young people's choice of marriage partners. The argument has also been applied to family extension, i.e., the coresidence of related adults beyond the nuclear core. However, historical and demographic research on family extension has shown very inconsistent results; many have concluded that there has been no change in the prevalence of family extension in the process of modernization (Laslett and Wall, 1972; Levy, 1975).

Increasing evidence has appeared recently that suggests that these conclusions may have been premature, and that real changes have occurred that were obscured by other factors. After World War II, an extremely rapid decline has been underway in the United States and Western Europe in the likelihood that unmarried adults will live with related persons, with a concomitant increase in the proportion of the population living alone (Young, 1983; LeBourdais and Goldscheider, 1986).

Some have argued that this recent increase in the likelihood of living alone simply reflects recent changes in a series of external factors--housing availability and increases in income and pension plans. Together, these have greatly increased people's ability to purchase the privacy that, according to this argument, they have always preferred (Michael, et al.,

1982). According to this view, no fundamental change in orientation toward family life has occurred.

In contrast to the economic argument, our interpretation of these recent changes is that they are part of a long term evolution in family structure, reflecting emerging new roles for women, the decline in the importance of marriage, and particularly early marriage, and, in turn, changing preferences for autonomy and independent living. Together, these changes have progressively reduced the likelihood of coresidence among related adults.

The analysis of long term change in living arrangements has been very difficult, since it has been greatly hampered by the lack of adequate, comparable data on households and on the relationships of the people within them (Smith, 1981). Further, two processes were going on at the same time that were obscuring the measurement of declining family extension. The long term aging of the population was increasing the pool of eligibles among the elderly population, offsetting any decrease in the proportion of families extended by an elderly relative (Kobrin, 1976). At the younger end of the adult life cycle, changes in the living arrangements were being influenced more visibly by fluctuations in age at marriage and changes in patterns of education. These two processes could well have obscured the long term decline in coresidence of unmarried adults with nuclear families.

This chapter seeks to clarify the changing family patterns associated with modernization by examining ethnic differences in family living arrangements in Israel in 1972, focusing in particular on the likelihood of living alone or with unrelated adults. These data provide a unique opportunity to examine whether there is any link between living arrangements and group patterns of family centeredness, since Israel at that time included large subpopulations from a wide variety of socio-culture areas, groups with very different exposures to the forces of modernization. There are Jews from European societies who have participated for several centuries in the long term rise in education, urban dwelling, and technology; Jews from Asian and African nations who were urban and town dwellers, but living in highly traditional societies; and Moslems who have only recently ceased highly agricultural-based, even nomadic, ways of life.

Yet this wide range of backgrounds can be measured with a common measuring instrument, a census with categories that were applied to all groups consistently, and the data refer to a single point in time, when pension systems were available for nearly all, and housing availability varied over a much narrower range, compared to differences across centuries or continents. Finally, access to financial resources for the purchase of privacy can be measured comparably. If group patterns of family living arrangements have responded to the forces of modernization, large differences should appear among these groups. Alternatively, if issues of pension availability, income, and housing have been the dominant factors in variations in family extension, then few differences between these communities should appear.

## Data, Hypotheses, and Operationalization

The data used in this analysis come from the 1972 Census of Israel, conducted in very much the same manner as their Census of 1961 (Nathan, 1977). A 20% random subsample of the population was asked more detailed questions (sample B), and a public use file of 10% of these records (2% of the total population), was prepared by the Central Bureau of Statistics, and made this analysis possible. We have included in the analysis only individuals aged 20 and over, since the focus is on adults, and their living arrangements.[1] The data file contained information on 33,612 persons aged 20 and over. Of these, 77% were married household heads (or wives of household heads). We have concentrated our analysis on the 7,867 unmarried adults.

Our guiding hypothesis is that Israeli ethnic subcommunities will vary in their likelihood of nonfamily living, net of resources and life cycle factors. Specifically, we expect that, net of other effects:

(1) Socioeconomic resources will increase the likelihood of nonfamily living.

(2) Life cycle factors will have a strong influence on nonfamily living, with older persons and formerly married persons less likely to live in family settings than the young or the never married.

(3) Ethnic communities will vary in their extent of nonfamily living, with Moslems the least likely and persons from Western societies most likely to live outside a family setting. Jews from Asian and African countries are expected to be intermediate between the two extremes. We further expect that these differences may be less among the second generation of each of the Jewish communities.

Most of the variables used in the analysis can be interpreted in terms of standard demographic categories, including age, marital status, and relationship to the head of the household. Measurement of the two major conceptual categories (ethnicity and socioeconomic status), however, requires more detailed specification.

*Ethnicity:* The ethnic categories normally constructed from the concepts measured in the Israeli Census of 1972 are based on religion,

---

[1] It is also important to study change in the living arrangements of children, but these change primarily in response to changes in marriage patterns, and the focus here is on the changing patterns for the unmarried.

national origin, and generation in Israel. Following this precedent, we have distinguished six basic groupings: NonJews (which we have restricted to Moslems, since the unmarried sample contains too few Christians and Druze for separate analysis); first and second generation persons from Asian and African societies; first and second generation persons from European and American countries; and the Israeli born of Israeli parents. In 1972, the majority of this last group were probably also of European origin, but this cannot be determined at the individual level. For the first generation born in Israel, origin was based on that of their father, the only information provided in the census. These categories allow us to examine the effects of both cultural variation and generational change, the two most frequently considered bases for ethnic analysis.

*Socioeconomic status:* Since those with more resources should be more able to afford separate living quarters, it is necessary to control for the effects of socioeconomic characteristics. We have, therefore, included educational attainment in the analysis. We would have preferred to use personal income, which would be a more direct indicator of access to such resources; however, the only information available in the 1972 Census on income other than wage and salary income is at the household level (total household income), which gives no indication of resources available should an individual not live with the others in the household. Education is a less valuable indicator of actual financial resources. Although education is highly correlated with income, it is less so for women and older persons, important groups in the move away from family living. On the other hand, the value of education is increased by the great restrictions on the housing market during this period, since access to housing was controlled to some extent, with preference given to those with greater need for space. Further, education is an important indicator of noneconomic dimensions of socioeconomic status, particularly those attitudes associated with a more "modern" orientation toward traditional roles and family-centeredness, and thus should reduce the likelihood that unmarried persons will live with relatives for this reason, as well. Education has been coded in single years of completed schooling.

The analysis will involve the estimation by OLS regression of the probability of living alone or with nonrelatives, testing the significance of ethnic, socioeconomic, and life cycle variation. While the use of a dichotomous dependent variable violates the assumption of heteroskedasticity, OLS regression is reasonably robust with regard to this assumption when the outcome being predicted is between 25% and 75%, as in this case (Goodman, 1975). There is little difference in this range between results estimated with OLS and those that would be obtained with logistic regression.

The portion of the population that must be studied most intensively for these hypotheses is that of unmarried adults, since married adults normally live with their spouse, and are thus not at risk to live in a nonfamily situation except for short-term separations for marital- or work-related reasons. The first set of entries for Table 9-1 shows the proportion of the

## Table 9-1

**VARIATION IN MARITAL STATUS AND LIVING ARRANGEMENTS BY AGE, SEX, AND ETHNICITY: ISRAEL, 1972**

|  | 20–24 | 25–34 | 35–44 | 45–64 | 65–74 | 75+ |
|---|---|---|---|---|---|---|
| Proportion not married family head | | | | | | |
| Male | 80.0 | 23.7 | 7.0 | 6.8 | 15.7 | 32.6 |
| Female | 48.5 | 16.3 | 9.5 | 21.3 | 54.9 | 81.3 |
| Living arrangements of the unmarried | | | | | | |
| One-person | 4.5 | 12.6 | 28.9 | 44.8 | 53.4 | 34.2 |
| Family head | 1.8 | 6.6 | 27.1 | 32.2 | 12.3 | 10.0 |
| Child of head | 89.9 | 75.1 | 35.2 | 2.5 | 0.3 | 0.0 |
| Other relative | 2.4 | 3.9 | 7.6 | 19.7 | 33.2 | 55.2 |
| Nonrelative | 1.4 | 1.8 | 1.3 | 0.8 | 0.8 | 0.7 |
| Total | 100.0 | 100.0 | 100.0 | 100.0 | 100.0 | 100.0 |
| (N) | (2,868) | (1,170) | (395) | (1,309) | (963) | (612) |
| Proportion of the unmarried living in nonfamily living arrangements | | | | | | |
| Total | 5.9 | 14.4 | 30.2 | 45.6 | 54.2 | 34.9 |
| Male | 4.1 | 12.5 | 35.7 | 53.8 | 58.4 | 36.1 |
| Female | 9.2 | 16.7 | 26.0 | 43.5 | 53.2 | 34.3 |
| NB Asian-African | 2.2 | 13.9 | — | — | — | — |
| FB Asian-African | 3.5 | 10.8 | 25.2 | 31.5 | 36.7 | 22.7 |
| Sabra 2 | 5.4 | 20.0 | — | — | — | — |
| NB Eur-N.America | 8.7 | 24.0 | 36.1 | — | — | — |
| FB Eur-N.America | 14.5 | 15.4 | 37.1 | 57.4 | 70.0 | 45.5 |
| Moslem | 2.8 | 2.3 | 16.7 | 14.8 | 21.8 | 9.3 |

NOTE: Dashes indicate fewer than 25 cases in that age group.

population that were not currently either a male married family head or a woman married to the head of the family, to give a clearer sense of the population being studied. Marriage for women was relatively early at this time, and more than half were married in the age group 20-24, leaving 48.5% available to live as an unmarried adult in a nuclear family (normally that of her parents), or to live alone or with nonrelatives. By contrast, 80% of males 20-24 were still unmarried. Marriage then greatly reduces the number of young men and women at risk to live outside a family setting through the middle years of adulthood. At the older ages, widowhood becomes an increasingly important factor, so that 21% of women aged 45-64 are not married, increasing to 55% among those 65-74, and reaching over 80% for those 75 or over. The male pattern differs substantially because of males' later age at marriage, their higher probability of remarriage at widowhood or divorce, and their shorter life expectancy. As a result, the nonmarried in the population aged 20 or more are primarily very young men and older women.

**Ethnic Origin and Living Arrangements**

With whom, then, does this population of unmarried persons live? The next panel of Table 9-1 shows the living arrangements of the unmarried, classified by relationship to head and household size. The first category is those who head a household containing only one person, i.e., they live alone. The last entry also includes persons living outside a family setting, since they are not related to the head of the household. Most of these are members of two-person households living with someone of the same sex and approximate age--roommates--but a few may be living with families. Such families could be one they are not related to, so that they are living as a boarder, lodger, or servant; or their own if they are living as an unrelated subfamily. This entire group, however, is very rare in these data. It seems likely that the preference given to families in housing allocation greatly reduced the ability of unmarried persons to form joint households as roommates.

The other three categories are the principal forms of family membership among the unmarried population: family head; child of head; and other relative of head (most frequently parent of head or head's spouse). This first group includes a wide variety of marginal family forms, including coresident siblings, two-adult parent-child pairs, and other combinations of related adults.[2] Since family headship among the unmarried is most common at the same ages that people normally are married, i.e., age 35-64, it is a very small fraction of the unmarried

---

[2] We have excluded formerly married persons living with minor children, who, like married persons, have much less of an option to live alone.

population. The most common family relationships are child of head and other relative of head. The two forms display quite predictable life cycle patterns, with the young extremely likely to be child of head and very unlikely to live with relatives other than parents, and with the old most likely to be other relatives, particularly the parent of the head or spouse, and extremely few having parents still alive with whom to live. These two categories combined, then, can be thought of as the opposite ends of "parent-child" or vertical family extension, in which unmarried adults continue to live with their parents well into adulthood, or live with their adult children in their later years.

For these reasons and for simplicity, we have combined the three family forms and the two nonfamily forms (one-person households and nonrelatives of head), as well. This summary version appears in the next panel of Table 9-1, showing, for example, that about 6% of those aged 20-24 in 1972 lived in nonfamily-based living arrangements (the total of the 4.5% who were heads of one-person households and the 1.4% who were nonrelatives of the household head.)

The level of nonfamily living shown here is an intermediate one, well below that found in the United States (Kobrin and Goldscheider, 1982) and even further below parts of Western Europe (Hecht, 1976); but above that of many other parts of the world (Burch, 1980). The impact of nonfamily living on the society is further reduced by the fact that the largest groups of unmarried persons (the young, not yet married adults), are the least likely to live outside a family setting. Nonfamily living is having a more substantial impact among older unmarried persons, who were relatively numerous, and likely to live alone. About half the unmarried between the ages of 45 and 74 are living alone or with nonrelatives, with some decrease for the oldest group, presumably because of increasing enfeeblement.

The final portion of Table 9-1 presents the proportion of the unmarried living in nonfamily quarters by age for the six ethnic groups. We separate for the Jewish population the native and foreign-born of Asian-African origin; second generation Israelis (Sabra 2); and the native and foreign-born of European or American origin, as well as Moslems.

These data show that overall, Moslems are far less likely to be living outside of a family-based household, while those of Asian-African origin are intermediate, and those of European or American origin are the most likely to live alone or with nonrelatives. The differences are quite substantial, with Jews of Asian-African background about twice as likely as Moslems to live away from family at most ages, and those of European or American origin often more than four times the Moslem level. These are very large differences, and suggest that despite the largely common pension systems and housing market, that there are major differences in group definitions about how people should live, if they are not currently married. However, these patterns are very similar to those that would be expected if the major factor influencing separate living were financial resources, since these groups also vary in the same way in terms of education, with those of European or American origin having the highest levels of education and the

Moslems having the lowest. To clarify this issue, we turn to a multivariate analysis of the probability of living alone or with nonrelatives.

**Life Cycle, Socioeconomic, and Ethnic Factors**

Table 9-2 presents OLS regressions to test the importance of all three sets of factors--socioeconomic, life cycle, and ethnic--in the pattern of nonfamily living arrangements. The variables presented are in the same form as in the bivariate analysis, with the exception of age, which has been recoded so that age 20 is zero, and the constant represents the level of nonfamily living among the youngest members of the three reference categories. Model 1 includes only life cycle variables--age, sex, and marital status--for these unmarried persons. The results indicate that all of these factors have a strong influence. The coefficients can be read as probabilities, or by moving the decimal two places, as percentage point differences. As in the crosstabulation, age has a very strong effect, with the probability of living in a nonfamily setting increasing by nine percentage points for each additional ten years lived after age 20, on average. Males are somewhat less likely than females (4.2 percentage points) to live outside a family group. It is not clear why this should be, when the major sex difference in the responsibilities of the unmarried has been removed (i.e., that of being a single parent with young children). It is

**Table 9-2**

**BASIC MODELS OF THE PROPORTION LIVING OUTSIDE OF FAMILIES: ISRAEL, 1972**

| Variables | Model 1 | Model 2 | Model 3 |
|---|---|---|---|
| Male | −.042* | −.042* | −.046* |
| Age | .009* | .008* | .009* |
| Divorced | .317* | .290* | .265* |
| Single | .072* | .058* | .019 |
| Moslem | — | −.219* | −.120* |
| FB Asian African | — | −.130* | −.067* |
| NB Asian African | — | −.119* | −.080* |
| NB Europe-American | — | −.020 | −.027 |
| Survivors | — | .076* | .069* |
| Sabra 2 | — | −.057 | −.051 |
| Education | — | — | .017* |
| Constant | .055* | .167* | −.127* |
| Adj. $R^2$ | .0937 | .1101 | .1211 |

* $p < .05$.

possible that a higher proportion of widowed and divorced males have more recently acquired that status, given the higher remarriage rates for males than females. If the normal pattern were one of not establishing a new home alone for a short period after divorce or widowhood, more men would be in that transitional stage. One the other hand, it is at the youngest ages, when both sexes are predominately single, that females are more likely to live separately. Young males may have the years of early adulthood more disrupted by higher education and military service than females, and so less willing than young females to assume the maintenance tasks normally associated with independent living. Further, the services provided them in the parental home may have been much greater than those provided to daughters, and their independence less curtailed, with the result that they were more willing to remain in the parental home than young women.

The results for marital status indicate that both the never married and the divorced are significantly more likely to be living outside a family setting than are the widowed (the reference category), with the biggest differences (32 percentage points) associated with having been divorced. This may suggest that there is some stigma associated with divorce in Israel, so that the traditional supports available to the widowed in terms of housing and family ties are less offered to the divorced. It is also possible that a strong selectivity is operating, in which married persons avoid divorce unless the likelihood is great that they can remain independent.

These results are very strong; much of the explanatory power for the set of models as a whole derives from these life cycle factors. Clearly, analyses that omit consideration of the life cycle pattern of living arrangements, and that ignore the consequences of the shifting age structure of populations, would have difficulty interpreting differences in living arrangements that emerge on other dimensions (including time). For this reason, we have introduced the ethnic subpopulations into the analysis after the effects of life cycle, and particularly of age structure, have been controlled, since these groups differ sharply in their age compositions.

Model 2 shows the effects of introducing ethnicity. The coefficients presented for each group test the difference between that group and the reference category (the foreign born of European or American origin) controlling for age, sex, and marital status. These data show that major differences existed among the ethnic communities in Israel in 1972. The overall order remains: Moslems are the least likely to maintain a nonfamily-based living arrangement and Jews from Asian and African countries are intermediate between them and Jews from European origins. Generational differences, however, failed to emerge. Both the native and foreign born Asian Africans have similar coefficients and are 12 to 13 percentage points less likely to live alone or with nonrelatives than the foreign born of European origin. There are also no significant generational differences for this group as a whole. Neither the native born of European or origin nor the third generation, who are largely of such backgrounds, are significantly different from the foreign born of European or American countries of origin. This suggests that the experience of living in Israel has had little effect on at least this dimension of ethnic difference, with little convergence between the two large groups of Jews observed by 1972.

A major and unexpected difference among those coming from Europe and American emerged, however, consistent with what had been observed in ethnographic studies but rarely distinguished in more statistical analyses. Among the immigrants from western countries were those who came from areas that were more directly exposed to the Nazi mass killings (Dawidowicz, 1975). These we have called "survivors" and are defined as those from the fifteen European countries that were estimated to have lost 20% or more of their pre-war Jewish population from the Nazi exterminations and entered Israel between 1942 and 1952. They were much more likely to be living alone or with nonrelatives than westerners who came to Israel at an earlier time, or from areas less affected by those events. Psychological factors may account for this pattern, but it is also the case that many of these people had fewer surviving relatives with whom to live.

The central question remains: Are these differences largely the result of socioeconomic differences among these groups? Model 3 introduces educational attainment into the analysis to address this question and the data show that the socioeconomic component is clearly a strong one, with an additional year of education having nearly twice as much impact as an additional year of age. Having more resources, and perhaps greater exposure to the world beyond the family and community that usually accompanies more education, leads to a substantial increase in the likelihood of living alone or with nonrelatives. And it is also clear that an important portion of the ethnic differences observed previously derived from their group differences in educational levels. Ethnic differences evident in Model 2 are much larger than those that appear in Model 3 (about 30 percentage points compared to about 20).

Nevertheless, nearly all the factors that had been significant in the earlier models (ethnicity and life cycle), remain so after controlling for socioeconomic status, and those that were not significant (generation) remained so. (The only exception is for the single, who were more likely to live separately than the widowed simply because of their higher levels of education.) Taken together, these data indicate strong ethnic differences in orientations toward family and in the importance of close kin ties. These differences are not simply due to the differences in economic resources or life cycle factors that characterize these communities.

### Age, Sex, and Education: Interactions with Ethnicity

More detailed analysis of these data suggest greater complexities in the ethnic patterns of living arrangements, relating to the ways that sex, age, and education affect living arrangements within each community. Table 9-3 presents these results, based on an analysis of ethnic interactions with these three variables. The first column, the "basic model," repeats the results from Model 3 of Table 9-2, except that the insignificant variables

## Table 9-3

### SIGNIFICANT ETHNIC INTERACTIONS IN THE PROPORTION LIVING OUTSIDE OF FAMILIES: ISRAEL, 1972

| Variables | Basic Model | Interactions with | | |
| --- | --- | --- | --- | --- |
| | | Sex | Age | Education |
| Moslem | −.107* | −.166* | −.080* | −.058 |
| Asian-African | −.056* | −.072* | −.007 | −.016 |
| Survivor | .078* | .077* | .048 | .209* |
| Divorced | .248* | .251* | .249* | .261* |
| Male | −.046* | −.064* | −.046* | −.045* |
| Moslem-male | — | .120* | — | — |
| Asian-African-male | — | .031† | — | — |
| Survivor-male | — | −.003 | — | — |
| Age | .009* | .009* | .010* | .009* |
| Moslem-age | — | — | −.005* | — |
| Asian-African-age | — | — | −.001† | — |
| Survivor-age | — | — | .000 | — |
| Education | .017* | .016* | .016* | .021* |
| Moslem-education | — | — | — | −.006 |
| Asian-African-education | — | — | — | −.004 |
| Survivor-education | — | — | — | −.014* |
| Constant | −.019 | −.012 | −.047 | −.066 |
| Adj. $R^2$ | .1211 | .1213 | .1227 | .1218 |

* $p < .05$.
† $.05 < p < .10$.

distinguishing the generations, and the single from the widowed, have been dropped. Each subsequent column focuses on a new set of interactions.

The results for the model interacting sex and ethnicity show that sex differences in independent living are much greater within the Moslem community than among Jews. The strong and significant coefficient that emerged for male Moslems indicates that whereas females are less likely to be living in a family setting for the country as a whole, Moslems men live more independently than Moslem women. This result reinforces other research about the strength of traditional sex roles and female seclusion in Moslem societies, and shows that these patterns carry over to living arrangements as well. In contrast, neither Jews from Asian and African origins nor those who were more likely to have experienced the Holocaust more directly appear to differ from other Jews in the strength of traditional sex roles, at least in terms of living arrangements. None of the coefficients for these groups of males was significant.

The third column repeats this exercise for age, and shows that again, Moslems differ from Jews in their life cycle patterns of living arrangements. Additional years bring only half as rapid an increase in the likelihood of living independently (although the relative effects might have been similar). Much smaller differences characterize the various groupings of Jews.

Finally, we interact education with ethnicity. This is a particularly important issue, since the effects of education, like those of time, or generation, are supposed to lead to convergence among ethnic groups, so that more highly educated members of different ethnic groups should resemble each other more than those with lower educations. Such convergence would appear in the analysis as significant positive coefficients for the variables measuring Moslem education and Asian-African education. This result does not appear, suggesting that education in Israel during this period was not serving to dilute ethnic differences in family patterns. Holocaust survivors again emerge as an unusual group, since education had much less impact on their likelihood of living alone or with nonrelatives. They are less likely to use the resources conferred by education to purchase privacy and independence from family. This suggests that some factor that characterized survivors as a group is influencing their living arrangements, particularly those at lower educational levels. It may be that their war-related experiences, which occurred for most after they had completed education, cancelled the educational effect on attitudes in some fashion. However, it is also true that many of this group had access to resources independent of education, through German reparations. These resources may be financing their independence from family, whether or not they have the educational level to command higher earnings. This non-educational related resource factor, rather than the absence of relatives or the psychological impact of the Holocaust experience may have increased their likelihood of living alone.

**Implications**

This analysis of ethnic variation in nonfamily living arrangements in Israel has shown that group level differences in family living patterns are strong and salient, even when other factors important in determining or limiting whether one can live alone or with relatives are taken into account. Consideration of life cycle effects is essential in the analysis of living arrangements, and the effects of resources are powerful in determining the likelihood that unmarried adults will extend the families of related persons. Nevertheless, most of the ethnic differences that appeared without these controls remained in the multivariate analysis.

The ethnic differences that appeared are those that would be expected to result from group adjustments to long-term change in social structure, the pattern of variation most consistent with the modernization theories of family change. This result argues strongly for a conclusion that there are strong, normatively-based forces underlying living arrangements decisions, leading to variation over time and between groups at the same time. Previous analyses of long term change in family structure were limited in their finding of little change, since so many of the other forces influencing living arrangements could not be controlled. This result reinforces the value of analyzing data from the State of Israel for general theoretical purposes, since the data available are of high, modern quality, yet are measuring groups that vary from the most traditional to the most modern. There is no other country in the world in which these conditions prevail to such an extent.

It is unclear how rapidly we can expect convergence among these ethnic and religious groups. The 1972 point in time is relatively early, and later data (i.e., 1983 Israel Census data) may show some tendency toward greater similarity. There has been rapid convergence among the Jewish groups on many dimensions, particularly those affecting younger people, such as fertility. The ethnic differences that appear in these data disproportionately reflect variation at the oldest ages. Nevertheless, neither the passage of generations nor the acquisition of education had yet led to greater similarity, a finding paralleling other research on the continuation of ethnic residential, occupation, and educational concentration (Goldscheider, 1983).

It is clear, however, that the incidence of nonfamily living can be expected to rise for all groups in Israel. Increases since 1972 in resources and housing availability should have led many to purchase privacy not previously available; the aging of the population will have increased the proportions in the ages in which more live alone. Thus, even if the more modern ideas that lead to increased separation from the family context do not spread far, the phenomenon should become more visible, although probably not to the extent that it has in Europe and North America. However, some convergence is likely to be underway, particularly for young adults. Moving away from parents before marriage allows the kind of autonomy and independence that is very attractive to young adults (and their parents) and both parents and children are likely to figure that out before long.

## REFERENCES

Burch, T. 1980. "The Index of Overall Headship: A Simple Measure of Household Complexity Standardized for Age and Sex." *Demography* Vol. 17:25-39.

Dawidowicz, L. 1975. *The War Against the Jews.* Holt, Rinehart, and Winston.

Goldscheider, C. 1983. "The Demography of Asian and African Jews in Israel." In J. B. Maier and C. I. Waxman, eds., *Ethnicity, Identity, and History: Essays in Memory of W. J. Cahnman.* Transaction Books, pp. 273-89.

Goodman, L.A. 1975. "The Relationship Between Modified and Usual Regression Approaches to the Analysis of Dichotomous Variables." In D. R. Heise, ed., *Sociological Methodology* Jossey-Bass, pp. 83-110.

Hecht, A. 1976. "Trends in the Size and Structure of Households in Europe, 1960-1970 and the Outlook for the Period 1970-2000." Paper presented at the Annual Meeting of the Population Association of America.

Kobrin, F. 1976. "The Fall in Household Size and Rise of the Primary Individual in the United States." *Demography* 13:127-138.

Kobrin, F. and C. Goldscheider, 1982. "Family Extension or Nonfamily Living: Life Cycle, Economic, and Ethnic Factors." *Western Sociological Review* 13:103-118.

Laslett, P. and R. Wall. 1972. *Household and Family in Past Time.* Cambridge University Press.

LeBourdais, C. and F. Goldscheider. 1986. "The Decline in Age at Leaving Home, 1920-1979." *Sociology and Social Research* 72:143-145.

Levy, M., Jr. 1965. "Aspects of the Analysis of Family Structure." A. Coale, et al., eds., *Aspects of the Analysis of Family Structure.* Princeton University Press.

Michael, R. et al. 1980. "Changes in the Propensity to Live Alone: 1950-1976." *Demography* 17:39-56.

Nathan, G. 1977. "Methodological Aspects of the Israel Population Census of 1972." In U. Schmelz, P. Glikson, and S. Della Pergola, eds., *Papers in Jewish Demography, 1973*. Institute of Contemporary Jewry, The Hebrew University.

Smith, D. 1981. "Historical Change in the Household Structure of the Elderly in Developed Countries." In R. Fogel, E. Hatfield, S. Kiesler, and E. Shanas, eds., *Aging: Stability and Change in the Family*. Academic Press.

Young, C. 1984. "The Effect of Children Returning Home on the Precision of the Timing of the Leaving Home Stage of the Family Life Cycle." Paper presented at the seminar on the "Demography of the Later Phases of the Family Life Cycle," International Union for the Scientific Study of Population, Berlin.

# 10

# Intergenerational Household Extension in Japan

## HIROSHI KOJIMA

While Japan has many demographic features in common with developed societies in the West, including low levels of fertility and mortality, it differs much more in the area of family demography, seeming to resemble more the newly industrializing and developing societies. Although Japan does not lag behind other developed countries in its socio-economic development, their more traditional family patterns have not responded in the same manner to development as have Western nations. Nor are the family patterns of the Japanese converging toward the nuclear family system as many sociologists had predicted (e.g., Goode, 1963). It is even possible that some aspects of socio-economic development facilitate the realization of the traditional family patterns that vary from society to society.

In many parts of prewar Japan, the intergenerationally extended (stem) family household was the normative living arrangement for the elderly parents and their eldest son. When the parents did not have any sons, they often lived with their eldest daughter and son-in-law. Coresidence was generally continuous from the child's birth or began again when the eldest child married or the parents retired, normally ending only with the death of parents. Coresidence with parents was usually an economic advantage to the married eldest son or daughter because he/she could obtain monetary and non-monetary assistance from them when they were younger and inherit much of their property, including the land and house. The prewar civil code prescribed unequal inheritance among children.

After World War II, there was a steady decline in the proportion of newly-wed couples coresiding with their parents immediately after marriage. However, the decline ended in the early 1970s and seems to have begun to increase (Atoh and Kojima, 1983). Data in Table 10-1 show the decline in extended family households since the mid-1950s. For the twenty year period to the mid-1950s there was an increase in nuclear family households but radical changes have occurred in the proportion of

## Table 10-1

### TRENDS IN HOUSEHOLD STRUCTURE: JAPAN, 1955–85
(Percent)

| Year | Total in 1000s | Family Households | | | One-Person | Non-Rel. |
|---|---|---|---|---|---|---|
| | | Sub-Total | Extended[a] | Nuclear | | |
| 1955 | 17,383 | 96.1 | 36.5 (38.0) | 59.6 (62.0) | 3.4 | 0.5 |
| 1960 | 19,678 | 94.9 | 34.7 (36.5) | 60.2 (63.5) | 4.7 | 0.4 |
| 1965 | 23,085 | 91.8 | 29.2 (31.8) | 62.6 (68.2) | 7.8 | 0.4 |
| 1970 | 26,856 | 88.9 | 25.4 (28.6) | 63.5 (71.4) | 10.8 | 0.4 |
| 1975 | 31,271 | 86.2 | 22.2 (25.9) | 64.0 (74.1) | 13.7 | 0.2 |
| 1980 | 34,106 | 84.0 | 20.7 (24.6) | 63.4 (75.4) | 15.8 | 0.2 |
| 1985 | 36,452 | 82.3 | 19.7 (24.0) | 62.6 (76.0) | 17.5 | 0.2 |

[a]Other related households than nuclear family households. Figures in parentheses are the shares within family households.

SOURCE: Institute of Population Problems (1986:90) (originally, Population Census, 1955–85, Bureau of Statistics).

## Table 10-2

### LIVING ARRANGEMENTS OF THE ELDERLY: JAPAN, 1985
(Percent)

| Age | One-Person | Married Couple Only | Coresidence with | | | Other Rel. | Non-Rel. |
|---|---|---|---|---|---|---|---|
| | | | Children | | | | |
| | | | Sub-total | Married | Un-married | | |
| Total | 8.7 | 25.8 | 61.8 | 42.2 | 19.7 | 3.5 | 0.2 |
| 60–64 | 7.3 | 31.9 | 55.7 | 29.1 | 26.5 | 4.9 | 0.2 |
| 65–69 | 9.1 | 29.9 | 57.4 | 38.0 | 19.4 | 3.4 | 0.2 |
| 70–74 | 10.0 | 25.3 | 61.9 | 46.2 | 15.7 | 2.6 | 0.2 |
| 75–79 | 9.7 | 19.4 | 68.2 | 55.5 | 13.3 | 2.5 | 0.2 |
| 80–84 | 8.6 | 11.1 | 77.7 | 62.2 | 15.5 | 2.4 | 0.2 |
| 85–89 | 8.0 | 6.8 | 82.4 | 64.4 | 18.1 | 2.5 | 0.2 |
| 90+ | 6.7 | 5.9 | 84.6 | 60.4 | 24.2 | 2.8 | — |

SOURCE: Institute of Population Problems (1986:93) (originally, Basic Survey of Health and Welfare Administration, 1985, Department of Statistics and Information, Ministry of Health and Welfare).

one person households, increasing five-fold between 1955 and 1985.

Moreover, most of the elderly live with their children (Table 10-2). Among older old persons the majority lives with a married child. While the proportion of elderly parents coresiding with children decreased during the period between 1975 and 1985, the proportion of married children aged 20-39 coresiding with their parents increased slightly (Hirosima, 1987).

What accounts for this pattern of intergenerational household extension in Japan? Some stress the importance of demographic factors. Martin and Culter (1983), for example, emphasize the increased survival of parents and children due to the postwar mortality decline; Hirosima (1984) stresses the increased proportion of eldest sons among the child generation due to the baby bust since the 1950s.

However, it may be that intergenerational household extension has new adaptive advantages over nuclear family living in contemporary Japanese society. For example, such household living arrangements can help the young couple to save housing and child-care costs (Morgan and Hirosima, 1983). Extended family patterns may also compensate for the changing inheritance system. Even though the postwar civil code stipulates equal inheritance among children, non-eldest children often give up their inheritance (especially immobile property) to the eldest child in exchange for the care of the aged parent(s) through coresidence. Hirosima (1987) argues that three generational coresidence is progressively changing its nature from a legal and normative obligation to a strategy of economic welfare.

While there may be specific factors particular to Japan in determining family extension, intergenerational household extension is also found in other contemporary societies. Coresidence of elderly or widowed parents with a married child is common in many parts of the world (Young, 1986). Short-term household extension after marriage is not uncommon in the West, including France and the United States (Roussel and Bourguignon, 1976; Cherlin, 1979). Short- and long-term coresidence after marriage is more common in some Asian societies, including Malaysia, Thailand, Taiwan and Korea (Palmore et al., 1970; Limanonda, 1979, Chamratrithirong et al., 1988; Freedman et al., 1982, Stokes et al., 1987; Morgan and Rindfuss, 1984).

An increasing number of studies analyzes the determinants of intergenerational household extension at both the individual and household levels using multivariate techniques. The earliest multivariate analysis of the determinants of extension seems to have been conducted for early postnuptial coresidence in Malaysia (Palmore et al., 1970). More recent studies on determinants of postnuptial coresidence have examined Taiwan (Freedman et al., 1982; Stokes et al., 1987), Thailand (Chamratrithirong et al., 1988), and the United States (Cherlin, 1979; Angel and Tienda, 1982; Anderson and Allen, 1984.)

Multivariate analyses of the determinants of the living arrangements of older persons, including intergenerational extension, are increasing rapidly in the United States (Soldo and Lauriat, Schwartz et al., 1984; Wolf, 1984; Wolf and Soldo, 1986; Mutchler and Frisbie, 1987.)

Comparative analyses of the determinants of the elderly's living arrangements have been carried out in six Latin American societies (De Vos, 1986) and in four Asian societies (Martin, 1988).

Many of these studies tend to emphasize economic and cultural factors as the major categories of determinants, especially income, race and ethnicity, although more attention has been given to demographic issues in recent studies. In several studies race and ethnicity have been found to have important effects on household extension. Although the interpretation of these ethnic and racial differences is not always clear, they suggest that even relatively affluent persons in highly industrialized and developed societies may choose intergenerational residence when they are members of traditional communities.

Although the specific ethnic and race findings from previous research are not directly relevant to the Japanese case, the theoretical emphasis on the continuing salience of cultural factors, along with demographic and economic factors, is an important insight. In one study of the relationship between age and assets of the elderly in Japan, using data derived from a small, regionally limited sample, self-employment and rural residence were found to increase the probability of household extension (Dekle, 1987). Research based on a larger, more representative sample in Japan (Kojima 1987b, 1988) analyzed the determinants of coresidence of young adults with parents before and after their marriage, and showed that demographic, socioeconomic, and cultural factors affected coresidence. The objective of this chapter is to analyze the relative importance of economic, cultural, and demographic factors in the household extension patterns in Japan from the perspectives of both child and parent generations.

**Theoretical Framework**

The framework used for analyzing the determinants of coresidence is a modfied version of the frameworks developed in previous research (Kojima 1987a, 1987b, 1988), which, in turn, builds on the framework for studying the determinants of nonfamily living proposed by Kobrin and Goldscheider (1982) as well as the framework for organizing the determinants of nuptiality proposed by Dixon (1970). Their components resemble those of the schemata of kin availability and observed household composition developed by De Vos and Palloni (1984).

Figure 10-1 shows the analytical framework for the determinants of coresidence in Japan, focusing on the married male household head (hereafter, "the head"). The analysis is limited to this category because female household heads tend to be unmarried and unmarried heads are much more likely to live alone. This limitation sharpens the comparison between the determinants of coresidence with parents and those of coresidence with a married child.

Coresidence either of parents or with a married child is assumed to be determined by three intervening variables: the availability of kin for

**Fig. 10-1—Analytical framework for determinants of coresidence of married male household head with parents and with a married child**

| Intervening Variables | Common Determinants | Independent Variables | |
|---|---|---|---|
| | | Coresidence with Parents | Coresidence with a Married Child |
| Availability of kin for coresidence | Head's Age (?) Migrant status (−) | Head's Eldest-son status (+) Sib size (−) | Head's Health status (ill +) |
| | Norms about choice of kin to co-reside with | Wife's Eldest-daughter status (−) Sib size (+) | Wife's Health status (ill +) |
| | | Parent's Survival (+) Marital status (widowed +) Health status (ill +) | Children's Number (+) Age (?) Sex (male +) Marital status (single −) |
| Feasibility of coresidence | Housing (owned +) Income (?) | | |
| Desirability of coresidence | Availability of alternatives { Education (?) Occupation (self-employed +) U/R residence (rural +) Region (+) Attitude (+)) } | | |

NOTE: Signs in parentheses show expected directions of effect.

coresidence, the feasibility of coresidence, and the desirability of coresidence. Each of these three is, in turn, determined by a set of independent variables.

Availability variables are also divided into two depending on whether the analysis focuses on coresidence of the head with his parent(s) or with a married child. The effects of feasibility and desirability are expected to be the same for coresidence both with parents and with a married child.

The availability of kin for coresidence is determined by the demographic characteristics of the head and his parents (both his own parents and his parents-in-law), those of his wife and children, as well as the norms about the choice of specific kin to coreside with. These norms can have either positive or negative effects on coresidence. Important demographic characteristics include age, sex, marital status, migrant status, eldest-child status, sib size and health status. (Since the age of the head would affect many of the other demographic and socio-economic characteristics, it is difficult to hypothesize the direction of its pure effect on coresidence a priori because they tend to influence it through other factors.)

The migrant status of the head is primarily hypothesized to exert a negative influence on coresidence with his parents and a married child by making himself less available, although some migrate to live with parents or a child (Shimizu, 1986). In those cases, migrant status would have a positive effect on coresidence. It is also possible that non-eldest sons and daughters migrate because they are not expected to live with their parents in the future (Itoh, 1984).

Coresidence with parents is expected to be influenced by several other demographic variables. Among them, the eldest-child status of the head and his wife, in conjunction with the norms about choice of kin to coreside with, is expected to have an effect on coresidence with parents because the norms give priority to the eldest sons and daughters in many parts of Japan. It should have opposite effects on coresidence with his own parents and coresidence with his parents-in-law because both sets of parents usually do not live together.

The number of siblings of the head and his wife is expected to exert an independent effect on coresidence from that of eldest child status through the availability of other siblings with whom parents can coreside. For example, being the eldest-child in a one child family (the only child) is qualitatively different from being the eldest child in a family of two or three children in the pressure for coresidence. The sib size of the head and his wife affects coresidence though the effects of both competition and crowding.

The effect of sib size is also hypothesized to be in the opposite direction for coresidence with the head's own parents and coresidence with his parents-in-law. The more siblings he has, the greater the chance of having a never-married sibling, whose coresidence with his parents should discourage his own coresidence with his parents. Similarly, the large sib size of his wife is expected to have a negative effect on coresidence with his parents-in-law.

The demographic characteristics of parents are equally or even more important for coresidence with parents. The survival of at least one parent is, of course, crucial. The survival of the head's parents is expected to have a positive effect on coresidence with his parents and a negative effect on coresidence with his parents-in-law.

However, the survival of two parents or the intact marriage of parents (or parents-in-law) may discourage coresidence with an adult child because each parent has another parent to live with, while the widowhood of one parent (or parent-in-law) should encourage coresidence. The poor health of parents (or parents-in-law) is expected to encourage coresidence for the possible assistance by the head or his wife in the care of the sick parent.

Several additional demographic variables should predict coresidence with a married child. The poor health of the head or his wife is expected to have a positive effect on coresidence through the need for care by the child or his/her spouse. The number of married children should exert a positive effect on coresidence with a married child due to easier access to an alternative married child. The presence of at least one never-married child should discourage coresidence with a married child, to reduce conflict between siblings-in-law.

The feasibility of coresidence is affected by housing conditions and by income. Although housing is often related to income, it exerts an independent effect on living arrangements (Wilk and Netting, 1984). Home ownership is expected to encourage coresidence because of very high housing costs both for buying and for renting in Japan (Morgan and Hirosima, 1982). Further, apartments and houses for rent are usually designed for a single person or a nuclear family with two children.

The effect of income cannot be determined a priori. Lower per capita income may encourage coresidence of parents and a married child in order to realize economies of scale in household expenditure, while higher income allows the purchase of privacy through separate residence as in the United States (Michael et al., 1980). However, it may also require more strongly the maintenance of good will and reputation through norm-conforming coresidence in a more expensive "three-generation" house.

The desirability of coresidence is generally influenced by norms and values concerning parent-child coresidence, inheritance rules, and arrangements for home making and for the care of the aged and of young children. These factors indicate the strength of social, economic and cultural alternatives to coresidence. In contemporary Japan they can be largely represented by factors like education, occupation, urban/rural residence and region, although these variables affect some of availability and feasibility variables. Norms and values are also reflected in attitudes toward three-generation family households.

The effect of education cannot be hypothesized a priori. While highly educated persons may have more non-traditional ideas and more resources to realize them, they are usually more susceptible to social pressures for conformity to the norms because they have more vested interests to protect in the society. Self-employed occupations (agriculture and small-scale family business) are expected to exert a positive influence on coresidence because they usually require family workers to live in the same building or on the same premises where the work place is located.

Rural residence is hypothesized to encourage coresidence because traditional norms may be stronger and housing for rent may not be readily available in the vicinity. According to Shimizu (1985), Tohoku and Hokuriku regions have higher percentages of the elderly in three-generational family households while Hokkaido, southern Kanto (Tokyo metropolitan area), central Kinki (Kyoto-Osaka-Kobe metropolitan area) and southern Kyushu regions have lower percentages. Tohoku and Hokuriku have long been characterized by extended family households, while southern Kyushu has been known for nuclear family households. Southern Kanto and central Kinki are largely urban. Finally, a favorable attitude toward the three-generational family is expected to have a positive effect on coresidence.

## Data and Method

The data analyzed in this study derive from a national household survey, the Demographic Survey on Changes in the Family Life Course and Household Structure (DSHH), conducted in June, 1985 by the Institute of Population Problems, in cooperation with the Department of Statistics and Information, Japanese Ministry of Health and Welfare. The survey was conducted for a sub-sample of subjects (8,900 household heads) in the Department's Basic Survey of Health and Welfare Administration (BSHWA). Two-stage systematic and stratified sampling was applied to all the ordinary census tracts in Japan. DSHH used self-enumerated questionnaires, while BSHWA was conducted through interviews. The results of BSHWA were matched and merged for selected variables. The response rate was 88%, yielding 7,708 usable questionnaires. The response rate was lower among single persons living alone.

DSHH gathered information on (a) characteristics of the household and its size, (b) recent changes in the household and its membership, (c) characteristics of the household head and his/her parents, spouse and children, and (d) attitudes of the household head toward issues about the family and population. However, it provides a limited amount of information on persons other than the household head (i.e., non-head household members and non-coresiding parents and children). DSHH included questions on the living arrangement of each parent of the household head and his/her spouse and that of each child.

For the multivariate analysis of the determinants of coresidence, logistic regression (the LR procedure in the BMDP package) is used to test the hypotheses summarized in Figure 10-1. It is most suitable for dichotomous dependent variables. In this procedure, the dependent variable is the log odds ratio of coresidence and each regression coefficient represents the additive effect of each variable on the log odds or, after exponentiation, the multiplicative effect on the odds.

As in OLS regression, the sign of coefficients for each independent variable represents the direction of effect. P-values for each independent variable as well as for the equation as a whole are provided. Where the independent variables are categorical, two or more categories within the variable are transformed into a set of "design variables" with one of the categories chosen to be a reference category. Dummy coding is used in this study.

Six separate regressions were performed predicting coresidence with mother, father, and two parents of the head and his wife. In each of these regressions, cases are restricted to those heads whose specific parent(s) are alive. For coresidence with a married child, separate regressions were prepared for coresidence with a child of either sex, a son and a daughter among those with at least one married child and those with all children married.

All these variables for the selection of cases are omitted from the independent variables in the regressions. Norms about the choice of kin to coreside with are not operationalized. Although the analytical framework includes the age of parents and children as independent variables, they are omitted in the empirical analysis because they have high correlation with the age of the head and can cause the problem of multi-collinearity. Thus the age effect of the head should be considered to include that of parents and children. As a proxy for per capita income, percapita monthly expenditure is used. This proxy, as well as the attitude variable, may incorporate, at least partly, the consequence of coresidence. Variables used in the regressions are summarized in Figure 10-2.

## Household Extension

Table 10-3 shows logistic regression results for the determinants of coresidence of the married male head with his own parents and parents-in-law. The mean value of odds is shown at the end of the table. The antilog of each coefficient represents the multiplicative effect of each variable on odds. For example, the coefficient for eldest-son status in the first column is 1.822, which means that those who are the eldest son have [exponential (1.822) = 6.184] times higher odds than those who are not.

In the regression for the heads whose own mother is alive (own father may or may not be alive), migrant-status, eldest-son status, mother's widowhood, home ownership, per capita spending, occupation and urban/rural residence have significant effects on coresidence with the head's mother. Among them, eldest-son status, mother's widowhood, home ownership, self-employed occupations and rural residence have positive effects and migrant-status has a negative effect, as expected. Per capita spending has a negative effect, possibly because lower income encourages the realization of economies of scale through coresidence or possibly because

### Table 10-3

**LOGISTIC REGRESSION COEFFICIENTS FOR DETERMINANTS OF CORESIDENCE OF HEADS WITH PARENTS: JAPAN, 1985**

| Independent Variables | Own Parents | | | Parents-in-Law | | |
|---|---|---|---|---|---|---|
| | Mother | Father | Both | Mother | Father | Both |
| *Availability* | | | | | | |
| Age | .014 (.009) | .024 (.015) | .025 (.020) | .012 (.013) | .032 (.020) | .033 (.023) |
| Migrant-status | ** −.594 (.135) | −.325 (.207) | −.484 (.252) | .043 (.219) | .008 (.341) | .168 (.391) |
| Eldest-son status | *** 1.822 (.153) | *** 2.173 (.260) | *** 1.935 (.304) | −.491 (.232) | −.811 (.382) | −.532 (.420) |
| Sib size | −.117 (.041) | .119 (.064) | .111 (.085) | .028 (.062) | .047 (.097) | .072 (.110) |
| Wife's eldest-daughter | −.141 (.215) | −.244 (.366) | −.484 (.455) | *** 1.886 (.269) | *** 2.275 (.389) | *** 2.178 (.435) |
| Wife's sib size | .017 (.019) | .011 (.058) | −.031 (.070) | ** −.253 (.077) | −.092 (.122) | .029 (.142) |
| Parents illness | .056 (.142) | .089 (.224) | .254 (.257) | .151 (.225) | −.408 (.430) | −.010 (.399) |
| Parent's widowhood | *** 1.337 (.143) | ** .939 (.254) | — | *** 1.452 (.236) | * 1.006 (.410) | — |
| *Feasibility* | | | | | | |
| Home ownership | *** 1.832 (.194) | *** 2.114 (.319) | *** 2.282 (.403) | * .638 (.274) | .494 (.396) | .169 (.434) |
| Per-capita spending | ** −.012 (.002) | ** −.011 (.003) | ** −.018 (.005) | −.003 (.003) | −.005 (.005) | −.019 (.009) |

## Table 10-3 (continued)

| Independent Variables | Own Parents | | | Parents-in-Law | | |
|---|---|---|---|---|---|---|
| | Mother | Father | Both | Mother | Father | Both |
| | | | Desirability | | | |
| Education | | | | | | |
| 1. Primary | −.069 | −.459 | −.352 | −.646 | −.552 | −1.158 |
| | (.161) | (.270) | (.331) | (.279) | (.482) | (.603) |
| 2. Higher | −.067 | .187 | .189 | −.376 | −.176 | −.344 |
| | (.160) | (.240) | (.290) | (.253) | (.375) | (.416) |
| Occupation | *** | *** | *** | * | | |
| 1. Agriculture | 2.016 | 2.045 | 2.105 | 1.074 | .777 | 1.236 |
| | (.236) | (.338) | (.379) | (.361) | (.594) | (.641) |
| 2. Self-employed | .400 | .481 | .267 | .506 | .420 | .917 |
| | (.161) | (.252) | (.315) | (.270) | (.435) | (.458) |
| Residence | * | *** | ** | | | |
| 1. Rural | .594 | 1.110 | 1.023 | .123 | .298 | .367 |
| | (.153) | (.244) | (.302) | (.263) | (.394) | (.450) |
| 2. Metro | −.100 | .084 | .108 | .546 | .453 | .533 |
| | (.191) | (.311) | (.373) | (.279) | (.469) | (.535) |
| Region | | | | | | |
| 1. Extended | .387 | .845 | .910 | .574 | .914 | 1.275 |
| | (.203) | (.309) | (.376) | (.336) | (.468) | (.545) |
| 2. Nuclear | −.015 | .223 | .552 | .292 | .160 | .741 |
| | (.146) | (.230) | (.285) | (.243) | (.380) | (.452) |
| Favorable attitude | .332 | .415 | .501 | .043 | −.160 | −.103 |
| | (.131) | (.206) | (.252) | (.216) | (.332) | (.372) |
| Constant | −4.438 | −6.938 | −6.599 | −4.416 | −5.537 | −5.631 |
| | (.415) | (.697) | (.858) | (.655) | (.981) | (1.138) |
| Log likelihood | −812.0 | −352.0 | −247.8 | −379.0 | −171.5 | −139.0 |
| N | 2,444 | 1,442 | 1,180 | 2,480 | 1,655 | 1,449 |
| Mean % | 24.4 | 14.2 | 11.4 | 4.8 | 2.8 | 2.5 |
| Odds ratio | .323 | .166 | .128 | .051 | .029 | .025 |

\* $p < .05$.
\*\* $p < .01$.
\*\*\* $p < .001$.
NOTE: Standard error in parentheses.

Table 10-4

## LOGISTIC REGRESSION COEFFICIENTS FOR DETERMINANTS OF CORESIDENCE OF HEADS WITH A MARRIED CHILD: JAPAN, 1985

| Independent Variables | 1+ Children Married | | | All Children Married | | |
|---|---|---|---|---|---|---|
| | Child | Son | Daughter | Child | Son | Daughter |
| *Availability* | | | | | | |
| Age | | | | | | * |
| | −.025 | −.012 | −.042 | −.027 | −.013 | −.049 |
| | (.012) | (.012) | (.022) | (.014) | (.015) | (.027) |
| Migrant-status | | | | | | |
| | −.145 | −.217 | .095 | −.163 | −.394 | .618 |
| | (.192) | (.207) | (.353) | (.258) | (.265) | (.471) |
| Illness | | | | | | |
| | −.296 | −.289 | −.060 | .074 | .074 | .079 |
| | (.184) | (.198) | (.359) | (.245) | (.251) | (.497) |
| Wife's illness | | | | | | |
| | .266 | .133 | .630 | .212 | .062 | .729 |
| | (.191) | (.204) | (.367) | (.245) | (.251) | (.503) |
| Number of married children | * | ***' | | | ** | ** |
| | .271 | .427 | .362 | .028 | .304 | .571 |
| | (.095) | (.095) | (.184) | (.130) | (.118) | (.235) |
| No sons | | — | *** | | — | *** |
| | .204 | — | 3.571 | −.039 | — | 5.070 |
| | (.241) | — | (.392) | (.333) | — | (.696) |
| No daughters | ** | *** | — | | *** | — |
| | .871 | 1.569 | — | .583 | 1.580 | — |
| | (.233) | (.231) | — | (.332) | (.310) | |
| No single children | *** | *** | | — | — | — |
| | 1.238 | .092 | .548 | — | — | — |
| | (.197) | (.204) | (.372 | — | — | — |
| *Feasibility* | | | | | | |
| Home ownership | * | | | ** | * | |
| | .797 | .608 | 1.303 | 1.166 | 1.174 | .791 |
| | (.325) | (.362) | (.690) | (.433) | (.480) | (.997) |
| Per-capita spending | *** | *** | *** | *** | *** | *** |
| | −.029 | −.026 | −.030 | −.038 | −.033 | −.046 |
| | (.003) | (.004) | (.007) | (.005) | (.005) | (.010) |

**Table 10-4 (continued)**

| Independent Variables | 1+ Children Married | | | All Children Married | | |
|---|---|---|---|---|---|---|
| | Child | Son | Daughter | Child | Son | Daughter |
| | | | Desirability | | | |
| Education | | | | | | |
| 1. Primary | −.444 | −.317 | −.631 | −.114 | −.041 | −.533 |
| | (.190) | (.203) | (.352) | (.263) | (.265) | (.514) |
| 2. Higher | .093 | .182 | −.302 | .092 | .011 | .808 |
| | (.303) | (.331) | (.601) | (.422) | (.456) | (.788) |
| Occupation | * | | | ** | | * |
| 1. Agriculture | .713 | .557 | .727 | .879 | .363 | 1.477 |
| | (.218) | (.227) | (.430) | (.305) | (.297) | (.647) |
| 2. Self-employed | .052 | .116 | −.047 | −.169 | −.208 | −.091 |
| | (.229) | (.248) | (.474) | (.308) | (.318) | (.653) |
| Residence | | | | | | * |
| 1. Rural | .024 | .229 | −.428 | −.633 | −.219 | −1.132 |
| | (.209) | (.226) | (.402) | (.288) | (.291) | (.580) |
| 2. Metro | −.001 | −.485 | 1.150 | −.323 | −.719 | .967 |
| | (.322) | (.398) | (.571) | (.448) | (.525) | (.939) |
| Region | | | | * | | ** |
| 1. Extended | .179 | −.062 | .538 | .512 | −.024 | .807 |
| | (.219) | (.232) | (.389) | (.310) | (.303) | (.519) |
| 2. Nuclear | −.290 | −.240 | −.548 | −.430 | −.294 | −1.173 |
| | (.201) | (.219) | (.421) | (.276) | (.287) | (.650) |
| Favorable | *** | *** | | *** | *** | |
| attitude | .796 | 1.017 | −.031 | 1.046 | 1.092 | .585 |
| | (.189) | (.213) | (.358) | (.249) | (.266) | (.517) |
| Constant | | | | | | |
| | −.262 | −1.932 | −2.038 | 1.998 | −.605 | −1.794 |
| | (.774) | (.837) | (1.492) | (1.065) | (1.094) | (2.211) |
| Log likelihood | −405.5 | 412.2 | −152.7 | −249.3 | −241.4 | −77.3 |
| N | 1,050 | 1,050 | 1,050 | 550 | 550 | 550 |
| Mean % | 28.7 | 22.8 | 5.9 | 38.9 | 31.1 | 7.8 |
| Odds ratio | .402 | .295 | .063 | .637 | .451 | .085 |

* $p < .05$.
** $p < .01$.
*** $p < .001$.
NOTE: Standard error in parentheses.

**Fig. 10-2—Definition of variables used in regressions**

| Variables | Description |
|---|---|
| Coresidence | 1: The head lives with parents or a married child |
| Age | Age of the head in single years |
| Migrant-status | 1: The head has a migration experience of 3+ months |
| Eldest-son status | 1: The head is the eldest son |
| Sib size | Number of the head's siblings plus one |
| Wife's eldest-daughter status | 1: The wife who is the eldest daughter without any brothers |
| Wife's sib size | Number of the wife's siblings plus one |
| Parent's illness | 1: The mother, the father, or either one is in poor health |
| Parent's widowhood | 1: The mother or the father is widowed |
| Illness | 1: The head is in- or outpatient |
| Wife's illness | 1: The wife is in- or outpatient |
| Number of married children | 1: Number of currently married children |
| No sons | 1: The head has no sons |
| No daughters | 1: The head has no daughters |
| No single children | 1: The head has no single children |
| Home ownership | 1: The house is owned by household members |
| Per-capita spending | Last month's household expenditure (in thousands of yen) divided by the number of household members |
| Education | 1: The head completed obligatory education<br>2: The head completed higher education |
| Occupation | 1: The head is self-employed in agriculture<br>2: The head is self-employed in non-agriculture |
| U/R residence | 1: Rural (non-DIDs)<br>2: Large urban (DIDs with a population of half a million or more) |
| Region | 1: Regions with higher percentages of the elderly in three-generation households<br>2: Regions with lower percentages of the elderly in three-generation households |
| Favorable attitude | 1: The head agrees with the statement, "Living in three-generation family is desirable" |

NOTE: All the categorical variables have an omitted reference category (otherwise) coded "0."

it represents a consequence of coresidence (increased household size). Other variables have expected effects on coresidence, although they are not significant.

In the regression for determinants of coresidence with the head's own father, the same set of variables, with the exception of migrant status, are significant. In the regression for coresidence with the head's two parents, parent's widowhood is not relevant but other variables, including eldest-son status, home ownership, per capita spending, occupation, and urban/rural residence are significant.

Therefore, these five variables remain significant in all three regressions pertaining to coresidence with the head's own parents. In addition, parent's widowhood is consistently significant when applicable. Migrant status is significant only for coresidence with his own mother. The sign of metropolitan residence is negative only for coresidence with his own mother.

On the other hand, some of independent variables lose their significance in explaining coresidence with the head's parents-in-law. Only wife's eldest-daughter status consistently has a strong positive effect as expected. Parent-in-law's widowhood also has a significant and positive effect on coresidence when applicable. Wife's sib size, home ownership and occupation have significant effects only in the regression for coresidence with the wife's mother. All of their effects are in the expected direction.

Table 10-4 shows regression results for determinants of coresidence of the head with a married child of either sex, a married son, and a married daughter for those heads with at least one married child and for those with all children married. Among heads who have one or more married children, the number of married children having no daughters or single children, home ownership, per capita spending, occupation and a favorable attitude toward family extension have significant effects on coresidence with a married child of either sex. The signs of these effects are as expected. The effect of favorable attitudes may be spurious because it may incorporate rationalization of actual behavior (coresidence).

When predicting living with a married male child, the significance of home ownership and occupation disappears. For living with a female child, having no sons becomes very significant, while have no single children and favorable attitudes are no longer significant. The signs of these coefficients are as expected.

When the cases are further restricted to those heads whose children are all married, some variables lose their significance while others gain it. Naturally, lack of single children becomes irrelevant. As for coresidence with a married child of either sex, the number of married children and presence of daughters lose their significance while region gains it. Home ownership gains significance in the regression for coresidence with a married son. Interestingly, age of the head, number of married children, occupation, urban/rural residence and region gain significance in the regression for coresidence with a married daughter. Age of the head has a negative effect, possibly because age is negatively correlated with headship.

Only per capita spending is consistently significant in the last three regressions as well as in the first three.

By comparing the data in Table 10-3 and 10-4, especially the third and sixth columns in the former and the second and third columns in the latter, one can conclude that the existence of a married eldest son consistently has a strong effect on the parents' coresidence with him, and that the lack of sons has a strong positive effect on coresidence with a married eldest daughter. Among other variables measuring availability, illness of parents does not seem to affect coresidence with a married child, while the widowhood of a parent does. Among feasibility variables, home ownership tends to have a positive effect on coresidence. In contrast, the proxy for per capita income, per capita spending, often has a negative effect on coresidence. Among desirability variables, education does not seem to have a significant effect on coresidence, possibly because of its opposing effects mentioned above. Self-employment in agriculture generally has a positive effect.

There are also differences between the two sets of regression results. The most conspicuous one is found in the effect of favorable attitudes. While it is significant for coresidence with a married son, it is not for coresidence with parents. This may be because coresidence with parents is more obligatory for the head than coresidence with a married child. Another difference is found in the effect of non-agricultural self-employment. It is positive for coresidence with parents but negative for coresidence with a married child when all children are married. This is understandable considering the decline of self-employment among younger generations.

## Discussion

Japan is a society characterized by a very strong tradition of intergenerational coresidence, typically involving a married, oldest son. However, it has also witnessed rapid industrialization, which in the West has been associated with decreases in household size through the nuclearization of families and increases in living alone among the oldest and youngest adults. The questions raised by this analysis are: How important is variation in indicators of norms in parent-child coresidence in Japan? How important are resources in reinforcing or reducing coresidence? And what are the implications of these variations for the future of intergenerational coresidence in Japan? Will it continue to resemble traditional cultures, with a strong emphasis on the family, or will it come more to resemble other industrialized countries of the West?

This research in Japan takes on added interest, since coresidence is analysed both from the point of view of younger adults, whose characteristics and attitudes are used to predict living with parents, and from the point of view of elderly persons, who also vary in their characteristics and in their likelihood of living with one of their adult offspring. Additional details are provided about factors leading to living with the wife's parents, as well as the husband's parents.

The evidence suggests that bases for continued intergenerational coresidence remain strong in Japan, but that fragmenting forces are not insignificant. There are clearly continuing economic structures that reinforce coresidence. The strong effect of self-employment in agriculture on coresidence for both generations suggests that economic ties continue to link parents and children. This interpretation is reinforced by the strong effect of homeownership on coresidence. The high costs of housing in Japan make homeownership almost impossible without the joint resources of both generations. Another piece of evidence suggesting the strength of attitudes supportive of coresidence is the lack of effect of education. While in other industrialized societies, the more educated are much less likely to live in extended families, there is little evidence of the growth of a "taste" for privacy as the result of increases in education.

On the other hand, other factors suggest that coresidence may decline. The migration of young people from rural areas to cities has clearly reduced intergenerational coresidence, although its effects might not last beyond the period of rapid urbanization. Migrant status of young adults decreases family extension, but not the migration of the older generation. This suggests that migration occurs early in the family building process, so that migrant parents are likely to have their children living with or near them in the new place, while migrant children are likely to have left their parents behind. Further evidence to support this interpretation is the finding that living in a rural area increases coresidence among young persons but has no effect among the older generation. Young people who remain in rural areas, then, coreside, while parents in rural areas have probably lost many of their children to out-migration.

Even stronger evidence that coresidence may decline further in Japan appears in the result for per capita spending. Clearly, both younger and older Japanese with more disposable income chose not to coreside; hence, as income rises, coresidence may well fall. A demographic factor that should also reduce coresidence in the long run is the importance of widowhood for coresidence in the parental generation. Young adults are more likely to coreside with members of the parental generation where the "parents" are really only a widowed mother. With the increase in longevity among older Japanese, particularly Japanese men, this route to coresidence will weaken.

Nevertheless, Japan clearly remains a society with a strong commitment to intergenerational coresidence. This is evident in the very strong effect on intergenerational living of being an eldest son. Where family extension is based on high fertility, or on a stem family pattern in which the youngest child remains indefinitely in the parental home, declines in fertility can have a major effect. But intergenerational coresidence in Japan is based on the eldest child--a son, preferably, but failing that, the eldest daughter--suggesting that intergenerational coresidence is likely to remain strong in Japan.

The evidence emerging from this study suggests that many factors that determine coresidence are shared by Japan with Western, industrialized nations. But the specifics of Japanese family structure, while being strained by processes associated with modernization, remain distinctive. Partly reflecting the cultural distinctiveness of Japan and partly the legacy of entrenched structures of economic, family, and intergenerational obligations, the Japanese family is unlikely to converge to the "western" model in the next generation.

## REFERENCES

Anderson, K. L., and W. R. Allen. 1984. "Correlates of Extended Household Structure." *Phylon* 45:145-157.

Angel, R., and M. Tienda. 1982. "Determinants of Extended Household Structure: Cultural Pattern or Economic Need?" *American Journal of Sociology* 87:1360-1383.

Atoh, M. N., and H. Kojima. 1983. "Attitudes toward Marriage among the Unmarried Japanese Youth." *Jinko Mondai Kenkyu* 168:30-57 (In Japanese).

Chamratrithirong, A., S. P. Morgan and R. R. Rindfuss. 1988. "Living Arrangements and Family Formation." *Social Forces* 66:926-950.

Cherlin, A. 1979. "Extended Family Households in the Early Years of Marriage: Some Longitudinal Evidence." Paper presented at the PAA annual meeting, Philadelphia, April.

De Vos, S. 1986. Living Arrangements of Older People in Six Latin American Countries." Paper presented at the PAA annual meeting, San Francisco, April.

De Vos, S. and A. Palloni. 1984. "Formal Methods and Models for Analyzing Kinship and Household Organizations." CDE Working Paper, 84-13.

Dekle, R. 1987. "Do the Japanese Elderly Reduce Their Total Wealth?" Unpublished paper, Reischauer Institute of Japanese Studies, Harvard University and Yale University.

Dixon, R. B. 1970. "The Social and Demographic Determinants of Marital Postponement and Celibacy: A Comparative Study." Unpublished Ph.D. dissertation, University of California, Berkeley.

Freedman, R., M.-C. Chang and T.-H. Sun. 1982. "Household Composition, Extended Kinship and Reproduction in Taiwan: 1973-1980." *Population Studies* 36:395-411.

Goode, W. J. 1963. *World Revolution and Family Patterns*. New York: The Free Press of Glencoe.

Hirosima, K. 1984. "A Basic Demographic Condition for Living Arrangements: Formal Demography of Parent-Child Coresidentiality." Paper presented at the IUSSP Seminar on the Demography of the Later Phases of the Family Life Cycle, Berlin, September.

Hirosima, K. 1987. "Recent Changes in Prevalence of ParentChild Coresidence in Japan." *Jinkogaku Kenkyu* 10:33-41. Institute of Population Problems, Japanese Ministry of Health and Welfare. 1986. "Social and Economic Implications of Aging Population." Paper presented at the International Symposium on Population Structure and Development, Tokyo, September.

Itoh, T. 1984. "Recent Trends of Internal Migration in Japan and Potential Life Time Out-Migrants." *Jinko Mondai Kenkyu* 172:24-38 (In Japanese).

Kobrin, F., and C. Goldscheider. 1982. "Family Extension or Nonfamily Living: Life Cycle, Economic, and Ethnic Factors." *Western Sociological Review* 13:103-118.

Kojima, H. 1987b. "Correlates of Postnuptial Coresidence in Japan." Paper presented at the IUSSP Seminar on New Forms of Familial Life in MDCs, Vaucresson, France, October.

Kojima, H. 1988. "Coresidence of Young Adults with Their Parents in Japan: Do Sib Size and Birth Order Matter?" Paper presented at the PAA annual meeting, New Orleans, April.

Limanonda, B. 1979. "Mate Selection and Post Nuptial Residence in Thailand." Institute of Population Studies, Chulalongkorn University, Papers, No.28.

Martin, L. G. 1988. "Determinants of Living Arrangements of the Elderly in Fiji, Korea, Malaysia, and the Philippines." Paper presented at the PAA annual meeting, New Orleans, April.

Martin, L., and S. Culter. 1983. "Mortality Decline and Japanese Family Structure." *Population and Development Review* 9:633-649.

Michael, R. T., V. R. Fuchs and S. R. Scott. 1980. "Changes in the Propensity to Live Alone: 1950-1976." *Demography* 17:39-53.

Morgan, S. P. and K. Hirosima. 1983. "The Persistence of Extended Family Residence in Japan: Anachronism or Alternative Strategy?" *American Sociological Review* 48:269-281.

Morgan, S. P., and R. R. Rindfuss. 1984. "Household Structure and the Tempo of Family Formation in Comparative Perspective." *Population Studies* 38:129-139.

Mutchler, J. E., and W. P. Frisbie. 1987. "Household Structure Among the Elderly: Racial/Ethnic Differentials." *National Journal of Sociology* 1:3-23.

Palmore, J. A., R. E. Klein and A. Marzuki. 1970. "Class and Family in a Modernizing Society." *American Journal of Sociology* 76:375-398.

Roussel, L., and O. Bourguignon. 1976. *La famille apres le mariage des enfants*. Paris: Presses Universitaires de France.

Schwartz, S., S. Danziger and E. Smolensky. 1984. "The Choice of Living Arrangements by the Elderly." Pp.229-253 in G. Burtless (eds.), *Retirement and Economic Behavior*. Washington, D.C.: The Brookings Institution.

Shimizu, H. 1985. "Regional Differences in the Family Structure." *Jinko Mondai Kenkyu* 176:33-37 (In Japanese).

Shimizu, H. 1986. *Sociology of Population and the Family*. Tokyo: Sai Shobo (In Japanese).

Soldo, B. J., and P. Lauriat. 1976. "An Analysis of Living Arrangements among the Elderly through Log-Linear Models." *Jounal of Comparative Family Studies* 7:351-367.

Stokes, C. S., F. B. LeClerc, and Y.S. Hsieh. 1987. "Household Extension and Reproduction Behaviour in Taiwan." *Journal of Biosocial Sciences* 19:273-282.

Wilk, R. and R. McC. Netting. 1984. "Households: Changing Forms and Functions." Pp.1-29 in R. McC. Netting, R. Wilk and E. Arnould (eds.) *Households: Comparative and Historical Studies of the Domestic Group*. Berkeley: University of California Press.

Wolf, D. A. 1984. "Kin Availability and the Living Arrangements of Older Women." *Social Science Research* 13:72-89.

Wolf, D. A. and B. J. Soldo. 1986. "The Household of Older Unmarried Women: Micro-Decision Models of Shared Living Arrangements." Paper presented at the PAA annual meeting, San Francisco, April,

Young, C. M. 1986. "The Residential Life Cycle: Mortality and Morbidity Effects on Living Arrangements." Pp.101-112 in United Nations, *Consequences of Mortality Trends and Differentials.* New York: United Nations.

# 11

# Ethnicity and the New Family Economy
## Synthesis and Research Challenges

### FRANCES K. GOLDSCHEIDER
### AND CALVIN GOLDSCHEIDER

What are the cumulative theoretical, methodological, and substantive lessons that we can extract from the nine research studies presented in this volume? What do we now know about ethnicity and about the new family economy, about residential and economic relationships between the generations? What are the more general conclusions we can draw about modernization and the family, about change in household structure and living arrangements, and about differences in these processes among ethnic, religious, and racial groups? How do these studies inform us about the changing family life course and how do the results help us to assess the value and the limitations of the available evidence? Most importantly, what new research questions are shaped by these research results?

In this chapter we address these questions by examining several themes that link the research studies to each other and, in turn, to broader theoretical perspectives and methodological strategies. Each research study is an important individual contribution; taken together, they gain in significance because they are part of a larger theoretical design. We return to the broader themes outlined in Chapter One, identifying the connecting threads and relating the specific findings to each other. New insights emerge that contribute to a fuller assessment of research on the new family economy and on the ethnic factor.

## An Emergent Research Model of Living Arrangements

The broader context of the research studies presented is the shift away from family centrality and tribal-ethnic-particularistic attachments in the transition to modern society. In the urban industrial societies of the late 20th century, extended families and intense community attachments are less conspicuous than in the past. These societies emphasize individualism, autonomy, and independence, not extended family obligations.

In the past, economic relationships were embedded in the family and in the attachments to local communities. In contrast, in modern societies such economic relationships have shifted to a broader market place, regulated more by impersonal institutions and bureaucracies, including the state, and are more dependent on technology and individual merit. These broader societal transformations have not, however, resulted in the demise of the family as an institution nor the end of ethnic or communal attachments. Research in the United States has shown that new processes are emerging that reinforce some aspects of ethnicity. Is this also the case for the family? Are the relationships between the economy and the family being transformed and realigned in new ways?

Several of these family processes have been studied in the research reported on in previous chapters. We have documented major changes in the living arrangements of older and younger persons, as greater individualism is translated into nonfamily living. Every study found that those with more resources and more education are more likely to live separately from other family members, and longer-term immigrant Asians and Hispanics are less likely to live with other family members than more recent immigrants. These cross-sectional results are consistent with other research showing increases in nonfamily living for adults in these ages, since over time, levels of income and education have risen and immigrant groups have been incorporated into their new society.

These patterns have resulted in new life course trajectories as young adults and older persons are less likely to live in a household with other family members. The increase in resources for the youngest and oldest adults, allowing them to purchase the privacy of a separate household, makes the coresidential family less necessary as a mechanism for the redistribution of resources to people at these ages. Thus, by focusing on the household context, these studies have shown that the family and household have become even less synonymous, increasing the need to distinguish between "households" and "families" as their relationships change over the life course.

However, the increase in the proportion of younger and older persons who live in nonfamily households does not imply that family relationships end with the formation of new households. Rather, these relationships are realigned, which is likely to increase the importance of financial flows between households. And as these flows become more common, nonfamily living may increase further, as the youngest and oldest adults come to expect such contributions, and as the middle generation expects to make them. Much more work is needed on the changing connections between household structure (intra-household relationships) and financial transfers (inter-household relationships) among family members.

Most of the research reported on focuses on the determinants of these new family-economic relationships. The studies address the fundamental question: what factors increase autonomy and independence between the generations at various stages of the life cycle? The basic framework, derived from the broader theory of the modernization of the family, serves as a general set of guidelines for these research studies on the residential and economic relationships between the generations. None directly tests this theory, since they do not focus on change over time. Nevertheless, judged by the research reported in the previous chapters, the theory leads to an efficient and organized set of linkages and (1) highlights the particular features of modernization have been important in the emergent new family patterns; (2) documents the specific features of the family that have been transformed; and (3) clarifies the mechanisms that relate these processes to each other.

The basic model of the modernization of family living arrangements assumes that peoples' choices represent the outcome of weighing preferences and constraints. An important constraint is resources, since shared housing is normally less expensive than separate housing. This implies that growth in income over time increases the extent of nonfamily living arrangements and that those with more income will have a greater likelihood of nonfamily living at any point in time. Why should this be the case? The simple and most direct reason is that more income allows the purchase of privacy and independence and that these "goods" are or have become valuable in modern societies. Hence, the greater the available income, the more likely it will be used to buy independence from family. This model also suggests that at given incomes, modernization increases the likelihood that these resources will be spent on privacy and independence, rather than on other goods, focusing our attention on the influence of non-economic or "taste" factors in living arrangement choices.

Sociologists have expanded this simple model of constraints and preferences in three important ways: First, taste factors were specified as important determinants of variation and change in living arrangements, rather than simply lumped into a residual category. Not all taste factors are the same, since tastes and preferences based on social class primarily influence individual and family life styles, while tastes rooted in ethnic affiliations more strongly influence group processes, from meals and holidays to job placements.

Second, the components of affluence have been identified, including private and public sources of financial support and in particular the in-kind and financial flows between the generations. The economic factor now takes into account a range of exchanges included in the broader concept of "resources." But we also know that the constraints on living arrangements are not simply economic. The third major expansion of the theory recognizes that structural factors, particularly demographic constraints, must be given a more prominent place in the analysis of living arrangements, since the potential persons available to extend a household have changed over time as families have become smaller and more persons survive to older ages.

These three expansions of the simple economic theory of family and household formation can be linked to three categories of factors that have been used to organize broader issues of family formation. These are demographic "availability", economic "feasibility," and preferences, or "desirability." We now highlight the ways the studies in this volume on new family patterns reinforce the importance of these issues. We start with the demographic.

## Demographic Constraints

The most important demographic constraint shaping choices about living arrangements is "availability". Numbers limit the range of persons available for given family configurations. These studies have revealed three ways that demographic constraints operate. Mortality changes play a key role. The decline in mortality (together with the decline in fertility) has led to dramatic changes in the structure of populations, increasing the possibility that older parents and grandparents, who are now more likely to survive, can live with a given child. This pattern has undoubtedly been a factor in the early increases in family extension in Japan, and has retarded its decline elsewhere.

Mortality decline also alters the relationships between the generations by increasing the joint survivorship of husbands and wives into old age. Typically, family extension is more likely when only one parent survives; couples are more likely to maintain an independent household. This is the case in Japan, and was also documented for older Portuguese and non-European ethnics in the United States. As couples begin to survive to a point long after their children have left home to start their own families and establish independent households, fewer become part of another household.

The role of mortality constraints emerges in more extreme form among selected segments of the Israeli Jewish population. Israelis of European origin who experienced major family losses in World War II and the Holocaust are more likely to live alone than Jews from other places. Although as a group, they had more access to outside resources than other Israelis (through German reparation payments), the absence of relatives is a significant and continuing constraint in their living arrangements patterns as they age.

Fertility is a second demographic process that has an important effect constraining living arrangements. The analysis of living arrangements of older adults both in Israel and Rhode Island showed that those who had fewer children ever born were more likely to live alone than those with more children. Fertility patterns at one stage of the life course therefore have an effect at a later stage through their impact on the number of potential households for unmarried adults to extend.

A third demographic process affecting living arrangements is migration. Although migration can bring people together, it normally operates to reduce access to households containing relatives. Young people often move away from their families in response to job opportunities or marriage needs. Retirees sometimes exchange areas of high economic opportunity for greater amenities and lower costs of living, leaving their children and grandchildren behind.

Migration was clearly a factor in the rural-urban patterns in Japan, since young adults left their parental home to find a job in a distant community. Migration of younger persons from rural to urban places in Japan has resulted in a pattern of greater coresidence with parents for young persons remaining in rural areas relative to young persons in urban areas, but lower coresidence for parents in rural areas, who have lost many of their children through out-migration to urban places. Many rural Japanese parents do not join their children to extend their children's households in urban areas and their children do not return rural areas to extend their parents' household.

Among young people in the United States, a similar pattern could be observed. Areas of high in-migration of young adults tend to have higher proportions living in nonfamily settings, controlling for other factors. Presumably this reflects the shortage of relatives with whom young people could live in such areas.

In general, the results of the research presented argue strongly for giving priority to demographic factors in influencing living arrangements. It cannot matter much how poor you are or how much you prefer to live with children or other relatives if there are no relatives accessible to you with whom to form a household.

## Economic Factors and Resources

Beyond demographic and life cycle constraints are the economic factors that facilitate nonfamily living throughout the family life course. As income rises, coresidence falls. Money also increases the probability of headship and hence the power of older persons within complex households. The effect of resources is not ambiguous, however, since these studies provide us with one clue that the choice between family and nonfamily living can be made even for those with relatively few resources. Areas with lower male incomes have lower rates of living alone, but they have higher rates of living with roommates, who are nonrelatives, not family members. Either way, the general effect of rising affluence appears to be to reduce family extension.

The effect of resources on decreasing family extension seems to be a general finding and characterizes ethnic and racial populations, e.g., Blacks and Hispanics, as well. Money buys privacy and independence for the unmarried, both among young adults and the elderly. For the married, however, at least among the elderly in Rhode Island, increased resources lead to more complex households, suggesting that while poorer older adults are more likely to extend a household, richer households are more likely to become extended as coresidence is used to redistribute resources from more affluent family members to those in need. If so, the analysis of factors influencing living arrangements should be careful to specify whose resources are being considered, since the effects of resources differ. However, this was not the case in Japan, where greater resources reduce coresidence both with parents and with children.

Wealthier persons can care for their relatives in other ways than through coresidence. One of the key insights drawn from the research reported here is the importance of extending economic analysis to consider inter-household transfers, whether for studying the nestleaving patterns of young adults or the maintenance of independence among the elderly. By taking into account intergenerational transfers for nestleavers, the sequence of education and leaving home can be disentangled. Modern nestleavers complete their education after leaving home; the traditional nestleaver completes education while living at home. The trade-offs between education and residential patterns, and therefore the links between the changes in living arrangements and stratification, provide an important and fascinating challenge for analysis.

Thus, resource transfers between the generations involve both in-kind and financial transfers. Children who complete their education after leaving home need subsidies from their parents. But resources can flow both ways. Just as young adults can stay at home until they complete their education or until they marry (usually receiving in-kind financial support from their parents), so older persons can be incorporated into the nuclear families of their children and extend those families (and children can contribute to the parental household). This represents a clear life course parallel between older and younger adults.

The substitution of inter-household financial flows for in-kind, intra-household financial flows is still quite rare at both ends of the adult life course, but it may be of critical importance for those involved. Among young adults, such contributions were associated at the group level with higher education: Jews and Irish Catholics were the most likely to support their children living away from home, while the Portuguese were the least likely, paralleling the extremes of educational attainment of these groups. And it is clear that for an important segment of the elderly, such family transfers allow them to live alone, contributing to the residential independence of the other family members, not only to the independence and privacy of the elderly person.

Another important economic dimension for the living arrangements of the elderly is the transition from family to public sector support. Considering public income as a component of financial resources reveals that older persons living alone use family transfers to raise income to an adequate level among those not eligible for public assistance and to supplement public income benefits among those who receive them. These findings reinforce the view that family transfers supplement public assistance. And just as family transfers and public sector transfers enhance the likelihood of living alone among the elderly in the United States, so government and extra government resources may facilitate the purchase of independence and privacy in Israel among Holocaust survivors.

## Preferences and "Tastes"

Having adequate funds is a necessary condition for living in a nonfamily household, just as having a given relative is a necessary condition for a particular form of family extension. But neither condition necessarily compels such a choice. There also has to be the desire or preference to do so. The extent to which nonfamily living is desired is a matter of "taste."

Although the taste issue is often examined simply as a residual--i.e., those factors that are not economic--some of the papers here went beyond this level, differentiating types of preferences, including gender, education, and particularly ethnicity. These are quite separate dimensions of preferences. Gender differences tap the extent of egalitarianism in the roles of men and women (and of children and their parents). Education normally connotes a more individualistic life style, in which family takes a less central role. And ethnicity relates to universalism, and the extent to which people's commitments and loyalties are focused on the local and particular as opposed to the broader national community, based on achievement-oriented values.

*Gender differences.* Women are generally less likely to live alone. This was the case among Blacks and Hispanics, particularly for Mexicans and Puerto Ricans; for all Asian groups; and among the elderly in Rhode Island. The same result appears at the areal level: areas with a high proportion female have lower levels of nonfamily living. This gender difference in living arrangements has almost always been interpreted as indicating a more traditional attitude toward women, in which women's lives and identities are more closely bound by family roles as daughter, wife, and mother than are men's. Hence, such differences are frequently stronger in more traditional subpopulations.

However, the extent of gender difference varied in these studies in ways that suggest that it is likely to be reduced in the future. There were no significant gender differences among White nonHispanics. In Israel, although Moslem women are much less likely to live independent of family than Moslem men, this is not the case for Jews. Finally, gender differences in the Asian American subpopulations were most pronounced for older people; there was much less gender difference among those 18-24, and for Koreans and Japanese, the youngest women were more likely to live independently than men of the same age. Other American research has also shown that young unmarried men are more likely to remain in the parental home than young unmarried women.

*Educational differences.* The effect of education on living arrangements reported in these studies also depended on context. The general pattern was that those with more education were more likely to live independently. This was the case among Blacks, Hispanics and others in the United States and among Jews and Moslems in Israel (with the exception of Holocaust survivors). Even at the areal level, standard metropolitan statistical areas with a higher average educational level registered higher levels of nonfamily living (although the effects were as strong for living with roommates as for living alone). These results suggest that education normally leads to exposure to life styles and preferences that favor individualism over familism. However, the level of education had no effect in Japan, either for living with married children or with parents. It is possible that education in Japan reinforces high traditional Japanese culture, which puts a strong value on maintaining such family extension. However, higher education did not increase the likelihood of coresidence in Japan. It is likely that education in Japan is also having the nonfamily effect found more generally, offsetting the effects of specific Japanese cultural patterns.

*Ethnicity.* The third major dimension of tastes in these studies is ethnicity. Differences by race, national origin, and religion appear throughout their results. Complex patterns appear that reinforce the importance of ethnicity as an indicator of culture, or "tastes." But the results also show how group differences can appear and be maintained through important institutional structures that go beyond preferences. There are clear indications that ethnic distinctiveness can be maintained over time, resisting pressures for assimilation--whether by minorities resisting a host culture or by national cultures resisting global trends.

A major challenge in disentangling ethnic effects is that ethnic groups are often "different" in ways that lead to economic deprivation, whether because they are new entrants into a society, and hence have not yet acquired the skills to function successfully in it, or because their "difference" leads to discrimination by the majority, blocking their access to economic opportunities and reinforcing ethnic residential concentration. As a result, what are often interpreted as ethnic effects may simply be the result of differences in resources. Hispanics and Blacks fit into the association of ethnicity with disadvantage and segregation, since they are disproportionately concentrated in the lower third of the class structure. Asian Americans, in contrast, have been more successful economically and have experienced less residential discrimination.

Patterns of differences are often additionally confused because culturally quite different groups are lumped together for discrimination. Blacks recently arrived from the West Indies are often treated in the same ways as Blacks who have lived many generations in the American South, creating important similarities as a result. And quite different groups can band together and create new ethnic formations, leading, for example, to "Italians" an identity that did not exist anywhere in the complex areas of the Italian peninsula from which they came, and to "Asian-Africans, a group formed out of diverse immigrant streams to Israel. Hispanics in the United States are culturally and economically quite diverse in terms of background, made up as they are of large groups of Cubans, Puerto Ricans, and Mexicans, as well as other smaller groups. Asians in American include large numbers of Japanese, Chinese, Koreans, Vietnamese, Filipinos, and Asian Americans, as well as other smaller groups. As a result, it is also important to examine the extent to which differences between related groups are being maintained.

These studies demonstrate the importance of taking into account class differences among groups when studying a phenomenon such as living arrangements, since separate housing normally requires more affluence than shared housing. Blacks and Hispanics are less likely to live alone, and those living in Black areas are more likely to live in families as well. In part, this is the result of their lower levels of income. But resources are clearly not the only cause of these group differences, since even controlling for income, some ethnic and racial differences in living arrangements remain. And it is also the case that Hispanics and Blacks use their resources in different ways from other groups, being less likely to purchase privacy as income rises than are those in other groups.

These studies also show the importance of carefully subdividing groups into specific ethnic communities. Among Asians immigrants to the United States, Japanese and Chinese Americans are more likely to live in nonfamily households than are Koreans and Vietnamese. There is also variation in the extent of female headed households, rare among Indian Asians and higher among Japanese and Vietnamese. Dramatic differences emerge when the unattached are examined: while five out of ten unattached Japanese males live alone, about two out of ten Koreans and Filipinos live alone, and only one out of ten of the Vietnamese live alone.

The evidence also indicates that Hispanic variation in living arrangements obscures substantial variation among Hispanics. Cubans are more family oriented than other Hispanics, such that Cuban widows are more likely to live with families, while Mexican and Puerto Rican widows are more likely to live alone. Even among those of European origin, some differences persist, with elderly Portuguese much less likely to live alone than those of Irish and Italian backgrounds. But for both Asians and Hispanics in the United States, it is clear that the subgroups are beginning to merge, as they have among most European groups. For each of the studies focusing on these groups, there appears to be a pattern that points to diminishing ethnic differences with duration of residence in the United States.

To some extent, ethnic or taste differences can be link to immigration and thus to differential exposure to modern family values. This allows us to use ethnicity as a window on a more traditional past. The living arrangements of Moslems in Israel and, to a lesser extent, the Portuguese and Hispanics in the United States resemble in some ways what can be gleaned from fragmentary data in the 19th century.

But ethnic change is not inevitable. The fact that Japanese immigrants to the United States are adapting rapidly to the family patterns of their new homeland poses an important challenge to the analysis of intergenerational living arrangements in Japan. Change has been relatively slow in Japan, and many scholars expect the strong pro-family Japanese pattern to prevail over the more nuclear, or even nonfamily forms characteristic of many western developed societies. These two differing patterns for Japanese who are culturally similar focuses our attention on context, and the structural supports that can maintain, or alternatively erode, cultural values. (It is also possible that those who immigrated were already different in some ways from those remaining behind.)

The patterns of change among women in Utah, Rhode Island, and California reinforce this interpretation. Rapid change in family patterns is epitomized by California, with large proportions of young women leaving home before marriage to set up an independent residence, long delays before getting married, relatively egalitarian marital roles, and high household headship rates. But these trends are also clearly visible in traditional Rhode Island, where the strength of Catholic social control over family matters has weakened in recent years. But this is not the case in Utah, where the Church continues to maintain a high level of involvement in peoples' lives. Change has been slower and nonexistent on some dimensions. Embedded in the social networks of the powerful Mormon community, Utah women have embraced the most traditional set of wife and mother roles and are resisting the trend toward nonfamilies.

Clearly, then, the extent to which given patterns are linked to other structures will influence the extent to which they are maintained. In this context, the link between living arrangements and intergenerational financial flows is particularly important. Among the Portuguese in Rhode Island, high levels of financial contribution by children to their parents is combined with their low levels of education and late nestleaving. These patterns suggest that Portuguese children are treated as a major family resource and that pressures on them to contribute to their parents may in fact lead to higher drop out rates and later nestleaving. Financial flows, living arrangements, and education are less tightly linked in the other communities in Rhode Island, allowing more rapid change. The opposite link actually characterizes the Jews, who combine high educational attainment, high levels of financial flows from parents to children, and an early residential break of young adults with the parental household.

## Modernization or Westernization?

As these studies seek clues to the broadly changing family economy, examining ethnic differences and speculating about longer term patterns of family change and living arrangements in a given society, it is often not clear the extent to which the patterns that are emerging are particular to that society. Most of the materials in seven of the nine research projects reported on in this volume are derived from United States data sources. But our theories are grander than one place and should be applicable to a wider range of processes in other places. If not, comparative analysis should point to what is general and what is particular about specific places.

The two case studies included here on other countries allow us to look at what is ethnic and what is Western among these patterns of family structure and change. They suggest that family transformation is cross-cutting religious and cultural groups, neither unique to American society nor the simple outcome of values that stress the independence and autonomy characteristic of the American national character. Instead, living arrangements and intergenerational relationships appear to be changing as part of broader processes of modernization, linked to the economic and demographic transformations that are increasingly separating family from the economic sphere and reflecting changes in the division of labor accompanying societal expansion and increasing complexity.

Clearly, many factors that affect coresidence in Japan and in Israel are similar to those in the United States. Demographic, economic, and preference differences in these contexts result in a somewhat different configuration of living arrangements, but the underlying processes appear similar. The similarity is striking particularly since Japan differs from western countries far more in the area of family demography than in the transitions in family size and death control. It may be that some of the affluence that has come to Japan may be used to reinforce the residentially extended family and to encourage multiple generational families in the face of the new demographic regime. Economic structures also powerfully reinforce coresidence. Housing is an important element, since housing is so costly that there is a need to pool resources to afford housing. And there is little evidence that higher levels of education change tastes for privacy and independence. Nevertheless, there is evidence that the extended family defined in terms of residence has declined in the recent period, despite the increased availability of older relatives with whom to coreside and the decreased number of children among whom to spread them around.

A similar conclusion emerges in Israel. Despite common pension systems and housing markets, there are major differences in living arrangements in Israel. Moslems are the most traditional in having the lowest proportion in nonfamily households, while the Jews from European origins are the most likely to live in nonfamily households; Jews from Asian and African countries are in an intermediate position. But the pressures toward a reduction of the power and centrality of the family appear to affect all these groups. Thus, while there continues to be distinctive family patterns in Japan and in Israel, there also appears to be increasing evidence of some common responses to the forces of economic and demographic changes.

## Methodological and Theoretical Conclusions

A variety of methodological strategies were used to arrive at these generalizations. In part these multiple strategies increase our confidence in the cumulative value of these studies as a base for further work, particularly since these studies have also used both census and survey data sources. Nevertheless, there remains a great need to move toward larger and more detailed survey datasets, to longitudinal measurement, and to the incorporation of contextual factors in order to measure more directly what is happening to the changing family economy.

A major challenge is to begin to measure the preferences and social structures underlying ethnic differences directly. Ethnic differences in living arrangements appear to reflect traditional values associated with family continuity. But they also should be the result of differential social structures, based on the institutions and associations that develop in ethnic communities. These studies had relatively little basis to study to distinguish these two processes directly. We need new data sources that measure ethnicity directly and tap values and preferences that underlie ethnic categorical differences.

A similar data shortage characterizes the whole area of interhousehold economic flows. Traditionally, datasets have emphasized individuals, with perhaps some information on the other members of the surveyed individual's household or coresidential family. But it is clear from the two studies in this volume that major influences on family patterns are lost by such a data collection strategy. A substantial portion of the elderly are being maintained in independent quarters through the contributions of family members who do not live in the same household. Who are these contributors? Why do they contribute? Are there family members who are similarly located in the family network who are not contributing, and, if so, why? And how do the families of the elderly who do not receive such contributions differ from those who do? Similar questions should be asked at the other end of the adult life course, as young people and their families confront choices about independence and parental contributions, as well as investments in the future.

A second major area for data development focuses on the longitudinal dimensions of these processes. Family change is linked to life cycle transitions that need to be studied as they unfold. The extent to which we can capture change over the life course by comparing ages remains a hypothesis to be tested when longitudinal life course data are obtained. Data with even greater longitudinal sweep--or historical depth--are needed to test the inferences drawn from these studies about the relationship between ethnicity and "tradition."

Third, areal data provide information about the community contexts-- economic opportunities and group norms--that influence individuals. The effects of rental costs can only be measured by collecting data at the community level. Such data can also tap levels of unemployment, extra-family community services, and other influences that operate on individuals outside of their immediate family.

It is also clear that there is a need to continue to focus on intergenerational relationships and to attempt to capture the points of view of both generations. New methodological strategies will have to be developed to assess how each generation within the same household and within the same family views the specific family patterns and living arrangements that are emerging. These intergenerational relationships will have to include both residential and economic components and will have to examine how these unfold over time as both generations age.

While the studies in this volume have not tested theories of modernization, family, and ethnic changes, the theoretical framework has been a useful map to direct us to research questions and to new research challenges. The research questions that we can ask are now sharper and clearer precisely because available data have been exploited and new variables have been considered. There are no perfect data sets available (or even that can be constructed that are not limited by the depth and time covered). We also cannot wait to analyze the "perfect" data set. Many of the conclusions that we have drawn seem to fit together and are drawn from diverse but complementary sources of data in diverse settings and addressed to different parts of an analytic puzzle. But there are other parts to the puzzle that have not been filled in and the puzzle is more complex than our data can address. Indeed these theoretical questions are continuously reshaped by the research that we carry out.

# Contributors

**Anne Castleton** is currently completing her Ph.D. in the Communications Department at the University of Utah. She received her M.A. in the Program in American Civilization at Brown University.

**Patricia B. Christian** received her M.A. degree from Brown University and is currently completing her Ph.D. in the Department of Sociology at Brown University.

**Zara Fisher** is affiliated with the NCJW Research Institute for Innovation in Education, School of Education, the Hebrew University Jerusalem, Israel.

**Calvin Goldscheider** is Professor of Sociology and Judaic Studies at Brown University and is affiliated with their Population Studies and Training Center. He is also a research consultant at The RAND Corporation.

**Frances K. Goldscheider** is Professor of Sociology at Brown University and is the Co-Director of the N.I.H. Training Program in Demography and the N.I.A. Training Program in the Demography of Aging. She is also a research consultant at The RAND Corporation.

**Luis Lazaro Hernandez** received his B.A. and M.A. degrees at Brown University and is currently a student at Yale University Law School.

**Mali B. Jones** is currently completing her Ph.D. in the Department of Sociology at Brown University.

Contributors

**Wilawan Kanjanapan** received her Ph.D. at Brown University and was a Postdoctoral Fellow at the Population Studies and Training Center. She is currently affiliated with the Institute of American Culture, Academia Sinica in Taiwan.

**Hiroshi Kojima** is completing his Ph.D. at Brown University and is currently associated with the Institute of Population Problems, Tokyo, Japan.

**Carol Shuchman** was a doctoral student in the Department of Sociology at Brown University and currently is associated with the Port Authority of New York and New Jersey.